THE FORBIDDEN WORLDS OF HARUKI MURAKAMI

The FORBIDDEN WORLDS OF HARUKI MURAKAMI

MATTHEW CARL STRECHER

University of Minnesota Press
Minneapolis • London

Published by the University of Minnesota Press
111 Third Avenue South, Suite 290
Minneapolis, MN 55401–2520
http://www.upress.umn.edu

Library of Congress Cataloging-in-Publication Data
Strecher, Matthew Carl, author.
The forbidden worlds of Haruki Murakami / Matthew Carl Strecher.
Includes bibliographical references and index.
ISBN 978-0-8166-9196-8 (hc)
ISBN 978-0-8166-9198-2 (pb)
1. Murakami, Haruki, born 1949—Criticism and interpretation. I. Title.
PL856.U673Z864 2014
895.6'35--dc23

2014015111

Printed in the United States of America on acid-free paper

20 19 18 17 16 15 10 9 8 7 6 5 4 3 2

FOR MY “BAOBEI”
AND IN FOND MEMORY OF THOSE IN OUR FAMILY
WHO HAVE GONE “OVER THERE” AHEAD OF US

CONTENTS

PREFACE

LIKE A LOT OF GOOD IDEAS, this book originated over a cup of coffee (or was it something stronger?) and an idle conversation with a friend. I was in Tokyo, getting some reading done after the departure of my language students, fourteen of whom had come with me for a two-week "travel study" program at Tōyō University. My friend, an NHK television producer who not only works on NHK's special programming on Murakami but is a serious fan in her own right, had just asked me whether I thought Murakami would win the Nobel Prize in Literature that year and what I thought of his latest novel, *1Q84,* which was still only two volumes at the time.

I must have talked for a long time, because at the end of my apparently endless commentary on Murakami, my friend opened her eyes wide and said, "It's time for you to write another book." She was right, of course. It *was* time. I had known it for a while but first had to get past the idea that it was somehow wrong—immoral, even—to write yet *another* book on this man. In the years since my *Dances with Sheep* was published in 2002, there have been no less than four new books written in English on Murakami Haruki (one of them a little reader's guide of mine that probably doesn't really count, but still . . .). At least once every year or two I am asked to sit on an examination committee for a master's thesis or Ph.D. dissertation on Murakami. I referee articles about him all the time. Part of me feels a profound sense of guilt at my energetic role in focusing so much attention on just one Japanese writer.

And yet . . . what a writer! Murakami's work has, in the past decade or so, gone completely global, and thanks to a small army of brilliant and dedicated translators he is now read in about sixty languages around the world. He has stirred up controversy, especially when critics try to categorize his work, but he has also bridged cultural and political divides. He is the first Japanese writer in a long while to develop major fan bases in countries like China and South Korea, where animosity to Japan runs as deep as memories of Japanese colonialist oppression run long. He is so big that Tokyo University hosted a gathering of his various translators from around the world for a symposium in 2006, inviting the public to come and listen in, and more than a thousand people turned up. In 2008, the University of California, Berkeley, held a symposium on Murakami and invited the author to speak; tickets to the event—held in a massive auditorium—sold out in fifteen minutes. And aside from the Nobel Prize in Literature, Murakami has won almost every major literary award the world has to offer. What was once facetiously called "Murakamimania" is quite real.

This being the case, immoral or not, it dawned on me in the summer of 2009 that I still have a lot of unfinished business with Murakami, partly because he continues to write so prolifically but also because my mind continues to work on him. And while I stand behind my various past writings on him—writing that has spanned nearly two decades—a great many fresh insights have occurred to me, not only about the author's recent works but about his earlier texts as well, and these are included in this monograph. I am also unwilling to rule out another book in ten or fifteen years. Murakami once told me that he considered Raymond Carver to be "his writer." Well, Murakami is *my* writer, in the sense that I feel a connection with his work that I cannot seem to break. I am, as I have admitted to more than one audience, a Murakami addict. This book reflects my ongoing fascination with his writing, along with my belief that Murakami's writing continues to develop and change and that these changes are important enough to the overall field of Japanese (and even world) literature to merit detailed description and discussion.

While the title of this book gives the name of its subject in Western order, that is, Haruki Murakami, in order to render it more easily recognizable to English readers on first encounter, Japanese names within the main text, both real and fictitious, are given in

Japanese order, surname first, given name second. Macrons over vowels indicate long vowel sounds, as in *Hādo-boirudo wandārando*.

As is my long-standing custom, I have worked from and quoted only original Japanese source materials. This means that all quoted passages, including those from Murakami's works, are my own English renderings, even when published translations exist. This is not intended as a slight toward the translators, whose renditions of Murakami's work in English are unvaryingly accurate and well wrought. But there are two good reasons to work from my own translations: first, it allows me to maintain a uniform style throughout the volume; and second, it helps to reduce the gap, or distance, between the texts and my analyses of them, which are, after all, based not merely on the words on the page but on how they reverberate in my head as I read them, rewriting in my mind as I go. Having taught courses in translation theory and practice, I am acutely conscious when working with translations of being at a third remove from the text, of interpreting an interpretation, and this is not ideal for the sort of close reading that grounds this work. I hope, then, as always, that Murakami's various translators will not take offense.

As a result, throughout this text readers will find that I have initially given the original title of each work, followed by its official translated title, except in cases where the work has not been translated or has been in some way combined with other works (as in Murakami's two nonfiction works on the Aum Shinrikyō incident and certain short story collections). Following the initial introduction of those works, they are mentioned in the text by their English titles. All citations are from the originals, including page numbers, and this is signaled in the notes by inclusion of the original title. The bibliography contains both versions.

ACKNOWLEDGMENTS

A GREAT MANY PEOPLE were helpful to me in the preparation of this book. Chronologically, I should begin with Honda Hiroko, the delightful NHK producer who first suggested it was time for me to write another book. Numerous friends and colleagues at Tōyō University also deserve mention: Satō Akira, Sugimoto Futoshi, Tsuchida Kensei, Katō Chieko, Murakami Makoto, Mochizuki Osamu, and Terada Nobuyuki, among many others. I thank the staff of the International Programs Office at Tōyō University (particularly Fukushima Narutoshi), as well as its library staff, for permitting me unfettered access to their excellent Japanese collections through the past five summers. Thanks also to Oikawa Masahiro at Ritsumeikan for arranging opportunities for me to present preliminary ideas about Murakami on his campus. At Tokyo University, I am grateful to Professor Shibata Motoyuki for including me in the 2006 symposium, and for his friendship and support since. I extend thanks to Professor Katō Yūji for his friendship, advice, and encouragement in completing this text. Finally, I offer profound thanks and warmest remembrance to Professor Ueda Yoshinori of Tōyō University, a dear friend and colleague, who lived almost long enough to see this text published.

Here at Winona State University in Minnesota many people have been helpful: Deans Ralph Townsend, Peter Henderson, and Holly Shi were all generous with funding at critical moments; Yogesh Grover was always generous with his time, listening patiently while I tried to explain what this book was really about. My lack of coherence in his office, happily, led to greater clarity in the present volume. I extend thanks as well to all the members of the Global Studies and World Languages department.

As always, deepest gratitude is due my friend and mentor Jay Rubin, who got me started on Murakami and continues to be the perfect model of what a mentor should be; and to John Treat, whose rigorous teaching has always remained in my mind. My debt to these two teachers can never be fully expressed in words. Sincere thanks also to Rebecca Suter, a fellow Murakami scholar and good friend, and to Ken Henshall, who has been a most supportive voice for many years. Thanks to Alex Bates for his help in locating a rare text on the 1923 Kantō earthquake, and to novelist Ruth Ozeki for sharing her knowledge, enthusiasm, and interest in Murakami with me. And finally, among the many professionals who have contributed, I wish to thank editors Jason Weidemann and Danielle Kasprzak at the University of Minnesota Press and the excellent readers of the first draft of the manuscript, whose comments and suggestions helped make this volume so much better. And also a note of gratitude to Mary Keirstead, who is one of the finest copy editors I have ever worked with.

On a more personal note, thanks to my parents, Victor and Barbara Strecher, who listened patiently to my weekly updates on the project and probably discovered the true meaning of the expression "at a glacial pace." Finally, love and gratitude to my wife, Mei, whose remarks about being a "writer's widow" were rare and always spoken with humor; and to Victor and Lizzie, who grew up alongside this volume and learned that the "monster living in the basement" was just their dad.

INTRODUCTION

The Power of the "Story"

> It is true, if you lose your ego, you also lose that consistent narrative that you call your self.
>
> —Murakami Haruki, *Andāguraundo*

IT HAS NOW BEEN MORE THAN THREE DECADES since novelist Murakami Haruki (born 1949) made his debut on the Japanese literary stage with the publication of his brief, almost laconic novella *Kaze no uta o kike* (1979; translated as *Hear the Wind Sing*). This work, along with his second, *1973-nen no pinbōru* (1980; translated as *Pinball, 1973*), has in fact been translated into English, but neither has been released outside Japan—according to popular rumor, because the author preferred it that way. His initial reception as a writer was somewhat mixed, despite his winning the Gunzō Prize for new writers with *Hear the Wind Sing,* and one suspects a fair number of established writers and critics of the time did not expect him to last long. Looking back on those times, Murakami admitted somewhat bitterly in 2005 that "'I was kind of an odd man out compared with other writers, and was almost totally shut out by the Bundan [literary guild] system in Japan. . . . The world of literary arts [in Japan] saw no value in me, and disliked me. . . . They said I would destroy the traditions of Japanese literature.'"[1]

Over the years, as Murakami's popularity as a writer has grown around the world, scholars and critics have been drawn increasingly to his writing style, his apparent rejection of belles lettres (literature as Art), his probing into the human psyche, his play with the metaphysical (especially through the literary trope known as "magical realism"), his peculiar take on history, and his encyclopedic knowledge of music (particularly jazz). Add to this a preoccupation, chiefly in Japan, with Murakami's so-called shift *(tenkan)* from social detachment to social commitment—commonly dated from 1995—and we have at least a partial picture of the types of critical discussions taking place with regard to this writer.

Around the late 1980s to early 1990s, a kind of "boom" in Murakami studies began to occur in Japan, an indication, perhaps, that reports of the death of modern Japanese literature had been somewhat premature. The "boom" in Japan was followed by the beginnings of interest in other parts of the world as well. In the United States, Murakami was being studied on university campuses from the early 1990s, and by 1995 his initial image as a "pop" writer had been overcome sufficiently that it was even possible for a graduate student—myself in this case—to submit a doctoral thesis on Murakami without going to unreasonable lengths to defend the importance of the topic to the overall field.

This is not to say, of course, that Murakami's reception was wholly positive even after the initially bumpy start. Many established critics were nonplussed from the beginning by his new style, or rather nonstyle, which signaled a rejection of the Modernist urge toward literary language, and some found his prose lacking in depth. Others found his characters' disaffected urban lifestyle too detached for their taste. Murakami was just a little too "cool" for their comfort and failed to measure up to standards of intellectual social critique that had marked Japan's great writers since the 1960s.

It must also be admitted, too, that a significant part of Murakami's difficulty in being accepted by the literary establishment lies in *his* refusal to accept *them*. If the Bundan gave him the cold shoulder, he has returned the favor tenfold, refusing to take part in the usual roundtable discussions with other established writers, choosing not to engage in *ronsō* (literary debates). Today it appears that Murakami and the Bundan, or whatever is left of it, have agreed to a peace of sorts; he has, after all, won most of the major literary awards (except the Akutagawa Prize, one of the most Bundanesque of them all) and has dutifully attended the awards ceremonies, managing a smile and a brief speech. In his work as a writer, however, he has determinedly remained as far as possible from the Bundan and its mainstream understanding of literature.

What few knew at the beginning, but many of us know now, is that this was a typical response on the part of this intensely individualistic man, who had attended Waseda in the late 1960s, at the height of the student riots in Tokyo, and joined in the violence but strictly as an independent; he refused to join any political group or faction but hurled stones at the police in his own right. Today we know Murakami as the man who went to Jerusalem to accept the Jerusalem Prize from the Israeli government and in his acceptance speech criticized the Israeli state for its military actions against civilians in Gaza, declaring to his hosts, in effect, that if they chose to bring their massive military and political power against the individuals protesting in the Gaza Strip, then, right or wrong, he would stand against them. This was his now famous declaration of the "wall and eggs" metaphor, in which powerful political systems are seen as a great stone wall, and individuals as eggs, hopelessly and rather suicidally hurling themselves against its implacable strength. In his own words:

> Each of us is, more or less, an egg. Each of us is a unique, irreplaceable soul enclosed in a fragile shell. This is true of me, and it is true of each of you. And each of us, to a greater or lesser degree, is confronting a high, solid wall. The wall has a name: It is The System. The System is supposed to protect us, but sometimes it takes on a life of its own, and then it begins to kill us and cause us to kill others—coldly, efficiently, systematically. . . . Between a high, solid wall and an egg that breaks against it, I will always stand on the side of the egg.[2]

This is highly characteristic of Murakami Haruki; in a fight between an egg and a stone wall, he will root for the egg. Yet, despite his rather humble and uncertain start as a novelist—more or less like all novelists—Murakami is now a favorite to be Japan's next Nobel laureate in literature, following Ōe Kenzaburō (1994) and Kawabata Yasunari (1968). Certainly NHK (Nippon Hōsō Kyōkai, Japan's national broadcast service) believes this to be so; they have been preparing for his anointing for several years already. The chief difficulty, according to the producer in charge of the preparations, is that Murakami will not do televised interviews, particularly with Japanese media.[3] Whereas past winners have always made the rounds of the talk shows and addressed the Japanese people, Murakami is likely, should he win, to make do with the release of a brief statement. He simply does not play the Japanese game by Japanese rules.

Perhaps this is why critics, from the very start, were uncertain what to do with Murakami. He did not really match any of the familiar "types" of contemporary Japanese literature. His writing style was odd—a point that will be revisited shortly below—and his fictional world was bizarre. Japanese readers and critics were not wholly unfamiliar with the bizarre; Abe Kōbō, Nakagami Kenji, even Ōe Kenzaburō had prepared them for surrealism, magical realism, and the grotesque. But serious writers in Japan, particularly in the postwar, had typically fit into one of two broad categories or occasionally both: they either had a serious social, political, or philosophical agenda, or they were pure aesthetes, out to create literary *Art* for its own sake. Younger writers (Ōe, Nakagami, Abe) tended to be chiefly the former; older ones, such as Tanizaki Jun'ichirō and Kawabata Yasunari, drifted more toward the latter. Mishima stood in both camps. And nearly all were good Modernists, in the sense that all understood the importance of pressing the field forward, innovating and experimenting, pushing language and literature to their very limits.

One Last Dance with the Sheep

But Murakami fit none of these patterns, and it was precisely this aspect of him that first drew me to his work in 1992. Worn down by a steady diet of so-called serious writers, I was drawn to the works of a novelist who had no regard for literary Art and, indeed, preferred the term *fiction* to *literature*. My initial approach, as a result, was to explore the issues surrounding genre, to determine, if possible, whether Murakami could be categorized. It was clear that he was not part of the *jun bungaku* ("pure literature") crowd that made up the Bundan, and yet, his writing was nothing like the "pop" fiction that made up the other end of that continuum, *taishū bungaku* ("mass literature"), whose chief quality seemed to be its endless repetition of predetermined formulas and, as a result, its easy predictability. Certainly there was nothing predictable about Murakami's novels. Or rather, it became clear over time that Murakami played with the formulas of mass literature—what is elsewhere termed *formulaic fiction*—but at the last minute subverted the expectations of those formulas and left the reader wondering what had just happened. This to some degree accounted for the peculiar sense of simultaneous thrill and discouragement one often felt at the end of some of these texts.

From the beginning it was clear that two principal elements informed Murakami's fiction: a focus on some internal being or consciousness that worked with the conscious self, sometimes in concert, other times antagonistically; and the nearly constant presence of a magical "other world" in which this internal being operated. As such, there was always a tension between the metaphysical—indeed, the magical—and the psychological in his work. Put another way, one was constantly in doubt as to whether Murakami's characters lived in a magical world or were simply out of their minds. This led me, at any rate, to hedge my bets; while exploring how and why Murakami developed an essentially "magical realist" setting for most of his novels, I also explored some of the deeper psychological underpinnings of his work, particularly how language and the unconscious combined to produce, through magical means, living embodiments of the Murakami hero's memories and dreams. This was my way of exploring characters in Murakami's novels that simply *could not* be real: people without names or past histories, fantastic animals or half-animals, talking machines and the like. Terming these "nostalgic images," I determined that they were projections from the protagonist's inner mind, whose relationship with their unconscious origins was metonymical, that is, based on chains of words that were closely related to one another but not the same. Precisely why these images took on forms so radically different from their origins was unclear, but it was one of the stated rules of the game for Murakami, who declared (ostensibly through Nietzsche) that "one cannot understand the gloom of the depths of night in the light of day."[4] From a more psychological perspective, one might simply say that the contents of the inner depths of the unconscious gloom are unfathomable, incomprehensible, as in dreams, and that they have no place in the conscious, physical world of the light. Their presence among us requires radical transfiguration.

And what was the purpose of these nostalgic images? To some extent this too was psychological: they existed in order to assist the protagonist in bearing up beneath the crushing weight of his nostalgic despair. Their task was to emerge into the light, to ease the burden of anguish and confusion suffered by the Murakami hero, who sought, unsuccessfully, the process by which he had lost his youth and become merely another cog in an unfeeling and dehumanizing social System that had appropriated his will, indeed, his very soul.

And the purpose of this overall structure, as I argued in *Dances with Sheep* (2002; my first full-length monograph on Murakami), was to expose, in fictional form, the threat posed to the individual core identity (the author was not yet using terms like *soul*), in constant danger of replacement by the artificially constructed ideologies (what Murakami now terms *monogatari*) of the consumerist Japanese State. In the course of this study it became clear that conclusions to the effect that Murakami had no social or political agenda in his writing were decidedly premature. One might say that readers and critics alike were deflected somewhat by the extraordinarily imaginative form that the author's stories took.

I continue to stand firmly behind the conclusions of *Dances with Sheep;* indeed, the idea of the "core identity" and the dangers it faces have been taken up by subsequent scholars more than once since the book came out, and Murakami's famous "egg and wall" speech, cited above, is merely another expression of the same notion; the egg is but the latest of many metaphors for the individual soul or core identity. At the same time, as is perhaps inevitable when working on a living, developing novelist, there continues to be much to say, and that is the purpose of this volume. Murakami has written four major novels since the publication of *Dances with Sheep,* and these need to be explored within the context of his earlier works, if only to highlight his development to this point.

There is, however, an even more important reason to be writing this current volume. Despite an almost dizzying array of critical writings produced on Murakami's fiction since the mid-1990s—much of it my own—there has yet to be, so far as I know, a concentrated exploration of the author's "metaphysical world" in its own right. Even *Dances with Sheep,* while acutely and constantly aware of the presence of the "other world" in Murakami's writing, is chiefly concerned with how that world manifested itself in *this* world—as image, as language, metaphorically and metonymically. Now, however, as Murakami's career reaches its thirty-fifth year, it is time to explore that "other world" in some detail, to examine its unique characteristics, and to determine, if possible, how it functions in the lives of the characters who access it, draw strength, knowledge, and a sense of identity from it. For those interested in the author himself, it should be noted that such an "other world," usually metaphorized by the author as some sort of "underworld" in his mind, seems to play an indispensable role in his own creative process as well. As Uchida Tatsuru has also recently noted, Murakami's metaphorical descriptions of the writing process invariably involve digging of some kind: "Murakami consistently uses 'digging a hole' as his metaphor for creation. Metaphorically expressing the act of building something, one could just as well say 'building a house,' or 'raising plants,' or 'making dinner,' but Murakami uses nothing but 'digging a hole.'"[5] His choice of metaphor is, I would argue, no accident; rather, it expresses his powerful and recurring image of going beneath the surface, burrowing into the mysterious depths of the inner consciousness, and rooting out things that normally remain hidden from our conscious, physical gaze.

This is an apt description of the author's writing process, but for how long has Murakami been aware of this inner consciousness that lurks beneath the physical? From the very start, it would seem, as one of the key scenes in *Hear the Wind Sing* depicts a boy's descent into a seemingly bottomless Martian well—the underworld—in search of some profound and essential part of himself. This "underworld," one suspects, represents something very real for Murakami, for it is, probably always has been, the source of his unshakable individualism, an essential part of his identity, whether he was aware of it or not. For despite the author's efforts (perhaps a little too insistent?) to present himself as a "normal" man, who had a "normal" childhood, such awareness of and access to the inner consciousness are, in fact, *not* normal; rather, they mark Murakami as an extraordinary person, a kind of genius who possesses the extremely rare combination of being a gifted storyteller and a man capable of seeing an inner world of which most people are only vaguely aware, usually when dreaming or daydreaming. Very likely Murakami was himself not aware of these two traits in himself for quite some time, yet we might see glimpses of them even in his life prior to taking up his pen to begin the novelist's craft.

From Reader to Writer in Twenty-Nine Easy Steps

Murakami Haruki was born in Kyoto on 12 January 1949, though his first memories are of Nishinomiya, a suburb of Osaka. Murakami's parents were both high school teachers, and both taught Japanese grammar and composition, which meant that they were considerably more familiar than most with Japanese canonical literature. Both encouraged their son to read and provided ample reading material—Jay Rubin notes that they collected a considerable body of classic works of world literature—and the young Murakami became acquainted with the greatest literary figures of Europe by the time he reached junior high school.[6]

He did not, however, read the Japanese classics of which his parents were so fond; perhaps in an unconscious act of rebellion—like the preacher's son who deliberately cultivates a reputation for being the worst kid in school—the teenage Murakami chose for his reading matter the novels of American writers such as Raymond Chandler, Truman Capote, and J. D. Salinger. This proved useful to him, for what he was not learning in the very dull English classes he endured in public school, he picked up on his own reading these works in their original English.

This was, then, the literary origin of the man who has since become such a key figure in Japanese literature.

Also in this period—high school—Murakami began what would become a lifelong interest in American jazz music, a subject on which he is now an acknowledged expert. Indeed, one of the more impressive sights I have seen is Murakami's record collection, which fills the custom-built shelves along the walls of his cavernous Tokyo office; it would be difficult to say how many record albums he owns (he collects the old vinyl LPs), but certainly there are many thousands. What is truly remarkable is that he seems to have intimate knowledge of every one of them. This much, at least, comes through in his writing as well, wherein music of various types—rock and roll, jazz, classical—plays a background role, if not a thematic one.

Other than his habit of voraciously reading American fiction in the original English, Murakami's youthful years appear to have had little to distinguish them from those of other Japanese teenagers in the 1960s. During the one interview with Murakami in which we discussed his life—in October 1994—the author rather insistently repeated this fact, perhaps concerned at the time that his novels, containing heavy doses of the metaphysical, the magical realist, were gaining him a reputation as some sort of nut. One item on the agenda for that meeting, for him at least, was to make clear that his work and his life were two separate subjects. Although he enjoyed reading and listening to music, he also had friends. "But I'm not the social type. I had four or five [friends]. But still, I was not a 'problem child.' Just a very ordinary kind of kid. I played baseball, and fished, climbed mountains. There were mountains and a beach. It was a perfect place. I was just an ordinary kid. I didn't work that hard, though my grades weren't all that bad, either."[7]

Rubin does point out that Murakami, like many people born and raised in Kansai (Osaka, Kobe, Kyoto), felt a powerful affinity to this region, to its special dialects of Japanese, to its flavors and cultural past.[8] This fact highlights the courage it must have taken, then, for Murakami to leave his hometown in 1968, at the age of nineteen, to attend Waseda University in Tokyo. Regional cultures aside, Murakami had placed himself into one of the greatest urban centers in the world. "Many people think of me as an urban type," he noted during our interview, "but that's just not so."[9]

Adding to what must have been a stressful transition into Tokyo life was the political turmoil that was reaching its climax on major university campuses around Japan in the late 1960s, but particularly in Tokyo, for this was the era of the so-called Zenkyōtō, the "united front" of students protesting—often violently—the U.S.-Japan Security Treaty of 1960, the continued presence of U.S. troops in Japan, the use of American military bases in Japan as a staging point for military activities in Vietnam, and the presence of nuclear-armed U.S. naval vessels in Japanese ports. The continued U.S. occupation of Okinawa was yet another point of contention. It was a time of political tension, a time when Japan's young people—indeed, young people throughout the world—were more involved in the political process than at any other time in history, before or since. In those heady days there was nothing particularly unusual about a dull lecture being interrupted by helmeted, masked student demonstrators, passing out leaflets and lecturing their fellow students—probably with equal dullness—on the merits of Marxist thought; about a university dormitory being taken over by student radicals; about campus closures.

Murakami, who majored in drama and once thought of becoming a screenwriter, found little to interest him in these political discussions, not because he found Marxism meaningless but because he could not respect the student radicals who professed it. "They had no imagination . . . Like, some of these guys were Marxists. I had nothing against Marxism at that time, but these guys weren't speaking their own words. They just talked in slogans all the time, excerpts from books, that sort of thing. I didn't like that. I mean, the words they used were strong and beautiful, but they weren't their own. So, since then I stopped believing in beautiful words, beautiful slogans, and beautiful theories. I just believe in honest words, from myself."[10]

Herein we see glimpses of the staunch individualist who would cultivate that trait in himself in a variety of ways as his life progressed. In 1971, while still a student, he married his wife, Yōko, against the wishes of both families owing to the fact that neither had yet graduated from college. Three years later, in 1974, the two of them opened a jazz café in Kokubunji called "Peter Cat." A year later Murakami graduated from Waseda University and devoted his time to running their café, which by now had moved to Sendagaya. Even then, it was his wife who had the business acumen, who actually ran the place; Murakami, by nature a shy man, spent his time in the back of the café preparing snacks for customers and chatting with the live entertainment they booked for the club, yet another outlet for his growing knowledge of and interest in jazz music.

So what caused him to begin writing? This is one of those bizarre stories that, in retrospect, seems to fit in with the way Murakami does a lot of things. In his twenty-ninth year, as he sat drinking beer at Jingū Stadium in Tokyo, watching a baseball game between the Yakult Swallows and the Hiroshima Carp, the batter Dave Hilton hit a double. At that moment it struck him: "'That's it. I think I'll write a novel.'"[11] Exactly what the connection is between Dave Hilton's double and Murakami's sudden decision to write a novel is unclear; most likely, it has never been clear to Murakami himself. Perhaps he had finally caught the sound of his own inner voice, one that still speaks to him and through him to this day. Somehow, out of this strange and fathomless epiphany experienced by the shy, yet individualistic owner of a jazz café, there emerged one of the most innovative and unusual writers Japan has ever known.

Murakami as Global Writer

Innovation begins and ends for Murakami with his use of language. His sense of rhythm seems at least partially attributable to his aforementioned knowledge of—and love for—music, particularly American jazz. The American "tone" of his work has been evident from the beginning, and he was initially compared to Kurt Vonnegut and John Irving.[12] This rhythm and tone were the beginning of what would become known as the author's "nationality-less" *(mukokuseki)* style,[13] an early manifestation of which, no doubt, led Ōe Kenzaburō to comment to British novelist Kazuo Ishiguro in 1993 that "'Murakami Haruki writes in Japanese, but his writing is not really Japanese. If you translate it into American English, it can be read very naturally in New York.'"[14] Ōe is not so much critiquing Murakami as expressing his wonder at how much Japanese writing has changed, at last reaching a stage of "internationalization" (to borrow a major 1980s catchphrase) of which writers in his generation could hardly dream.

This *mukokuseki* style has proved an effective passport for Murakami's entry into cultures around the world, particularly those in East Asia. Critic Chang Mingmin states that Murakami caused the first revival of interest in Japanese literature in Taiwan since Japan's recognition of the People's Republic of China in 1972,[15] and Kim Yang-su notes that Murakami has (partially, at least) overcome half a century of Korean animosity toward Japan following half a century of colonial rule, and now stands at the forefront of a new body of East Asian writers—many of them influenced by Murakami himself—who are poised to develop "a cultural autonomous zone in which the weight of nationalism is eliminated . . . where [these writers] will be able to interact freely."[16]

The *mukokuseki* style both influences and is influenced by Murakami's long-standing relationship with translated literature. It is well known that the author taught himself to read English through American popular fiction during his adolescence and that his style and approach to writing, as noted above, owe much to writers like Vonnegut and Irving, as well as Raymond Carver, Raymond Chandler, Truman Capote, and J. D. Salinger, among others. He admits to having experimented early in his career with writing in English and translating himself back into Japanese in an effort to simplify his style.[17] His ultimate goal has been to reinvent the Japanese literary language in a manner that suits him, and this new style filters into his own translations into Japanese of Capote, Fitzgerald, and Salinger. Numano Mitsuyoshi, one of the more prolific Murakami critics, comments on the peculiar effectiveness of Murakami's use of pronouns like *kimi* ("you," familiar, referring to the implied reader) in translating Holden's monologue in *Catcher in the Rye*.[18] Kazamaru Yoshihiko similarly notes Murakami's violation of certain key sociolinguistic rules in Japanese (again, mostly centering on pronouns), but his more significant analysis focuses on the rhythm of the author's prose; this rhythm, grounded in the skillful use of connective terms like *soshite* and *keredomo* ("and then" and "however," respectively), forms the basis of what he terms Murakami's "translationese tone" *(hon'yakuchō)*.[19]

This atmosphere of translation is undoubtedly one major reason Murakami's works read well in other languages, as Ōe's comment above suggests. And while some Western critics have been irked by the absence of anything "quaintly Japanese" in Murakami fiction, there can be little doubt that his *mukokuseki* style plays an important role in the attention he has received outside of Japan.

Murakami as a Japanese Writer

Nevertheless, Murakami is deeply committed to Japan, to his readers and their welfare. While the first fifteen years or so of his career were spent telling the stories of detached, disinterested young men who did not seem to care much about anything (written by a novelist who preferred living in Europe, the Mediterranean, or America, anywhere but Japan), a change seems to have come over Murakami in the early to mid-1990s. There are a number of likely reasons for this. First and foremost has to do with Murakami's years spent abroad. It is not uncommon for persons living abroad for extended periods to rediscover their identity as a member of the culture they have left behind. Having essentially "escaped" his homeland—ostensibly to get away from the pressures of being a famous writer in Japan, with all the responsibilities that come with it—Murakami very likely came to recognize himself, perhaps for the first time in his life, as a Japanese and to feel some sense of responsibility for his land and people. This was very nearly what he tried to tell me, though not in so many words, in October 1994 when he said that he was beginning to feel a sense of responsibility to his readers and to Japanese literature. "I am forty-five years old, you know, and I can't be a rebel all my life. I think right now may also be a turning point for me."[20] Interestingly, this comment came at a point when the third volume of *Nejimakidori kuronikuru* (1994–96; translated as *The Wind-Up Bird Chronicle*) was approximately two-thirds completed, and the author appeared uncertain himself how the novel would end; would the protagonist's wife, Kumiko, trapped in the metaphysical world, be permitted to escape her prison? In the end she does escape, but it is unclear whether she ever manages to recover her missing sense of individual self. This in itself seems to express some of the ambivalence Murakami felt, or perhaps even his precarious position, poised atop the dividing line between self-absorption and social commitment, at that precise moment.

Given that Murakami's suggestion of a "turning point" came more than two months before the Hanshin-Awaji earthquake of 17 January 1995, and almost exactly five months prior to the Aum Shinrikyō subway attack of 20 March that same year in Tokyo, it would be in error to suggest that those two incidents were what finally prompted Murakami to take up a more proactive role in his society. It would, however, be reasonable to suggest that these two incidents confirmed in Murakami his sense of commitment to the Japanese people and his own sense of duty to play a role in the improvement of that society.

Whatever the cause of Murakami's greater interest in doing something for his homeland, it is safe to say that his narrators/protagonists gradually gave up their frustrating habit of saying "Whatever!" (or as a Japanese might say, *yare yare*) each time they encountered the inexplicable and of putting their faces back into their mugs of warm beer and tears. In fact, with the publication of *The Wind-Up Bird Chronicle* the Murakami hero acquires not only a new name (Okada Tōru) but a new attitude that sustains him to the completion of his quest, which in this case is to rescue his wife, Kumiko, from the clutches of her evil brother, Wataya Noboru. Not only does Tōru complete his task, but he goes so far as to bash in the brains of his archenemy with a baseball bat in the process. This was decidedly a first in Murakami fiction.

One aspect of Murakami's writing that has not changed, in its essence at any rate, is its emphasis on the "inner self" or "core self" of the individual, as we see reflected in the author's Jerusalem speech as well. This concern for the "soul," as he termed it in that speech, has been a central facet of his writing from the start, when in *Hear the Wind Sing* a boy enters a deep Martian well, wanders around for 1.5 billion years, and then emerges to have a nice little conversation with his own inner self, here taking the form of the wind. The next few novels—including *Pinball, 1973*, and the first of Murakami's works to be released in English, *Hitsuji o meguru bōken* (1982; translated as *A Wild Sheep Chase*)—also included movement in and out of the protagonist's inner mind, where he meets people and things once lost and believed gone forever. These early protagonists—universally known to us as "Boku," the first-person familiar pronoun "I"—somehow seem to represent lost souls in Murakami's universe. They are young men in their late twenties or early thirties, trying to figure out how they managed to get to where they are, and yet having virtually nothing to show for it. These young men either invent quests for themselves or have such quests thrust upon them, but invariably their adventures end up little more than the aimless pursuit for self-understanding. This is not to say that such efforts are without value, but until the mid-1990s, it would be safe to say, the insights gained by the Murakami protagonist tended to be rather minimal.

That protagonist's lot improved, however, as Murakami's self-confidence as a writer grew, along with his gradual understanding and acceptance of what had happened to his generation following the collapse of the 1960s student movements and the general spirit of activism that seemed to electrify Japan at the time. If the 1960s were a kind of day-to-day thrill ride for the author's generation—raised in the affluent 1950s and gripped by the worldwide revolutionary spirit of the 1960s during their late teens—the 1970s were a time of comparative lethargy and confusion; early Murakami fiction sought to make some sense of how they had lost their way. "We needed ten years to turn around," Murakami once commented. "Our generation was confused, so it took us the ten years of the 1970s to get back to real life."[21]

Since those early days, Murakami has expanded his fictional landscape considerably, writing novels that combine the basic tropes of magical realism with science fiction *(Sekai no owari to hādo-boirudo wandārando,* 1985; translated as *Hard-Boiled Wonderland and the End of the World),* with romance *(Kokkyō no minami, taiyō no nishi,* 1992, translated as *South of the Border, West of the Sun;* and *Supūtoniku no koibito,* 1999, translated as *The Sputnik Sweetheart),* with the psychological thriller *(The Wind-Up Bird Chronicle),* and even with the quasi-spiritual *(Umibe no Kafka,* 2002, translated as *Kafka on the Shore; 1Q84,* 2009–10, translated as *1Q84).* Clearly the author's reputation for being Japan's premier writer of magical realist fiction—that is, fiction in which the setting is realistic yet contains definite elements of the supernatural that call attention to themselves, but must be accepted by readers as part of the "normal" world—is well deserved. From talking pinball machines and grubby little men running around in even filthier sheep suits in his early works, to an unconscious hotel that can only be reached through magical means, from walking and talking spirits who take on the forms of "Johnny Walker" and "Colonel Sanders" (of Scotch whiskey and KFC fame, respectively), to time slips that leave us in a world that contains two moons, the author simply does not seem capable of resisting the paranormal, the bizarre, and at times the utterly funny. Even the one work Murakami himself likes to claim as a "realistic" novel, *Noruwei no mori* (1987; translated as *Norwegian Wood*), has points at which, as will be shown later in this book, the magical makes a subtle appearance.

Enter the "Other World"

The mechanism by which the magical is presented in Murakami's fiction is what has been called the "other world," sometimes called "over there." Murakami himself chooses not to define—or even properly name—this realm, and Japanese critics, depending on their approach, have used a variety of terminology, from *naibu* (the interior) to even more abstract expressions, such as *achiragawa,* or "over there." From a psychological perspective, it is an obvious representation of the unconscious, though not every critic is prepared to make that case; Tanaka Masashi prefers the terms *gaiteki genjitsu* and *naiteki genjitsu* ("external reality" and "internal reality," respectively) and moreover argues that what Murakami means by terms like *jiga* and *jiko* (roughly equivalent to "ego" and "self," respectively) is not the same thing the psychoanalyst means.[22] This is probably true, but we would be wise to recall that Murakami represents concepts like these very differently from specialists in the field and makes no pretense of attempting psychoanalytical "cures" in his fiction; he is, rather, concerned with portraying the inner mind—the realm to which we retreat when we dream—in visual terms his readers will understand, and in philosophical terms that will establish its purpose, both for his characters and for his readers. Jungian scholar Kawai Toshio has no difficulty in calling Murakami's metaphysical realm the unconscious (using the standard term *muishiki*) but warns that any attempt at actual psychoanalysis through these fictional works is pointless.[23] Kawai's sentiments echo those of his father, the late Kawai Hayao, credited with introducing Jungian theory to Japan, who argues that Murakami's stories give us "not so much the analytical results of scientific investigation, but a plenitude of hints about life."[24]

Whatever our terminology, this "other world" or "metaphysical realm" (the expression I have elected to use for the remainder of this book) is in my view the most recognizable and critical aspect of Murakami Haruki's fiction, for the simple reason that it leads us to what the author has termed the inner *monogatari,* or "narrative," a key part of the inner "core self" that grounds and informs the conscious self, while simultaneously tapping into *the* collective Narrative, with a capital *N,* that results from the entire history—even the prehistory—of human experience. This realm, as the most central and significant facet of Murakami's fictional landscape, is the principal topic of this book. My ultimate purpose in this monograph is to offer as detailed an explication as possible of that metaphysical realm, to understand what it looks like, how it has evolved over the years, how it is accessed, how it functions in the lives of the characters who populate the Murakami fictional landscape.

As we do this, however, we are likely to find ourselves discussing how this metaphysical realm, potentially, affects the very real people who read Murakami's books (and perhaps those who do not), as well. What I mean is that fictional though Murakami's portrayals of the metaphysical realm unquestionably are, they are also tied inextricably to the notion of the inner self and the inner "narrative" that feeds and nurtures the development of that self in the real world.

Murakami first began talking about the inner narrative, what he terms the *monogatari,* in the afterword to *Andāguraundo* (1997; Underground), a collection of interviews with survivors (or families of nonsurvivors) of the "sarin incident," in which members of the Aum Shinrikyō,[25] a radical cult led by Asahara Shōkō, released liquid sarin (a nerve agent with similar effects to the mustard gas used in World War I) into selected subway stations and trains in Tokyo during the morning rush hour of March 20, 1995. The attack killed a dozen people outright and physically and/or emotionally injured thousands more—many were left with permanent damage to their brains and nervous systems. As we shall see in greater detail in chapter 4, dealing with the journalistic aspects of this text, Murakami's purpose was to restore individual human faces and personalities for the victims, who had for the most part been presented by the media as a faceless mass of people. The media sought to develop a simple opposition between "good" and "evil" in discussing ordinary citizens versus the Aum Shinrikyō, Murakami argues, and "it was probably easier to present the circumstances with victims who didn't have any faces."[26]

In restoring those lost faces to the victims of the sarin incident, Murakami needed first to hear their individual stories about the attack, what they saw and what they felt, and in this way he hoped to reconstruct them as three-dimensional people in his text. But Murakami's interest lay not merely in the content of the stories he was told but rather in the unique manner in which a story expresses something unique that lurks inside the storyteller. His awareness of this function of narration did not come about as a result of the sarin incident; indeed, fully half a year before the incident, during our 1994 interview, Murakami spoke about the "power of the story," suggesting that it possessed for him the ability to express things beyond mere words:

> Like, in *Norwegian Wood,* there is a part where Midori asks the protagonist, "How much do you love me?" And he has to make up a story. If he just says, "I love you very, very much," she will not be impressed at all, right? So he has to make up a story. Just like, "Oh, I was walking in the woods in springtime, and then a bear came along. . . ." *[laughs]* Just like that. Then she is impressed. That scenery, that dialogue, that feel . . . everything. In that way, he expresses how he loves her. *That's* the power of the story.[27]

It must have been around this time that Murakami was thinking with some intensity about the inner narrative as a vastly powerful element in the human ego, one that not only serves to construct/define the self but also sustains and is fed by the self. In October 1994 Murakami could still joke about this aspect of the human mind, for the tragedies of January 17 and March 20, 1995, were still months away. Writing of this inner narrative in *Underground,* on the other hand, the author is considerably more serious:

> It is true, if you lose your ego, you also lose that consistent story that you call your self. But people cannot live long without a narrative. That is because the narrative is the means by which you transcend the logical system (or systematic logic) that surrounds and limits you; it is the key to sharing time and experience with others, a pressure valve.
>
> Of course, a narrative is a "story," and "stories" are neither logic nor ethics. It is a dream you continue to have. You might, in fact, not even be aware of it. But, just like breathing, you continue incessantly to see this dream. In this dream you are just an existence with two faces. You are at once corporeal and shadow. You are the "maker" of the narrator, and at the same time you are the "player" who experiences the narrative.[28]

Is Murakami here describing what psychology terms alternately the "mirror stage," or "individuation," in which we become conscious of our subjectivity by imagining our objectivity in the gaze of an other? Perhaps, but analysis of Murakami's writing has a tendency to get murky when we start attempting to apply hard-core psychological theory to it, as noted above by both Kawai Hayao and Kawai Toshio, and my inclination is to comprehend this statement in terms of the symbiotic relationship between experience and memory. What I mean by this is that, using the author's own terminology, we possess a core inside our metaphysical realm—if we insist on a metaphor, we could perhaps think of it as a computer's hard disk drive. Into this hard disk drive we constantly input everything we experience through our various five senses. Much of this is too inconsequential for our conscious mind to notice; some is repetition of previous experience ad nauseum—the taste of orange juice, the experience of telling time—but it all goes into the hard drive just the same. (Repetitive activities are, incidentally, constantly being measured against past experiences; aberrations are noted.) However, like any good computer system, our hard drive encodes the data we give it, orders it according to its own system; it is not meant to be viewed as raw data, nor is it comprehensible as such. (Anyone who has "opened" an executable [.exe] file on a computer knows what this looks like; yet "run" the program, and it can become a word processor, a photo organizer, a game, an Internet browser, and so on.)

But this is not all. Our "hard drives"—our narratives—are not isolated. At least, within the literary framework of Murakami Haruki they are not. Instead, like computers connected to the Internet, all of our individual inner narratives are linked to and feed into one great narrative, what I will call *the* Narrative, the story that has been written and continues to be written constantly, incessantly, from the time when humans had only just evolved. This master Narrative belongs to everyone, yet it cannot fully be pinned down, for it never stays quite the same. In some ways it is like Carl Jung's "collective unconscious," and in other ways it is like the anima mundi—the world soul—of which mystics speak. In *Star Wars* it would be "the Force," a vast, endlessly changing field of energy and experience that is constantly fed with new data from billions of individual narratives, while at the same time making itself (in minute doses) available to our individual narratives for, returning to the computer metaphor, "updates."

But herein lies a problem: just as users of the Internet find it difficult to judge "good" information from "bad," real e-mail from spam, our narratives cannot always be certain they are tapping into *the* Narrative. In fact, our world is filled with group narratives—systems of thought, ideologies—that claim to be *the* Narrative, yet are not. When the individual is fooled into believing that these group narratives are *the* Narrative, they are easily tempted into surrendering their individual narrative to the demands of the group one. This happens, for instance, when organized religion, political ideologies, or philosophical ideas become too powerful, especially when they are centered upon one charismatic individual or idea.

Whether he realized it or not, Murakami spent the first fifteen years or so of his career writing about characters whose individual narratives are threatened with being subsumed into a group narrative (but not *the* Narrative). In the so-called Rat Trilogy—which includes *Hear the Wind Sing, Pinball, 1973,* and *A Wild Sheep Chase*—the *group* narrative is "Japan, Inc.," and it demands from its participants a wholehearted abandonment of individual values in favor of those determined by the group narrative. Seen from this angle, the Rat Trilogy is actually a tetralogy, since the fourth and final work dealing with this protagonist, *Dansu dansu dansu* (1988; translated as *Dance Dance Dance*), really brings to a fine point Murakami's attack on late-model capitalism, which fuels and drives forward the "Japan, Inc." model.

Later novels deal with different collective narratives, but most have something to do with control over the ability or right or simply willingness of the individual to continue developing his or her own inner narrative. How that "narrative" is depicted, not surprisingly, changes over time: a tiny mechanical implant in the protagonist's brain in *Hard-Boiled Wonderland and the End of the World,* a sort of fetal blob in *The Wind-Up Bird Chronicle,* a disembodied voice in *Kafka on the Shore.* In each case, an individual does battle with an apparently invincible foe in order to maintain individual autonomy or to restore this autonomy to others. This is what Murakami means when he speaks of individual eggs hurling themselves at a solid wall; yet in the conflicts that are joined in these works, particularly during the past decade or so, the eggs do seem to be holding their own.

This began with *The Wind-Up Bird Chronicle,* in which Okada Tōru, the work's mild-mannered protagonist, actually succeeds in his quest of drawing his kidnapped wife out of her unconscious prison and in the process beats her brother, Wataya Noboru, to death with a baseball bat. This was the signal from Murakami that some of his protagonists were about to drop their nice-guy facade and start kicking some ass. Later protagonists commit even more shocking acts in the name of self-preservation. Fifteen-year-old Tamura Kafka, by the end of his narrative, will have hacked his father to death with a kitchen knife (albeit by proxy), seduced a woman he imagines to be his mother, and forcibly raped a girl he thinks might be his sister (in the metaphysical realm, but still . . .). The heroine of *1Q84* is a professional assassin and seems quite prepared to kill as many as she must to protect the man she loves and the baby growing in her womb. There can be no doubt that the Murakami hero/heroine has both grown up and grown tremendously strong in the thirty-odd years since the hero of *A Wild Sheep Chase,* following a singularly unsatisfying quest to find his best friend, sits weeping on a beach, inconsolable, filled with his own sense of longing and loss and, yes, even self-pity.

Into the Cellar of Our Minds

For Murakami, the development of this stronger, more self-reliant protagonist has been a long and arduous process involving years of digging into his own inner self, exploring some of the darkest reaches of his soul. In an interview shortly after the publication of *Kafka on the Shore,* the author described the human mind in the terms of a two-story house, complete with basement. His comment is somewhat long but interesting enough to merit being quoted in full here:

> "I think of human existence as being like a two-story house. On the first floor people gather together to take their meals, watch television, and talk. The second floor contains private chambers, bedrooms where people go to read books, listen to music by themselves, and so on. Then there is a basement; this is a special place, and there are a number of things stored here. We don't use this room much in our daily life, but sometimes we come in, vaguely hang around the place. Then, my thought is that underneath that basement room is yet another basement room. This one has a very special door, very difficult to figure out, and normally you can't get in there—some people never get in at all. . . . You go in, wander about in the darkness, and experience things there you wouldn't see in the normal parts of the house. You connect with your past there, because you have entered into your own soul. But then you come back. If you stay over there for long you can never get back to reality.
>
> My sense is that a novelist is someone who can consciously do that sort of thing."[29]

Looking at Murakami's model, we see that the ground and second floors of his house represent consciousness, the physical realm, clearly enough. The first level of the basement is a shallow level of the metaphysical realm and is accessible both awake (as memory) and asleep (as dream). This is where we store memories, let our (conscious) imaginations wander, and in the most general sense of the word, "think."

What, then, is the basement level beneath the first basement? This, I think, is where the "narrative" of which Murakami speaks is kept, and he is quite correct in saying that we do not normally enter this room—at least, not by our own will or volition. However, it also must be said that just as the computer's CPU continually accesses the hard disk drive for information needed to deal with each electronic impulse that runs through itself and its memory chips, we are in constant unconscious contact with this deepest level of our "soul" *(tamashii),* as Murakami terms it, for this is how we constantly apprehend the world, take in its sensations of every type, and make sense of them.

The part that Murakami leaves out of his model, of course, is the underground plumbing, and this includes both the "water supply," through which all psychic/metaphysical input is imported, and the "drainage system," through which our psychic/metaphysical output is exported back to the collective whole, *the* Narrative. Murakami claims to climb down into this second-level basement each time he writes, to touch base with the source of his imagination and bring back to the surface—in narrative form—whatever can be carried. At the same time, it is precisely this second-level basement wherein the drama of the Murakami novel is enacted, to where his characters must go in order to confront themselves and those who seek to appropriate their selves. It is, therefore, the primary topic of this monograph, whose purpose will be to help readers to understand how that metaphysical realm works.

This topic does lead to some interesting challenges for this book. How does one make sense of the "metaphysical"? For that matter, what does the word *metaphysical* even signify for us? In the context of Murakami fiction, it really has two primary meanings: first, and most literally, it refers to that which is beyond the physical. In this sense it covers things that are part of our own everyday parlance as well, from the "paranormal" (in which many people do not believe) to "the mind" (in which most people do). That which is metaphysical is "real," in the sense that we can see its effects, feel its effects, yet it does not have a (comprehensible) physical state.

The second meaning for *metaphysical,* in the Murakami fictional world, is that which actually appears to have a tangible element but exists inside some realm that does not. In this case I refer to the inner mind, which for Murakami's characters is more than simply vague mental images, as it is in our nonfictional world, but which contains apparently tangible things as well. It is in this realm that Boku can drink metaphysical beer with his dead friend Rat, can play a metaphysical game of pinball on his dead girlfriend Naoko, where Okada Tōru can beat his metaphysical brother-in-law to death with a metaphysical baseball bat, and Tamura Kafka can rape his would-be sister. These things really happen, and yet they happen in a virtual world that happens to feel quite as physical, as tangible, as our own waking, conscious world.

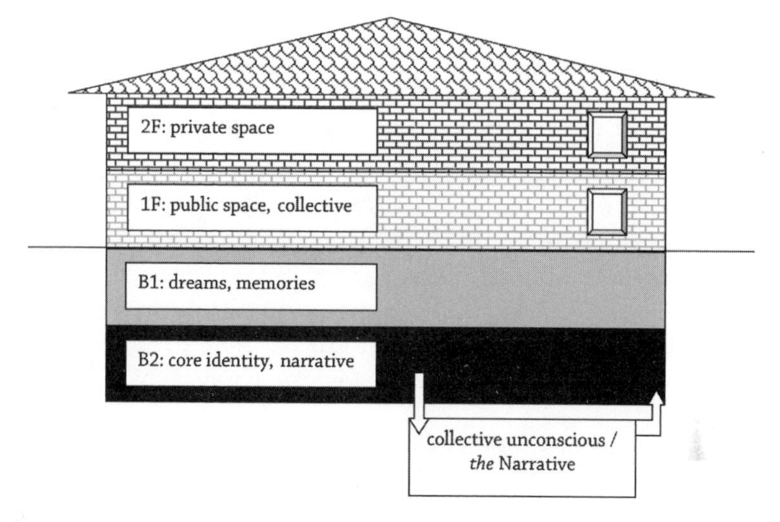

The two-story house metaphor

This, however, is finally an illusion; the inner mind has no true physical body, no tangible reality, but only deceives us into believing these things are there. Such concepts put us into contact with a very traditional Japanese view of the spirit world. Mythologist Kamata Tōji, writing of ancient Japan and its Shintō traditions, divides these realms into those of the "visible" and "invisible":

> Since ancient times, engaging in various religious mysteries and ascetic devotions, it was understood that we are not limited merely to these physical bodies that we can see with our eyes, touch with our hands. In other words, in addition to the body we can see and touch, people thought there was another, more exquisite and detailed body, invisible to our eyes.[30]

Casting Kamata's use of the terms *visible* and *invisible* into a somewhat more modern form, psychologist Iwamiya Keiko notes that "the world is not constructed merely of reality we can see with our eyes; different worlds (other worlds) are layered on top of it. . . . this 'invisible body' is profoundly linked to the invisible functioning of our minds, our souls."[31]

Kamata's and Iwamiya's way of characterizing the metaphysical realm as one in which the "invisible" self lurks is useful in that it reminds us of the constant presence of the metaphysical world around us. It may be tempting to view these realms as mutually exclusive, but in fact, just as psychoanalysts speak of the barrier between conscious and unconscious being permeable, seldom fixed or firm, we should recognize that the physical/visible and metaphysical/invisible realms are a symbiotic structure; neither is capable of existing wholly on its own, and neither ever achieves total dominance over the other. To repeat my earlier statement, the physical self is responsible for perceiving and experiencing the world around itself; it is the task of the metaphysical to process, store, and explain those perceptions and experiences. This is the purpose of Murakami's metaphysical realm as well.

This monograph examines Murakami's portrayal of the metaphysical world and its various manifestations chiefly as functions of language. The initial chapter explores the function of language, how it grounds, expresses, and most importantly, *constitutes* both the physical and metaphysical worlds. The strategy of this maneuver is to deconstruct the privileging of "physical" over "metaphysical" (as, for instance, "real" and "unreal," or, more pertinently, "true" and "false") to expose the fallacy of objective reality and argue that *all* realities are grounded in perception, language, experience, and culture. This is more than simply an exercise in skepticism, for my task is not to deny reality but to understand better what reality is, how it comes into being and how, in too many cases, we fail to comprehend that realities pressed upon us as "absolute" are all too often nothing more than constructs of language, whose certainty breaks down under more careful scrutiny. This subject has been of particular significance to those writers whose interest lies in the realm of semiotics, and it has proved an important facet of Murakami's writing as well.

The second chapter provides a detailed look at the metaphysical realm as a central feature of the Murakami literary universe, exploring its principal characteristics, how it is accessed, what its various functions are. We will discover, among other things, that Murakami's metaphysical realm shares numerous points in common with the unconscious as it was envisioned by both Freud and Jung, not merely as a repository for memories or a source of libido (à la Freud), but also as a sort of spirit world, a dwelling place for the souls of the dead, and a source of connection to a more collective sphere of human spiritual experience (Jung). Like the theoretical unconscious, the metaphysical realm as portrayed in Murakami fiction is freed from the constraints of time and space, permitting visitors to travel freely not only across vast distances in an instant (via a kind of metaphysical "wormhole") but also across the temporal boundaries that divide historical epochs, indeed, that separate past from present from future. In fact, we will find that in Murakami's idea of the metaphysical world there is no "past" or "present," only an endlessly self-replicating *now*.

The uses for this metaphysical realm, as we will see, are varied, but virtually all are tied to the idea of establishing, maintaining, or otherwise protecting individual identity—the internal narrative—while at the same time establishing contact with others. In early works, as noted above, this may amount to little more than a character rooting around in his inner mind, rediscovering things he has lost or forgotten; in later works the metaphysical becomes a sort of battleground on which a guerilla war is fought between the System and the individual, the prize being control of the individual soul. This is highlighted in the third chapter of this volume, dealing with concepts such as fate and free will, and establishing—partially via the arguments of chapter 1—that "fate" itself is by no means absolute; rather, as yet another construct grounded in language (which is itself always grounded in culture, in human perception), ideas like "fate" and "determinism" are used to deceive the individual into imagining he or she has no room to maneuver. Chapter 3 looks at the recognizably mythological undertones to Murakami's fiction, from beginning to now, in order to see how the Murakami protagonist has struggled with each successive attempt on his or her autonomy, culminating in the use of some fairly unexpected tactics on the part of the most recent heroes to overcome fate, or at least to turn it to their advantage. The chapter also examines the author's most recent depictions—in the context of a post–sarin incident and post-9/11 world—of the relationship between true spirituality and organized religion.

In a somewhat logical fashion, this will return our attention in the fourth chapter to questions of representation, of reality versus imagination, and permit us to consider some of the formalistic tropes of representing either. In this chapter we will explore in particular Murakami's forays into the world of current events, his contributions to the largely unremarked genre of literary journalism, and a related new one we will call *journalistic fiction*. My argument in this chapter will be, in a rough nutshell, that although objective fact is a fallacy, always grounded in the subjective perception of the writer, there are nonetheless degrees of subjectivity/objectivity, and that by shifting emphasis from a largely objective mode of reporting to a largely subjective one, we open the door to entirely new ways of representing actual events, through creative nonfiction and through fiction that contains recognizable elements of current events, thus bringing to the fore elements of those events that had not truly come into existence via mainstream reporting.

The volume concludes with a close reading of Murakami's most recent novel, *Shikisai o motanai Tazaki Tsukuru to, kare no junrei no toshi* (2013; translated as *Colorless Tsukuru Tazaki and His Years of Pilgrimage*). In some ways this chapter will prove an anomaly to the rest of the volume, in that it focuses not on a particular theme but rather on a particular text. I do this partly to acquaint readers with this new work, which hopefully will be available in English translation by the time this monograph is released, or at least shortly thereafter, but also to provide a sense of closure for the discussion *up to this point*, for as we will see, *Tazaki Tsukuru* expresses a great many of the critical themes that will be discussed in the four chapters that precede the final one.

Let us, then, embark on our exploration of the "other world" of Murakami Haruki, a world made up of language and of memory, less tangible yet no less "real" than the world we inhabit every day ourselves. For, as we are shortly to discover, some of the answers to our most vexing questions about consciousness, about existence itself, lie just beyond the border between physical and metaphysical, just "over there."

ONE

New Words, New Worlds

> When I write, I'm kind of like a god, creating everything. I create what looks real to me.
>
> —Murakami Haruki

IN ONE OF HIS VERY FIRST SHORT STORIES, "Binbō na obasan no hanashi" (translated by Jay Rubin as "A Poor Aunt's Story"), Murakami Haruki's ubiquitous nameless protagonist "Boku" explains the pale image of a middle-aged woman clinging to his back as *tada no kotoba,* or "just words." In this one brief statement, Murakami sums up a facet of his fiction that is both simple and yet deceptively complex. It is simple in the same sense that God's declaration in the opening lines of Genesis is simple: "Let there be light," says God, and sure enough, light comes into being. But therein lies a multitude of complex questions. We are not gods; can we, therefore, merely speak (or write) and cause new realities to come into being? Is the reality that exists outside our minds and our consciousness truly there, does it exist? If so, *how* does it exist? How do we comprehend its existence? And if, as a result of our speaking, some new reality comes into being, what qualities must that reality possess for others to accept its existence as legitimate? Who, in fact, is qualified to speak, and who is not?

Some of these questions lie within that branch of philosophy known as phenomenology, the chief interest of which is how the sentient human being perceives and makes sense of the world external to his or her mind. My own phenomenological approach—one supported by the texts that will be treated below—is grounded in the idea that nothing *meaningfully* exists outside the human mind that has not first been passed through the filters of language, experience, and culture. At the same time, as a linguist and a humanist I cannot help but be skeptical—even seriously doubtful—about the ability of language and experience to mediate effectively between my thoughts and the world I perceive around me through my senses. It is from this essential point of skepticism and doubt that I approach my world, and from which, I believe, Murakami's protagonists approach theirs.

In this chapter, we will examine several of Murakami's most recent works, particularly *Kafka on the Shore* and *1Q84,* in order to see how he places words and language *first,* and existence *second,* thus positing for language a clearly constitutive function, that is, the power to create new realities. We will also look at several early Murakami texts that reveal the roots of this concept.

At this point it is useful to retrace briefly the theory of the "nostalgic image" to note the metonymical connections between images of the inner mind and the realities that flow from it. As noted in the introduction, the Murakami protagonist, caught in the grip of a nostalgic obsession for things and people he has lost, unwittingly "conjures" the unconscious objects of his obsession (memories) into the conscious world as "nostalgic images," persons and objects that are (mostly) solid and (almost) real, yet not (entirely) real. These nostalgic images are linguistically grounded; like clever wordplays, they are linked to their unconscious origins via one or more words.

A useful case in point is *Pinball, 1973,* a sequel to *Hear the Wind Sing,* which explores its protagonist's sense of loss as he ponders the death of his girlfriend, Naoko, and the disappearance of his best friend, Rat. Boku is comforted along the way by "the Twins," identical girls whom he discovers sleeping on either side of himself one morning after a night of heavy drinking. Despite their insistence that they are totally different from one another, physically the girls are indistinguishable but for their sweatshirts, emblazoned with the numbers "208" and "209." Even more confusing is the fact that the girls have no names. Prompted to choose names, the girls suggest a series of binary oppositions—"up and down," "left and right," "vertical and horizontal," and so on. Boku's suggestion is "entrance and exit," which leads him to consider things that have entrances but *not* exits, such as mousetraps. And this leads us to Boku's best friend, Rat. The Twins are, in fact, nostalgic images who stand in for the missing Rat; their identical surface features mask their opposite natures beneath, much as Rat and Boku look similar yet are quite different.

Midway through *Pinball, 1973* Boku takes it into his head to go hunting for a pinball machine known as "the Spaceship," on which he often played during his time with Naoko. He eventually traces the machine to a collector in Tokyo and arranges to visit the machine. Upon locating it, locked up with hundreds of others in a freezing cold storage facility, he does not play it but instead holds an intimate lover's conversation with it—we are perhaps mildly surprised that the pinball machine talks *back* to him. He then returns home with a vague sense of comfort. The name *Spaceship* is key, for it connects with *Naoko* as a storyteller. As a young man, Boku spent a lot of his time listening to stories, some told to him by Naoko, others, according to his narrator, by people from on other planets. "Spaceship" connects to "other planets," which leads to "stories" and finally to "Naoko." Given the somewhat fantastical nature of Boku's encounter with the machine, it is no great leap to see the machine as a nostalgic image for Naoko herself. Like the Twins, however, this connection is grounded in linguistics, in wordplay.

Nostalgic images, conjurings of the protagonists' tormented minds, form one important and largely unremarked facet of Murakami's work as a writer: namely, to expose the potential power of language—our internal language—to constitute the *real* world around us. In that same gesture, however, such images force us to question the existence of objective reality.

The Ontological Status of Language

One need not suppose that such skepticism toward the external world is always such a bad thing. Indeed, having once accepted that there is no *absolute* reality in the world external to our minds (the conscious world), none, at any rate, that is not filtered through the medium of language, we recognize that language fulfills the extraordinary and necessary function of constituting reality nonstop, creating it anew in our minds from moment to moment. The first premise of our reading strategy for this chapter will therefore be to state clearly that everything we believe ourselves to see "outside" ourselves is created first on the "inside"—in our minds—through language.

But language does not exist in a vacuum; it is, rather, dependent on two fundamental factors: experience and culture. Both of these factors come (perhaps a bit paradoxically) from the world around us. Anyone looking at his or her own life can draw the same conclusion: we move through the world, perceiving phenomena, reacting to them (as they react to us), storing the results—our experiences—in our minds via language. The sum total of these collective experiences, conscious and unconscious (including those contained in what Jung describes as the collective unconscious), is culture; the sum total of our individual experiences, taken in conjunction with culture, results in the self. As we move through the world, performing these operations more or less constantly, we both act upon the culture around us and are acted upon *by* that culture. And as we do so, we ceaselessly make and remake the world around us in our minds through language. But the world we make is never any better or worse than the language at our command. Infants and small children create simplistic visions of the world because their command of the language is only barely formed. I am not thinking here of vocabulary so much as of the ability to conceptualize, for not all language is words; from gestures, facial expressions, and seemingly meaningless sounds to symbolic logic, musical notation, pure mathematics, and scientific symbols, all of these are forms of language. Language, for the purposes of this chapter, is best understood to be a symbolic or representational system by which intelligent beings order the world around them in their minds, and communicate that order (as far as possible) to others and to themselves.

Linguists and language-based philosophers have understood for some time—followed, a little reluctantly, by members of other fields—that language is more than simply a tool for describing things the way they are, or even for communicating those descriptions. At one theoretical extreme, thinkers like Michel Foucault and Jacques Derrida have constructed complex arguments questioning the structure of power, of subjectivity, of the privileging of one side of a binary opposition ("up" is better than "down," "true" trumps "false," and so on), grounding their critiques of social systems in how language is manipulated. Such ideas have exerted considerable effect on virtually every field of discourse that relies on language to present its case (and what field of discourse does not?), proving to be a source of liberation for once peripheralized areas of social politics and theory—feminism, postcolonialism, and queer theory, to name a few. At the same time, given that these theories also imply a powerful subjective element in language, they prove unnerving to those fields that traditionally place a premium on objective and detached inquiry.

As recently as 1987, for instance, intellectual historian John Toews remarked on the "linguistic turn" and the gradual acceptance among historians that "language can no longer be construed as simply a medium, relatively or potentially transparent, for the representation or expression of a reality outside of itself."[1] This is most encouraging. At the same time, however, Toews betrays his uneasiness about the apparently bottomless relativism of Derrida, Foucault, Habermas, and others. "If we take them seriously," he argues, "we must recognize that we have no access, even potentially, to an unmediated world of objective things and processes that might serve as the ground and limit of our claims to knowledge of nature or to any transhistorical or transcendent subjectivity that might ground our interpretation of meaning."[2]

Toew's resistance is not unreasonable, given that discourses such as history—any discourse, in fact, that seeks to establish a detached and objective approach to its subject—will face considerable hardship once we undermine the credibility of the very medium in which their discourse is couched. It is also true that the work of Foucault and Derrida in particular is aimed, among other things, at exposing the gross manipulations of language in the various struggles of power politics.

Exciting as such inquiries are, they are not what I seek to probe in this chapter. My interest lies, rather, in a less complicated epistemological concern for "existence" itself, that is, of what "reality" actually means. While I cannot claim to be free of politics—no epistemology is ever truly free of politics, for language is always political—my inquiry stems less out of the political than the aesthetic and ontological aspects of language and its construction of reality. For a starting point we might leap back almost four centuries, to Descartes's efforts to prove his own existence—efforts that were met with mixed results, for Descartes had better success proving that he was conscious than he did proving that he truly existed. In the end, *cogito, ergo sum* proves only that Descartes could think; his act of thinking, however, insofar as it represents a subjective act, must be viewed in terms of interpretation of the things he perceived around him, as well as the fact that he can think.

Such inquiries continue to occupy us today, usually in the application of specific fields of discourse. From the more practical side of linguistics, for instance, Willis Barnstone, a theorist of translation, argues a fundamentally hermeneutic line for all acts of perception, even (or perhaps especially) in our daily lives, when he says that

> there is unending process of rewording, retelling, translation, transmutation, and wherever we turn, where meaning is sought, where mental activity takes place, we are living inescapably in the eternal condition of translation . . . every perception of movement and change, in the street or on our tongues, on the page or in our ears, leads us directly to the art and activity of translation.[3]

Herein we find echoes of reception theory (sometimes called "reader response"), and it is true that such a reading strategy, in which the reader, in the act of reading, *rewrites* the text through the filter of his or her own language, experience, and culture, is grounded in the idea that the reader plays the fundamental role of breathing life into the text; indeed, the text remains only potentially meaningful until this occurs.

While hermeneutics (in its simplest form understood as the "theory of interpretation") is, to be sure, a basic grounding factor in my own argument for this opening chapter, I propose to carry the question beyond textual exegesis, wherein we permit the reader a voice in rewriting the text; rather, I propose, following Barnstone (whose "translation" might be viewed as "interpretation" here), that we "read" the world (within our minds) and "write" the world (external to our minds) all the time, and moreover, that the realities we construct are not merely virtual, nor even potential, but as real as it gets. Stated another way, there is no reality perceptible to us that we do not create ourselves through language. Among other things, this means that we can formulate an answer to the age-old question, if a tree falls in a forest and no one is there to hear it, does it make a sound? The answer is no, it makes no meaningful sound, because no one is there to recognize it as such and thus "concretize" it with the meaning that our minds construct; at the same time, the answer is yes, because I can imagine the sound a tree makes when it falls (I am imagining it as I write this line, in fact, and perhaps some of my readers are doing the same as they read it), and somewhere in the world, in some forest, a tree surely *is* falling at this moment. . . .

For those who choose not to follow me into the solipsistic tunnel, let us propose a less unnerving proposition: that language is frequently assigned a constitutive role in literary works, by which I mean simply that it is given the power to create realities within the fictional framework. Such an idea, no doubt, arose in part out of the more sophisticated theories of language that attended the 1960s and beyond, particularly as linguists probed ever more deeply into how language and words actually managed to carry meanings, more or less intact, from one person to another; it is also, however, a first principle for anyone who approaches a text as a series of critical decisions made by its writer *and* (often unconsciously) by its reader.

If such ideas have been with us since Genesis, they continue to find modern-day expression in literature and film. These range from the absurd—popular films such as *Ghostbusters* (recall the arrival of the giant marshmallow man near the end) and *Jumanji* (wherein drawing a card from the deck brings into reality whatever it says)—to more sophisticated works of fiction. A number of writers from the past three decades, including Murakami Haruki, have addressed the question of whether language, in addition to describing reality, is in fact capable of creating it as well. We will explore this important facet of Murakami's writing, but before that, let us examine the works of other novelists who have given language a dominant role in the construction of reality.

Ecos of the Past

In pursuit of fiction in which great events and realities are hinged upon the apparently nondescript or insignificant, one comes across a number of interesting works. Thomas Pynchon's 1973 novel *Gravity's Rainbow,* for instance, follows the movements of one Tyrone Slothrop, a U.S. Army lieutenant, the locations of whose sexual exploits in London appear to match the German V-2 missile strikes near the end of World War II, raising the question: are the Germans targeting Slothrop (or his dates)—unlikely, since the V-2 were unguided and fell more or less at random—or do Slothrop's sexual conquests cause the unguided rockets to land on those spots?

A similar motif is seen in Salman Rushdie's *Midnight's Children*

(1980), in which children born at the stroke of midnight on August 15, 1947—the precise moment at which India's independence from Britain began—seem to determine their nation's development. The work focuses on Saleem Sinai, one such child, who believes that his personal destiny somehow guides greater India's destiny, and therefore sees the occurrence of great events as somehow originating with himself. Referring to the India-Pakistan War of March 1971, for instance, he notes that "the purpose of that entire war had been to re-unite me with an old life, to bring me back together with my old friends." As in Slothrop's case, one cannot be certain whether Saleem causes these events in India to occur, but clearly in his own mind things happen because he needs them to happen.

In terms of declarative language constituting new realities, however, the Italian writer and semiotician Umberto Eco surely has produced the most intriguing narratives. Beginning with *Foucault's Pendulum* (1988), Eco explores what happens when one tells just the right story to just the right people and waits for them to bring it to life. At its heart the novel centers on three men—an elderly book editor named Belbo, his assistant Diotallevi (a cabalist who fancies himself a lost Jew), and the young Casaubon, a recent college graduate who invents for himself the vocation of "information detective." As these three men begin to solicit authors for a series of books on the history of the occult, the three editors begin to discuss what they know about the connections between the Templar Knights and the occult, particularly rumors that the Templars had discovered the secret to immortality. As they pursue some of the more colorful characters in the Templar story, and what Belbo and Casaubon (facetiously, at first) term "the Plan," some of their writers—whom they now term "the diabolicals"—appear to assume those identities, as though *they* were immortal. It would be comic, except that Belbo goes too far in trying to discover "the Plan," losing his life in the process.

But *Foucault's Pendulum* is less about Templars and the occult than it is about the credulity of those who would attempt to force connections between things that have nothing to do with each other, to invent realities where none existed. Eco's satirical view of such things finds voice time and again in Casaubon's character, whose view of his peculiar vocation is strictly cynical. "I knew a lot of things, unconnected things, but I wanted to be able to connect them after a few hours at a library. . . . It was a little like that game where you have to go from sausage to Plato in five steps, by association of ideas."[4]

Such gestures, ultimately, are without much merit, and Casaubon's work represents for Eco not the emancipation of unfettered intertextuality, of free association and interpretation, but rather the hazards of uncritical association, of letting one's imagination run wild and free. A pattern is discerned, it matches what one wishes to see, and soon it takes on the illusion of reality, of fact. Games like this are almost irresistible, and the more unfathomable they appear, the more readers are inclined to play. "'Whenever a poet or preacher, chief or wizard spouts gibberish,'" Casaubon reasons, "'the human race spends centuries deciphering the message. The Templars' mental confusion makes them indecipherable. That's why so many people venerate them.'"[5] And yet, there is no denying that the patterns constructed between writer and reader have a tendency to take on lives of their own, to escape the control of their creators. "'Matthew, Mark, Luke, and John are a bunch of practical jokers who meet somewhere and decide to have a contest. They invent a character, agree on a few basic facts, and then each one's free to take it and run with it. At the end they'll see who's done the best job. . . . Actually, though, the books have an appeal, they circulate, and when the four realize what's happening, it's too late.'"[6]

What strikes one as odd in this tale is that so down to earth a character as Casaubon, by novel's end, appears to believe in "the Plan" himself, and yet, what other options lie open to him? Though it may well be a figment of the collective imagination of "the diabolicals," it is nonetheless a lethal figment; it has already claimed the life of Belbo and threatens that of Casaubon as well. By novel's end he cannot even bring himself to leave a final note explaining how things have come to this pass; he will only be misunderstood yet again, for "if They were to read it, They would only derive another dark theory and spend another eternity trying to decipher the secret message behind my words. It's impossible, They would say; he can't only have been making fun of us."[7] Ultimately, however, this is exactly what Casaubon does, and he mirrors the fun Eco pokes at those who read far more into a text than it can possibly hold. And yet, the "reality" Casaubon is so determined to reject is undeniably there; it has killed Belbo, and it soon will kill him. It does not get much more "real" than that.

Eco's later books bring this point to the fore as well. *Baudolino*

(2000) concerns a young man with a gift for languages and storytelling, who attaches himself to Frederick the Great during his days of conquest in Europe, helping the king to speak with the various villagers and burghers they encounter in Italy, interceding when Frederick is inclined to get too rough. Seeking to assist his king in gaining equal footing with Pope Alexander III, Baudolino enlists the help of several friends, and they begin to fabricate Christian "relics" that will gain Frederick the prestige he requires to achieve this aim. Baudolino discovers his gift for creating realities out of words during a visit to Rome after Frederick has declared himself the new emperor, and he convinces the emperor's soldiers that certain relics exist in the city:

> Everyone hung on my lips. If I felt like saying I had seen a sea siren—after the emperor had brought me there as one who saw saints—they all believed me and said good boy, good boy. . . . After all, I thought, *whatever I say is true because I said it.*[8]

Throughout the story Baudolino defends his brilliant ability to lie, arguing that he simply brings into actuality things that lie dormant for want of proper narratives to support them. As he prepares to construct a story by which to transform three mummified corpses into the Magi who, according to legend, brought gifts to the baby Jesus, Baudolino rationalizes his actions:

> "I also thought that a relic is valid if it finds its proper place in a true story. Outside the story of Prester John, those Magi could have been the trick of some rug merchant; within the true story of John they became genuine testimony. A door is not a door if it does not have a building around it; otherwise it would be only a hole—no, what am I saying?—not even a hole, because a void without something surrounding it is not a void."[9]

In the end, after transforming the simple wooden cup that had belonged to his peasant father into the Holy Grail of Christ—again, simply by declaring it to be so and constructing a narrative to make it so—Baudolino spends fifteen years traveling to the ends of the earth, seeking the fabled kingdom of Prester John, the so-called earthly paradise, where the language of Adam is still spoken in all its purity, and immortal creatures from the age of the Garden of Eden still live. He finds this land and dwells there for a time, but readers are uncertain whether this is (for him) a true story or a fabrication that, like Casaubon's, has simply gone too far. It might also be the result of the "green honey" (apparently a type of hallucinogenic) that Baudolino and his friends ingest for inspiration. Indeed, Baudolino himself seems uncertain.

More recently, Eco has written *The Mysterious Flame of Queen Loanna* (2004), the story of a modern-day bookseller who, following some sort of cerebral incident (perhaps a hemorrhage), loses his memory, yet can remember every line he has ever read and quote whole passages from thousands of books, all from memory. His wife, a psychologist, brings to his attention the case of a mental patient who, having lost his memory, allows his hand to write his life story, gradually recovering it: "'It was as if his hand, with its automatisms, was able to put in order what his head couldn't. Which is like saying that what he wrote was more intelligent than he was.'"[10] Traveling back to his childhood home, the narrator seeks out his past in the books, comics, and notes of his childhood, eventually rediscovering himself in these written texts. In the end, however, having again entered the fog of a coma, he begins to doubt both his memories and his perceptions, concluding finally that reality is a subjective matter, a personal choice: "In order to survive (odd expression for someone like me who may already be dead) I must decide that Gratarolo, Paola, Sibilla, my studio, all of Solara with Amalia and the stories of Grandfather's castor oil, were memories of real life."[11] Ultimately, every reality is always already grounded in perception, language, and narrative, and so the choice lies with the perceiver whether to accept this reality or that.[12]

This sentiment is—dare one say it?—echoed in Eco's most recent novel, *The Prague Cemetery* (2010), as well. In it, a man calling himself "Captain Simonini," suffers (like the narrator of *The Mysterious Flame of Queen Loanna*) from partial amnesia and reconstructs the missing elements of his memory by carrying on a diaristic "conversation" with one of his alter egos, the persona of a man he has already killed. The reconstruction of his memory takes place through the writing of his life story, but this story in itself is strongly reminiscent of *Baudolino,* for in it Simonini explains his lifelong work as a creator of documents that help to guide the political movements of the various political factions at work in late-nineteenth-century Europe. He gets the idea for this from a charlatan lawyer who cheats him out of his inheritance when his grandfather dies, then employs him to help produce documents. Interestingly, his employer insists that his work lies not in forgeries but in the "recovery" of documents that *ought to have* existed but do not. "'What I produce,'" the man explains to Simonini, "'are not forgeries but new copies of genuine documents that have been lost or, by simple oversight, have never been produced, and that could and should have been produced.'"[13]

As the novel progresses, Simonini works for a variety of political entities, first in Italy, later in France, and somehow his work in constructing documents is always tinged by his memories of his grandfather's anti-Semitic leanings, leading him to construct an elaborate narrative about a worldwide plot on the part of Masonic lodges and the Jews to ruin Europe's economy ("It didn't occur to me that a conspiracy of five continents might be an excessive way to change constitutional rule in France,"[14] he admits), a theme—particularly the involvement of the Jews—that seems to attract interested parties in the same way that Casaubon and Belbo drew in their "diabolicals." Simonini's own narrative, however, contains the seeds of a much more frightening aftermath than anything we find in *Foucault's Pendulum,* as is clear when the German agent "Goedsche" (meant to remind us of Goethe) explains to Simonini how German Jews had been handled in Luther's age, using expressions that ring a disturbingly familiar bell: "'all their gold, money and jewelry was to be taken from them, and their young men given axes and spades and their women flax and spindles. That is because,' said Goedsche, sneering contemptuously, '*arbeit macht frei,* work sets you free. The final solution, for Luther, would have been to drive them out of Germany like rabid dogs.'"[15] In the end, Simonini realizes that "[t]he Prague cemetery was slipping out of my control, but I was probably contributing to its success."[16] His memory also returns; it seems that his amnesia may have resulted from mental strain caused by the men and women he has killed in the course of protecting his position as government agent. In a sense, however, Eco seems to suggest that Simonini's trauma is also the result of the innumerable killings yet to come, clearly set into motion by the scribblings of this seemingly insignificant person. Through the construction of his narrative—a fabrication—on the Jews, Simonini is given de facto credit for the

Holocaust. This is the true (and, here, the truly terrifying) power of language.

Of Dogs and Men

As noted earlier, this powerful aspect of language is clearly evident in Murakami's first works of fiction, particularly from *Pinball, 1973*. One of the more striking examples comes up early in that work, shortly after the character "Naoko" has been introduced. Naoko's role in the narrative is to tell Boku stories, in a sense to help him envision the "other world," of which she is already to some extent a part and to which she will soon return permanently in death. Naoko's character is only barely developed in this work, but the story she tells to Boku in this instance, a description of her hometown, is interesting for the fact that it later comes to life:

> "You could barely even call it a town," she continued. "There's one road, and a train station. The kind of pathetic station the conductor might forget to stop at on a rainy day."
>
> I nodded. For a full thirty seconds we were silent, watching the cigarette smoke moving in a shaft of light.
>
> "A dog keeps walking from one end of the train platform to the other. That kind of station. Get it?"
>
> I nodded.
>
> "In front of the station is a little rotary and a bus stop. A few shops. . . . barely conscious places. If you go straight through it you run into the park. It has a slide and three swings."
>
> "How about a sandbox?"
>
> "Sandbox?" She thought about that for a while, then nodded in confirmation. "It has one."
>
> We were silent again. I put out my burnt-down cigarette in a paper cup.
>
> "It's a horribly boring town. Like, you can't even imagine why they'd build such a boring town."
>
> "God reveals himself to us in many forms," I suggested.[17]

Naoko offers this description of her hometown to Boku in the spring of 1969, as a new school year begins for them. Interestingly, her description, which does not end with the passage above, contains semipermanent aspects, such as the fact that the town is known for its tasty water, and momentary ones, such as the dog pacing the train platform. Yet it is this momentary aspect that Murakami's protagonist latches onto and seeks out when he visits the town some ten pages—and an unspecified period of time—later:

> I waited for exactly one hour, but the dog did not appear. . . . Then, under that vague spring sunshine, a white dog—he looked like he had been brought by one of the men fishing—appeared, diligently sniffing at the clover.[18]

Is this the same dog described by Naoko in her narrative? In the end it does not matter; Naoko has declared that a dog paces the train platform, and so Boku must find a dog there, or he cannot trust the reality of what he has been told. In short, Naoko has created this "reality" in which a dog perpetually paces a train platform, and Boku, out of an urge to confirm this fact, goes to visit it. It would be more accurate, however, to say that in responding to the narrative constructed by Naoko and the world it describes, Boku in fact *concretizes* this world, constructs it, brings it into actuality by the very act of acknowledging it.[19] For reality, like the narrative, is a discursive act, one that connects and requires mutual acknowledgment from both maker and viewer, the latter of whom in turn becomes maker.

Prophesy and Prediction

One of the more common mechanisms by which language constructs reality in Murakami fiction is the use of prophesy and prediction, and while it is easy enough within the fictional landscape to attribute this to magical forces, it also represents a manipulation of time by the author, either by its apparent suspension altogether (as occurs in the so-called other world) or through the introduction of multidirectionality. As one of the central defining aspects of the "other world," time will be discussed at some length in the chapter that follows; here I will note only that time, commonly taken to be an objective fact of the natural universe (chiefly due to the incontrovertible effects of deterioration and decay), is in fact a construct like any other, bound to language and culture and by no means absolute. We are fooled by time into granting it greater ontological status than it deserves because it may be divided and expressed uniformly through the symbolic system of mathematics. We speak of how long "a day" is on other planets and make adjustments for the rate of rotation and circumference of those planets, and yet in the end we are still playing with the clumsy tool of our arbitrary divisions of time, with hours and minutes, which can be made to divide one year on earth into 365 (almost perfectly) even days. But why not measure time in sticks of incense, as used to be done in Asia, or by the occurrence of the full moon, as ancient humans did and some modern people still do?

Time may be looked at culturally as well, in terms of human historical development, as Jean Baudrillard does, and when it is viewed in this way, something interesting occurs: we see that time is not necessarily linear nor even unidirectional but may well move the way the wind does, now in this direction, now in that. Near the end of his admittedly esoteric work *The Illusion of the End,* in which he confronts the massive wave of revisionist history that accompanied the closing years of the twentieth century, Baudrillard has this to say:

> We have to accord a privileged status to all that has to do with non-linearity, reversibility, all that is of the order not of an unfolding or an evolution, but of a winding back, a reversion in time. Anastrophe versus catastrophe. Perhaps, deep down, history has never unfolded in a linear fashion; perhaps language has never unfolded in a linear fashion. Everything moves in loops, tropes, inversions of meaning, except in numerical and artificial languages which, for that very reason, *no longer are* languages.[20]

But there is, lying outside the boundaries of the artificially constructed time that divides our daily lives, a more permanent, all-encompassing Time that binds the vastness of all human experience, a realm of Time that contains no directions, that is eternal and always a single, unified whole. In this mode of Time there is no past or future, only an endless present, constantly renewing itself. Japanese critic Shimamura Teru examines the Greek myth of Cronus swallowing his children in order to clarify the presence of both forms of time ("time" and "Time") in Murakami fiction. Alarmed by the prophesy that he would one day be dethroned by one of his children, Cronus swallows each of the children his wife, Rhea, bears him, until, fed up, she hides Zeus and substitutes a stone for her husband to swallow in his place. Eventually Zeus returns, and having arranged for his father to vomit up his siblings (Hades and Poseidon among them), he leads a rebellion against Cronus. Shimamura's point is that even as Cronus attempts to extend his own reign as king at the expense of his children, he not only disrupts the forward movement of time, but he also postpones or even negates his eventual inclusion in the more permanent timelessness of what Shimamura calls "the chronicle" and what I am terming Time:

> For Cronus, to change places with his son as successor represented the end of his "time." As each previous father/king was killed by his son/prince, so too was history/chronicle constructed, and the father/old king would be bound up into that chronicle.[21]

In other words, until he is succeeded by the next generation, Cronus effectively remains a part of *living* time, thus causing a stagnant present and depriving the future of its rightful ruler, but at the same time he prevents himself from joining the narrative—the chronicle—of Time, which, unlike living time, constantly constitutes and is constituted by all collective memory.

It is precisely this sort of linearity, this forward progress in time, that is so frequently disrupted in Murakami fiction. What we see instead is the apparent *disappearance* of time, as in the "other world," where it cannot exist in its regulated, divided form. Thus we have what seems to be the temporary *stoppage* of time, as in *The Wind-Up Bird Chronicle,* in which moments the cries of the semimythical "wind-up bird" signify that the world's springs have run down. At such moments physical time is briefly supplanted by the metaphysical Time, causing past, present, and future to collide with one another, opening a new dimension in which time and space seem to disappear, allowing certain characters to see "backwards" into the future.

A moment like this occurs in Aldous Huxley's novel *Time Must Have a Stop* (1945), in which a young man—who might remind us just a little of Joyce's Stephen Daedalus—is taken from his dull life in London to live with his Uncle Eustace in Florence. Near the end of the novel, however, Uncle Eustace, all alone in his bathroom, suffers a fatal heart attack, and while his life ebbs from his body on the bathroom floor—and presumably beyond, as well—he hears and joins in the laughter of the universe around him, seeing visions of the things past, present, and future:

> Yes, the whole universe was laughing with him. Laughing cosmically at the cosmic joke of its own self-frustration . . . . A counterpoint of innumerable hilarities.[22]

> There was a kind of side-slip, a falling, as it were, through the intricacies of the lattice—and he knew himself remembering events that had not yet taken place.[23]

As part of the cosmos itself, the world soul, Eustace has jettisoned the bounds of physical life and of the limitations of its time and space, though for him it is a disconcerting feeling, and at one point, when he is brought back into a medium's body during a séance, he experiences pleasure at emerging from "mere incoherent succession into the familiar orderliness of time. . . . It was enough just to have this feeling of space and time and the processes of life."[24] This "incoherent succession" is, of course, the movement of the universe *outside* the boundaries of human time and space, and it permits Eustace to see everything at once, as a great and terrible simultaneity. This, too, is seeing the future, but only insofar as the future is a never-ending present.

This conception of Time may assist us in making sense of the frequent prophesies that occur in Murakami fiction as well, a motif that should and will be discussed in terms of its quasi-spiritual qualities in chapter 3 of this text. But prophesy also has an important linguistic aspect to it, for it is one of the more dramatic examples of how *speaking* the future can *create* the future. Put another way, one can never be certain whether the prophet is *reading* what is to be, or *writing* it.

At the beginning of *A Wild Sheep Chase,* for instance, the sequel to *Pinball, 1973,* in which the protagonist searches for a semimythical, all-empowering sheep—and at the same time, for his missing friend Rat—Boku reminisces about a woman he slept with in college, who told him, rather matter-of-factly, "'I'm going to live to be twenty-five . . . and then I'll die.'"[25] The following sentence informs us that she died just a year later than predicted, at twenty-six. Did this woman predict her death, or did she bring it about? We cannot be certain. In the same novel, the protagonist is assisted by his clairvoyant ear model girlfriend, who informs him that a telephone call will soon come, one that has to do with a particular sheep, and that this will be the start of a great adventure. Sure enough, the man's business partner telephones ten minutes later with the news that someone has come around asking what they know about a certain sheep. It would be natural enough to assume that the girlfriend is simply reading the future, but can we really be certain that she is not arranging the circumstances by which Boku's great "sheep chase" may begin?

Dance Dance Dance, which narrates Boku's quest to find "Kiki"—the same ear model, who disappears near the end of *A Wild Sheep Chase*—raises similar questions through the thirteen-year-old Yuki, yet another clairvoyant companion to Boku, who expresses profound uneasiness about her ability to see things that are about to happen, for she comes to feel responsible in some way for the events she predicts. "'Sometimes I have these periods where I'm sort of blank, like in a dream,'" she tells Boku. "'And when those come, it happens. It's not a premonition. It's more vague than that. But it happens. I can see it. But I don't say anything anymore. Whenever I do, everyone cries "witch".'"[26] In the end Yuki is uncertain whether she is seeing the future or making it happen, and does all she can to block her visions out. Boku experiences something like this himself when he reflects on those who have died in his life and those who appeared likely to do so. In one unnerving scene, while chasing Kiki, he enters a room—part of the "other world," which will be explained in the next chapter—and sees a group of skeletons. Are these people who have died, or those who are yet to die? He has no way of knowing. "In my mind I went over the list of those who might die. I felt like the Angel of Death. I was unconsciously choosing the order in which they would die."[27]

Reconstructing the Self through Words: *The Wind-Up Bird Chronicle*

As noted earlier, the great majority of Murakami's characters concern themselves with preserving or recovering their threatened or lost individual identity. Until the mid-1990s and publication of *The Wind-Up Bird Chronicle,* they employed two common approaches to this end: (a) the protagonist would enter his own mind and reencounter elements of his previous experience, in a sense, reminding himself of where he came from; or (b) the protagonist would draw elements of that past out, as the aforementioned "nostalgic images," into the conscious world, using them as direct links to his past and also as an emotional salve while confronting his past. This task is for these protagonists an intensely personal operation, for this was the period in which both Murakami and his protagonists were still maintaining distance—both physical and emotional—from the rest of Japanese society.

Whereas this earlier model was, as we have seen, linguistically grounded in metonymical connections between objects and words in Murakami's early texts, the concept of (re)constructing oneself through the act of writing a story (and having it read by another), something like what we saw in Eco's work, is first seen as a concentrated theme in *The Wind-Up Bird Chronicle,* particularly the later chapters. *The Wind-Up Bird Chronicle* is essentially a quest novel in which the work's hero, Okada Tōru, seeks to rescue his missing wife, Kumiko, from the clutches of her evil brother, Wataya Noboru. Structurally, the novel shifts frequently between the present narrative of Okada Tōru, Kumiko, and Wataya Noboru, and the brutal history of the Japanese Imperial Army in Manchuria during World War II. As with previous Murakami fiction, the work's central theme is the loss of individual core identity, whether to the amnesia of history or by its being forcibly stripped away by another.

An example of the former is "Lieutenant Mamiya," a survivor of Japan's disastrous clash with the Soviet Union at the largely forgotten 1939 battle of Nomonhan near the Mongolian border. Captured while on reconnoiter, Mamiya is dropped into a deep Mongolian well and left to die but is rescued instead. Yet, it is only his physical body that is saved; his inner self, his soul, is left behind in that well, and now he leads only a half existence, a metaphor for the collective Japanese amnesia that has forgotten all those who fought at Nomonhan, whether they survived or not. Mamiya, however, unlike his forgotten comrades, has the opportunity to recover at least some part of himself by telling his story to Okada Tōru, some in person, the rest through a series of letters that detail his experiences. In having his story heard and recognized by Tōru, Mamiya in some small measure is reconstructed by Tōru.

Others—generally those who have confronted death in some manner—find their inner selves threatened through violence in the present era: Kumiko, her older sister (who committed suicide), and a clairvoyant named Kanō Creta are assaulted by Wataya Noboru, though our only account of this comes from Kanō Creta, who throughout her life suffered from severe, unexplained physical pain and eventually attempted suicide. Following this attempt, which resulted in the disappearance of her mysterious malady, Kanō Creta became a prostitute, and one of her customers was Wataya Noboru. During one of their sessions, she tells Tōru, Noboru reached into her body through her sexual organs and "'removed something wet and slippery'" from her.[28] This was her core identity, something akin to her soul, and without it, like Lieutenant Mamiya, she leads only a partial existence. This will likely be the fate of Kumiko as well, should Tōru fail to rescue her from the metaphysical prison in which her brother keeps her.

Herein we see the true function of Okada Tōru in this novel: to read (or listen to) the stories of the afflicted and, in doing so, to recognize them as individuals and thereby restore some small part of their core identity to them. He does this with his neighbor, the sixteen-year-old Kasahara Mei, who survived a motorcycle crash that killed her boyfriend (a symbolic splitting of inner and outer selves) and now spends her time chatting with Tōru, whom she has nicknamed "Mr. Wind-Up Bird." Somewhat less directly he also does this with "Cinnamon," the mute son of "Nutmeg," the latter of whom employs him to use his special connection to the "other world" in order to help women who have become disconnected from their own core identities. All of these instances highlight the crucial importance of language, for it is through the construction of these narratives, and their reconstruction through the reading/writing process, that identities are created. Each character who shares his or her story with Tōru is both recognized by him and in that act of recognition re-created—"concretized," in the terminology of reception theory—as a viable ontological presence.[29]

This process is best illustrated through the narrative of Cinnamon. We learn late in the novel that Cinnamon, following a bizarre encounter with the "other world," lost the ability to speak. Cinnamon's affliction begins when, as a small boy, he awakens one night to what sounds like a spring being wound—the springs of history, of time, are actually being wound up here—and happens to look outside his bedroom window, where he sees a man who looks like his father climb a tree in the garden but never come down, while a second man buries a mysterious bundle. Later, the boy dreams—or believes he has dreamed—of going outside to dig up the bundle, which turns out to contain a human heart, still beating. When Cinnamon returns to bed, he finds a perfect replica of himself sleeping there and forces his own way into the bed, awakening the following morning all alone but completely mute. What has happened is that the conscious Cinnamon and his inner self have changed places during one of those brief periods when time stops and the passages between conscious and unconscious are unblocked. As noted previously, it is the inner (unconscious/invisible) self that contains memory and experience, while the outer (conscious/visible) self provides fresh experience, living the story. What it means, then, for the two to switch places, in brief, is that the Cinnamon living in the conscious world—who remembers all but does not speak—must keep the record of his experiences, while the Cinnamon living in the unconscious realm (who, presumably, can still speak) must feed new information to the mute Cinnamon, who will (silently) put it down in writing. The fact that most of Cinnamon's chronicle deals with past events stems from the fact that the "speaking" Cinnamon lives in the unconscious repository of (collective) memories, the unchanging and unchangeable past itself, and thus has no "present" that may be distinguished from past; or rather, we might say he lives in an endless present.

This comes to the attention of Okada Tōru when Cinnamon deliberately leaves his computer running, giving Tōru access to a series of memoirs he has been writing about himself and his mother, all under the general title of "The Wind-Up Bird Chronicle." This is certainly disconcerting for Tōru, given that it repeats a nickname that he believes is strictly between himself and Kasahara Mei. Does it mean that Kasahara Mei and Cinnamon are connected in some way? Or is Cinnamon somehow tapped directly into Okada Tōru's own memory banks? This is merely one of the many riddles for which Murakami is famous, and readers may turn gray attempting to decipher them. We might conclude, for instance, that Okada Tōru is himself nothing more than a character in "Cinnamon's" narrative (and thus, mere words), a figment of his imagination, like the Cartesian "evil genius."[30] (No doubt many readers of Murakami's various works have, at some point or another, wondered whether the entire narrative they read is not simply a figment of the protagonist's overactive imagination.) Such a scheme, in narratological terms, at least, would shed light on Cinnamon's inability to speak: as the author of the text, his "voice" would necessarily be reserved for the narrative itself, rather than for direct, vocal interaction with the characters in his work. It would also be compatible with our contention that actual worlds can be and are created from words. In fact, this is more or less what happens in *1Q84,* wherein a world created within the confines of a novel comes into actual being, encompassing its authors and all those connected with it.

Perhaps a more useful reading of this point within the context of the present text is that Cinnamon, closely connected to the "other world" of Time as a collective unity, has direct access to *all* human memory and experience, past, present, and future, and thus is not only aware of Okada Tōru's nickname and its meaning—as "the bird who rewinds the springs of time"—but is eager to make this fact known to Okada Tōru as well. Why? Perhaps it may be read as a distress call from the Cinnamon, who has remained trapped "over there" since the night when he wrestled unsuccessfully with his inner self for control of the outer body. Cinnamon's "Wind-Up Bird Chronicle" would then be an SOS directed at Tōru, who alone possesses, as Cinnamon knows perfectly well, the ability to "read/write" him back into existence.

In this sense Cinnamon succeeds; Tōru reads the narrative he has constructed, interprets it against what he already knows, what he has conjectured, and what he has guessed, and in the end constructs his own "Cinnamon," *in the reflection of which* Cinnamon then views himself as an autonomous being. It is, ironically, the same process by which Kumiko herself attempts to catch Tōru's attention; the recurring calls from the "telephone woman" early in the novel are actually from Kumiko, who is doing all she can to let Tōru know what has happened to her. Out of his natural prudishness, and of course his inability to recognize her voice, altered by the "other world," however, Tōru completely fails to catch her signals and thus does not "read/write" Kumiko until it is too late. Indeed, whether Kumiko *or* Cinnamon can actually be saved by Tōru's "reading" of their texts is left unclear by the end of the novel.

Reconstructing the Self through Words: *Kafka on the Shore*

Nearly a decade before *The Wind-Up Bird Chronicle,* Murakami played with the idea of the inner mind as a construct of language in *Hard-Boiled Wonderland and the End of the World,* the author's only quasi-science fiction novel to date. Its parallel narratives—one representing the outer mind, the other depicting the inner—create a powerful tension between the individual Will of the conscious world and the somnambulant repose of the unconscious state. The conscious protagonist (Watashi) is a hard-boiled operative who works as a human information encoder for an organization calling itself the System. As part of an unauthorized private experiment carried out by the lead scientist in charge of programming Watashi's brain, however, a third circuit is added to the structure, one containing an approximation of his inner mind, constructed out of words and images found in his actual inner mind. This third circuit, known as "the Town," is a walled enclosure containing a bucolic sort of village, and as the circuits in Watashi's brain begin to fuse together, he is threatened with permanent imprisonment in "the Town."

Hard-Boiled Wonderland and the End of the World is actually a useful representation of how characters like Kumiko and Cinnamon get to be the way they are, for it begins with the forcible removal of the protagonist's "shadow" *(kage)*, a recurring image in Murakami fiction that can represent, all at once, the soul, memory, self, identity.[31] Without the shadow, a Murakami character becomes quite literally mindless, without memories and without a sense of individual identity. At novel's end, the protagonist and his librarian friend, both of whom retain traces of their shadows but not enough to be considered "whole," are given the opportunity to escape the Town, presumably back to the conscious world, but elect not to do so. At the same time, not wishing to return to the mindless stagnancy and control of the Town, they choose a third option: to stay in the forbidden forest outside the Town, where they will, presumably, attempt to reconstruct (or construct anew) their lost selves.

Nearly two decades after completing this work, feeling a sense of responsibility about what had happened with those people,[32] Murakami set to work on *Umibe no Kafka* (2002; translated as *Kafka on the Shore*), a lengthy and complex work to which we will have occasion to return in greater depth later in this volume. *Kafka on the Shore* concerns a fifteen-year-old boy named Tamura Kafka who seeks (unsuccessfully) to escape his father's prophesy that he will one day kill his father, then locate and copulate with his long-lost mother and older sister. Fleeing to Takamatsu City in Shikoku, several hundred miles away from his home (and father) in Tokyo, he believes he has avoided his fate, until he awakens from a deep trance one night behind a Shintō shrine, covered in blood. Initially he takes refuge in the apartment of a young woman named Sakura, whom he met on the bus to Takamatsu and who is, coincidentally, just the right age to be his missing sister. Later he finds his way—or perhaps is led by fate itself—to the Kōmori Memorial Library, a small, private library managed by "Miss Saeki," a woman with a mysterious past who is, also coincidentally, just the right age to be Kafka's missing mother.

The flip side of Kafka's movements is a parallel narrative that features "Mr. Nakata," a man of approximately sixty, who describes himself as "not very bright" but has the peculiar ability to speak the language of cats. This makes him popular with cat owners in his neighborhood, who frequently call upon him to help locate their missing pets. While on such a mission, Nakata encounters a kind of spirit or deity calling himself "Johnny Walker"—a perfect replica of the Scotch whiskey icon, complete with top hat—who has taken over the body of Kafka's father. While in Johnny Walker's home, the normally mild-mannered Nakata becomes suddenly enraged when the other man shows him his collection of captured neighborhood cats and then proceeds to vivisect them one by one, swallowing their internal organs afterwards. Nakata kills him with a kitchen knife, then (without really knowing why) heads for Takamatsu City in Shikoku himself, aided by a cynical truck driver he meets along the way named Hoshino. Once in Takamatsu, with the help of another spirit/deity, taking the form of "Colonel Sanders" (the Kentucky Fried Chicken founder), they locate a stone known as the "Gateway stone" *(iriguchi no ishi)*. They "open" this by lifting it up, thus opening the passage between the worlds of the physical and metaphysical, permitting movement between them. Not long after this Nakata finds his way to the Kōmori Memorial Library, where he meets Miss Saeki, who seems to recognize him, takes her by the hand, and sends her peacefully into death.

Saeki and Nakata actually share the same crippling debilitation: like the protagonist who is trapped in "the Town" in *Hard-Boiled Wonderland and the End of the World,* both have lost their shadows and must now live in the conscious world—on *this side*—while their other halves go on existing "over there." Nakata's story begins in the closing days of World War II. For reasons that are never made clear—perhaps it was to escape the rampant violence that surrounded him in his own world—Nakata entered the "other world" as a child, emerging some weeks later without his "shadow." Along with his shadow, he has lost the ability to remember anything from his past or to form new memories. Put in a slightly different way, he is no longer a being in "time," divided into past, present, and future, but of Time, that unified eternity in which past and future are bound up in an endless present. Saeki, on the other hand, having once entered the "other world" as a teenager in the mid-1960s, appears to have returned without her complete physical self. Today she has the appearance of a woman in her midforties, but she is, almost literally, a mere shadow of herself with nothing but memories to sustain her. Much like Cinnamon, she spends her time writing memories in a notebook.

Owing in part to his liberation from the snares of the human construct of time, like Yuki in *Dance Dance Dance,* Nakata is able to sense when certain things are going to happen. And yet, again like Yuki, he cannot be certain whether he is merely seeing what will happen or is actually making it happen. Following his murder of the spirit known as "Johnny Walker," Nakata visits the nearest police box and confesses what he has done, but he is taken for a senile old man and told to go home. As he prepares to leave, Nakata helpfully suggests to the officer that he bring along an umbrella should he be on duty the next evening, even if the sky is clear, because "'fish will fall from the sky like rain. A lot of fish. Probably sardines, though there may be a few mackerel mixed in among them.'"[33] The following day, as he predicted, a great plague of fish rains down upon that section of Tokyo. Somewhat later, at a rest area on the way to Shikoku, Nakata observes a man being beaten to death by a biker gang in a parking lot. As when he witnessed Johnny Walker's cruelty toward the neighborhood cats, Nakata's inner self reacts to this brazen violence and rises to the surface of his consciousness, incensed:

> Nakata closed his eyes. Something in his body was quietly boiling over, and he was powerless to hold it back. He felt faintly nauseated. . . . Nakata looked up at the sky, then slowly opened his umbrella above his head. Then, carefully, he took several steps backward. . . . At first it was just a few spatters, but soon the numbers swelled and it became a downpour. They were pitch-black and about an inch long. Beneath the lights of the parking lot it looked fascinating, like black snow. This unlucky

> snow stuck where it landed on the men's shoulders, arms, and necks. They tried to pull them off, but this was not easily done.
>
> "Leeches," someone said. (1:332–33)

Does Nakata open his umbrella because it is about to rain leeches, or does it rain leeches because Nakata opens his umbrella? Even Nakata appears uncertain. Later in the novel he confides to Hoshino that he is afraid of being used for some terrible evil: "'Suppose, for instance, that what falls from the sky next time is ten thousand knives, or a huge bomb, or poison gas? What would Nakata do then?'" (2:140). The truth is that Nakata, by his own admission, is an "empty shell"; we might say he is a mere vessel through which ideas—words—pass at the whim of others, and it is this, rather than any willpower of his own, that brings these new realities into being. He has never truly been in control of his life or of the things that happen in this world through him.

It is, instead, Saeki who represents the more active aspect of the two characters, for in contrast to Nakata's "pure flesh" existence, Saeki is something closer to "pure thought," or "pure spirit." Like all Murakami characters—like the "poor aunt"—she has a corporeal form but one that can change; her true existence is bound up in the pages of manuscript paper on which she scribbles, virtually nonstop, with her fountain pen. In response to Nakata's admission, late in the book, that he understands nothing but the present, Saeki declares to him that she is the opposite, that "'I haven't had anyone I could call a friend for a very long time . . . except for my memories'" (2:286–87).

But what exactly *has* Saeki been writing on her manuscript paper, so much that it fills many large file folders? "'Since returning to live in this town, I have been sitting at this desk, writing this manuscript,'" she explains to Nakata. "'It is a record of the life I have followed'" (2:290). Her final request to Nakata, before he touches her hand and sends her "over there" for good, is that he burn the entire manuscript, so that not a single fragment remains. This collection of manuscript pages thus stands in for the physical remains of Saeki; its burning will be her cremation.

Though he is unable to read or write himself, Nakata intuitively grasps the importance of both, for as Saeki tries to explain to him, the process of writing is synonymous with the act of living, of existing meaningfully, something about which Nakata has had no firsthand knowledge since his childhood:

> "It is a very important thing, the act of writing, isn't it?" Nakata asked her.
>
> "Yes. That's right. It is the act of writing that is so very important. There is nothing meaningful in what has been written, in the result itself."
>
> "Nakata cannot read or write, so I cannot leave any records behind," said Mr. Nakata. "Nakata is just like a cat." (2:292–93)

Stated another way, words—spoken or written—create a new reality for themselves. The act of writing, rather than *what* is written, is important because through this means we create a new, often tangible, reality. And Saeki is correct in stating that what is written is meaningless, but fails to add, "*until it is read by another.*" It is the acknowledgment of another that brings the reality of all words to fruition. For Saeki, however, the only person she might wish to read her words is long gone from this world, so she directs Nakata to destroy them.

The most important reality generated through words in this novel, of course, occurs for the title character, Tamura Kafka himself, whose solution to the Oedipal prophesy/curse that governs his life is to *create* the reality he desires by fulfilling every last detail of that prophesy as it was spoken by his father. In so doing, as we shall see later, Kafka uses his oracle to *construct* a world in which he regains not only his mother and sister but a renewed (and for him, more acceptable) sense of identity.

A Question of Subjectivity

As we have noted in the case of Nakata, who struggles to cope with the responsibility of this power he possesses to create realities, yet whose control appears to rest in the hands of others, the issue of who narrates—that is, for us, who creates the world—comes more into play in these later Murakami texts. This becomes an issue in the short story "Hibi idō suru jinzō no katachi o shita ishi" (2005; translated as "The Kidney-Shaped Stone That Moves Every Day"), which appears as part of the collection *Tōkyō kitanshū* (2005; Strange tales of Tokyo). In "The Kidney-Shaped Stone," a young writer named Junpei has a brief romantic relationship with a mysterious woman named Kirie. Here, as in *Kafka on the Shore,* Junpei's father has burdened him with a haunting prophesy: in his entire life he will meet exactly three women, neither more nor less, who will be important to him. This pronouncement, however, while lurking all the while at the back of Junpei's mind, proves to be less central to the story than the actual relationship between Junpei and Kirie, who maintains a playful but determined sense of mystery about herself. In response to Junpei's repeated queries about what she does for a living, she invites him to guess—but in the end she never reveals the answer. From her side, rather unfairly given her own reticence, she demands that Junpei reveal something that is, for him, even more personal: the plot of the story he is currently writing. For Junpei this is a serious thing, the violation of a strict personal rule, but his reluctance to comply is more than a writer's quirk; rather, it lies in his recognition of the power of words and the potential risk that attends relinquishment of that power:

> He made it a rule never to tell anyone the contents of stories he was still writing. It would be like a jinx. The moment the words left his mouth, a certain something would vanish like the morning dew. Subtle nuances would become superficial scenes. Secrets would no longer be secrets.[34]

The Chinese have a saying: When once a single word escapes, four horses cannot draw it in *(Yi hua ji chu, si ma nan zhui).* It reminds us that something said cannot be unsaid, and by extension, when once a reality is created, it cannot be uncreated. For Junpei, the risk is that a thought, an idea, once spoken aloud, becomes something *real,* and when this happens, that something will cease to be within the speaker's (or writer's) power to control but will instead belong to the public at large. In the end Junpei does tell Kirie the basic plot of his story, up to the point where he has stopped writing. His story began life as a psychological thriller about a female doctor who brings a kidney-shaped stone back from vacation, only to find that it changes positions in her office every night when she is away. Once Kirie has heard this much, however, she comments to Junpei that the woman is perhaps not being tricked—either by a malicious prankster or even her own psyche—but rather that the stone possesses a will of its own. She envisions the stone to possess a divine force, for it is part of the natural world, like the wind. "'The wind, for instance, has its own will. Normally we live our lives without noticing it. But then, one day, we are made aware of it. The wind purposely envelops you, shakes you. The wind knows everything that's inside you. And not only the wind. All things. Stones, too.'"[35]

As these words take root in Junpei's mind, his story is inexorably changed into one of fantasy, and he does indeed lose control of it. "As he wrote the short story, Junpei thought about Kirie. She (or something inside of her) seemed to be pushing the story forward."[36] As Junpei writes, his drive to complete the story reinvigorated, he gives himself wholly over to the narrative, in which his doctor-protagonist at once abandons her lover. Junpei intends to call Kirie after the story is completed, but when he does, rather predictably in Murakami fiction, he finds her number has been disconnected. Like other Murakami characters of this type, Kirie is both a part of Junpei's own inner mind—a projection from the dark recesses of his imagination—and also part of the actual, physical world. Her purpose is to turn the story down a new path, to create a scenario in which the doctor casts aside her lover, just as Kirie will now cast aside Junpei. In this scenario, Kirie is able to "take control of the story" from within Junpei's mind, but she is also part of that narrative—may, in fact, be its protagonist.

In this sense, Kirie is rather like "the Twins" from *Pinball, 1973,* who emerge from the protagonist's mind to help him deal with the loss of his girlfriend, or like "the Sheepman" in *A Wild Sheep Chase,* who assists him in locating his missing best friend "Rat" in that novel. It is unclear whether Kirie has, like the Twins and Sheepman, gone back "over there" once her task is completed, however; Junpei's next encounter with her comes when he chances to hear her being interviewed on the radio and discovers she is a high-wire walker, hence her intimate knowledge about wind. But on a deeper level, Kirie's sense of oneness with the wind as she walks high wires strung between skyscrapers comes into better focus when we reflect that she belongs "over there," where the wind (as expression of the inner mind) originates, and is herself thus a pure embodiment of language, with no more permanent corporeal existence than the words themselves, despite the powerful effects she generates. Perhaps this is why Murakami names this character "Kirie," a homonym for the Greek *kyrie* (κύριε, "lord"); for if words are ultimate constitutive building blocks of reality, then Kirie proves herself not only to be constituted by words but to be a master of them as well. In this sense, we might also say that she resembles the inner mind, constituted of language, yet also using language to constitute and project its own realities.

"The Kidney-Shaped Stone" is not the only story in the *Tōkyō kitanshū* collection to suggest a direct connection between tangible reality and words. In "Shinagawa saru" (2005; translated as "A Shinagawa Monkey") we encounter the peculiar tale of Andō Mizuki, who has the misfortune of suddenly forgetting her own name at odd moments. She can remember everything else, including lists of telephone numbers, important dates, addresses, anything, but not her own name. The root of her problem, it turns out, goes back to her school days, many years earlier, when a schoolmate, Matsunaka Yūko, entrusted her school name tag to Mizuki, asking her to prevent its being stolen by a monkey while she went away for the weekend. While Mizuki takes this for a joke, she fails to question it further even when the school learns some days later that Matsunaka Yūko committed suicide over that weekend.

Yūko's plea to protect her name tag comes back into play in the present time when a local mental health counselor, who has been helping Mizuki deal with her memory problem, informs her that she keeps forgetting her name because her own name tag has been stolen from her bedroom by a monkey. Upon restoration of the name tag, Andō Mizuki's problem disappears. While the monkey (who can speak) never fully explains why he steals people's names, he insists that the act benefits its victims in some way. "'I steal people's names, it is true. But when I do, I can also carry off a certain amount of their incidental negativity. . . . Had I been successful in stealing Matsunaka Yūko's name, I might have been able to carry away with it some of the darkness that lurked in her heart.'"[37] Here we see the beginnings of a new perspective on names in Murakami fiction, namely, that they now form a direct connection with something more essential in the subject's identity. No longer merely an arbitrary signifier by which to delineate one person from another, the name becomes a distinct entity in itself, a word that somehow contains the essence of that person. Murakami returns to this theme briefly in his most recent novel, *Shikisai o motanai Tazaki Tsukuru to, kare no junrei no toshi (Colorless Tsukuru Tazaki and His Years of Pilgrimage),* when his protagonist Tazaki Tsukuru reflects that he was nothing before being named:

> In any case, that was how he had become the individual person known as "Tazaki Tsukuru." Until that point he had been nothing, a nameless little bit of predawn chaos. Barely capable of breathing in the blackness, a wailing, not-quite-three-kilogram lump of pink flesh. First a name had been given. Then came consciousness and memories, and finally his self was formed. The name was the starting point for everything else.[38]

That a single word can contain the essence of the individual, or even the soul, is a provocative idea, for, if true, it ought to follow that one could evoke the totality of the individual merely by uttering his or her name. But this also highlights the vulnerability of the individual soul; if the name has a physical presence, then—like the soul taken from Kanō Creta—it is vulnerable to corruption at the hands of those who would abuse it. This is essentially what happens in "A Shinagawa Monkey," and while we can never know whether the monkey truly was attempting to help Andō Mizuki, the fact that the physical presence of her name is something that can be lost or stolen (a literal case of identity theft) is extremely unnerving and once again demonstrates the awesome power of words.

Colorless Tsukuru Tazaki and His Years of Pilgrimage will receive full attention in the final chapter of this volume. Here I would like to turn to its predecessor, *1Q84,* to discuss how its construction of a fictional world in a work of literature is projected out into the actual world as a new reality.

A Whole New World: *1Q84*

At just under 1,700 pages in three volumes, *1Q84* is Murakami's longest novel to date, though by no means his most complex. The work may be summed up quite simply as the story of two soul mates, Kawana Tengo and Aomame Masami, who were separated at the age of ten, and the process by which they are reunited as adults some twenty-five years later. Tengo and Aomame are in certain ways polar opposites to one another: as a child Tengo was popular, got excellent grades, and was widely recognized as a math prodigy; today he is a literary stylist par excellence, as well as a celebrated math teacher at a cram school. By contrast, Aomame was a virtual outcast as a child, owing to her parents' activities (as well as her own) as Jehovah's

Witnesses; today she works as a martial arts instructor at a fitness club, moonlighting as a uniquely talented assassin, targeting men who abuse their wives and children.

Despite the difference in their status at school, however, Tengo and Aomame shared one significant characteristic as children that might be termed traumatic: both were raised by zealots, humiliated by their parents' adherence to beliefs they themselves could not share and that were not accepted by the communities around them. Aomame's case is not surprising; as a child she was taken with her mother "witnessing," visiting strangers' homes in the hopes of converting them to Christianity, an activity she found deeply embarrassing. Tengo, for his part, was raised by a man who collected monthly dues for NHK (Nippon Hōsō Kyōkai, or Japan Broadcasting Corporation), Japan's government-sponsored broadcasting service, which since the advent of television in Japan in the late 1950s has collected "voluntary" monthly dues from every household in Japan that possesses a television set. In an age when television is broadcast into homes whether they pay dues or not, and in which many channels besides NHK are now available, not a few Japanese have come to wonder why such dues are still required, and some avoid paying the dues altogether, recognizing that NHK has no special power to force compliance. NHK collectors have therefore become a widely disliked symbol of unwanted government intrusion into people's lives. To make matters worse for Tengo, his father insisted on bringing him along on collection rounds on Sundays. Occasionally Tengo and Aomame would pass one another on the street during these Sunday ordeals, so each developed an unspoken understanding of the other's sense of humiliation and isolation.

The two never really got to know one another as children, however. Their interaction was limited to just two face-to-face encounters. The first occurs after Aomame has been shunned by the other children in their science class; "they referred to her as 'The One,' not so much to bully or humiliate her, but rather to indicate that she simply 'did not exist.'"[39] Tengo comes to her rescue and becomes her lab partner, carefully explaining the experiment they are doing until she understands it. "They had been in the same class for two years, and this was the first time (as well as the last) that Tengo had spoken to her. . . . As a result of having stood up for 'The One,' however, without any words being spoken, his status in the class dropped a step.

In their minds, his association with the girl had caused some of her pollution to be transferred to him" (1:274).

Their second meeting is more significant. One day, after school has finished, Tengo and Aomame find themselves momentarily alone in their classroom. Without a word Aomame takes Tengo's hand and holds it tightly. At that moment, it seems that something crucial—but not as yet understood—is passed between them. This is one of the central moments in the novel:

> There was no one else there. As if she had made up her mind to do it, she quickly crossed the classroom, stood beside him. Then, without hesitation, she grasped Tengo's hand, and looked up into his face (he was about four inches taller than her). Tengo, surprised, looked back down at her face. Their eyes met. Tengo could see in her eyes a transparent depth he had never seen before. The girl held his hand tightly in hers for a long time. Strongly, without slackening her grip even for a moment. Then she suddenly let go his hand, and with the hem of her skirt flaring, she trotted out of the classroom. (1:275)

Precisely what was exchanged between the two of them is impossible to say, but only a few chapters later, the present-day Aomame tells a friend about him, that he is the only person in the world she loves and that she will wait—for the rest of her life if necessary—for fate to bring him back to her. She will not, however, seek him out herself. "'What I want is to run into him by chance one day,'" she tells her friend. "'For instance, we pass each other on the street, or happen to be riding on the same bus'" (1:340).

The novel begins with Aomame on her way to a kill, getting caught in a traffic jam on one of Tokyo's elevated highways and leaving her taxi to climb down the emergency ladder to the ground level below, from where she plans to take a train the rest of the way to her destination. When she climbs down the ladder, however, she unwittingly leaves the familiar world of "1984" behind her and enters the almost—but only *almost*—identical world of "1Q84." In this peculiar realm, more of a "time slip" than another physical dimension, the Tokyo Metropolitan Police have exchanged revolvers for automatic weapons, the world is invaded by metaphysical creatures known as "the Little People," thunder booms without lightning, and most prominently, there are two moons in the evening sky—one normal, the other smaller, "slightly misshapen, with a greenish color, as though growing with a thin layer of moss" (1:351).

Various conflicting elements—and perhaps fate itself—combine to bring Tengo and Aomame onto a collision course with one another in this strange realm. A seventeen-year-old girl known as "Fukaeri" (short for Fukada Eriko), who has run away from a religious cult headed by her father, known to all simply as "the Leader," dictates the story of her adventures to another, who writes the story down and submits it to a literary magazine, for which Tengo works part-time as a copy editor. At his editor's suggestion, Tengo rewrites the story, and they publish it in Fukaeri's name, winning for her a prize for new writers of literature and creating a major best seller. Meanwhile, Aomame's attention is drawn to the cult because "the Leader" is rumored to be sexually abusing the preteen *miko* (something like vestal virgins) in his cult. She is therefore dispatched by her controller, an old woman who arranges her targets for her, to "convey him to the other world" (2:17), as they euphemize their assassinations.

Aomame is initially not aware that Tengo is in contact with the Leader's daughter, nor does she realize that her actions will eventually lead her to him. Rather, through a lengthy conversation with the Leader, just before she ends his life, she learns that the cult's grounding in the spiritual world is not feigned and that the Leader himself truly is a holy man, whose function is to hear the voices of the Little People, forest spirits who maintain balance and order in the world. For Fukaeri, the Little People represent the danger of unwanted control in human affairs, and to escape their influence, she flees the cult and tells her story to another. The Leader, feeling similarly used by the Little People and suffering from considerable pain, actually welcomes the death Aomame has come to deliver, but upon hearing his story, Aomame is no longer inclined to complete her mission. In the end she does so only after the Leader assures her that it is the only way to save Tengo from the wrath of the Little People, even though he warns her that Tengo's salvation will likely require her to sacrifice her own life as well.

Following completion of her mission, Aomame's original plan is to alter her appearance through plastic surgery and flee the city, but spotting Tengo at a park visible from the safe house where she hides from the cult's vengeance and also realizing that she is mysteriously with child, she abandons this plan, electing instead for a chance to meet him again and perhaps rescue him—along with herself and her unborn child—from the world of "1Q84."

This is the basic plot of *1Q84*, whose mythological and journalistic aspects will be explored in greater detail later in this volume. Here we will examine the function of Fukaeri and Tengo's narrative, *Kūki sanagi* ("air cocoon," rendered as *Air Chrysalis* in the English translation of the novel), and how it functions to create a new reality not only for Aomame but for all the characters in the story. This embedded narrative recounts Fukaeri's experiences within the compound of her father's cult, centered chiefly upon the Little People, whom I have described as forest spirits but Murakami describes as "'something like messengers from a primitive, underground world,'"[40] and how those Little People teach Fukaeri to spin a cocoon out of the air. When the cocoon is finished, it contains a perfect replica of Fukaeri, permitting one of them to remain behind in the cult's compound while the other makes her escape.[41] Fleeing to the home of a family friend, Fukaeri, who suffers from severe dyslexia and has great difficulty writing, relates her story verbally to her benefactor's daughter, who then writes it out and submits it to the magazine edited by Tengo's boss, Komatsu, who then passes it along to Tengo for rewriting.

But how, precisely, does this embedded narrative come to be the reality of "1Q84"? This is a complex question and returns us to Murakami's notion of the "internal narrative." Tengo, who is a brilliant literary stylist, struggles at the beginning of the text to produce a surpassing novel of his own because, as his editor Komatsu notes, he has not yet managed to access his inner narrative. "'What you need to be writing is inside you somewhere for sure, but it's like a scared little animal that's burrowed its way into a deep hole and won't come out'" (1:49). As Tengo recrafts Fukaeri's narrative in his own words and style, however, his own internal story awakens as well. "As Tengo wrote he sensed the birth of a new wellspring inside himself. No great rush of water bursting forth from this spring, it was rather like a tiny trickle of water coming out of a rocky fissure. The volume of water was minute, yet welled up ceaselessly, droplet by droplet" (1:354).

From this perspective *1Q84* may be seen as a novel about writers and writing, and it is in this context that the obvious and oft-noted references to (if not actual parody of) George Orwell's *Nineteen*

Eighty-Four (1948) come into play. Late in the first volume, Tengo attempts to explain the basic plot of the Orwell novel to Fukaeri, focusing particularly on the function of protagonist Winston Smith's work at the "Ministry of Truth," which is revising history to match the current political stance of the government. His description of Smith's task—which is undeniably and uncomfortably similar to revisionist efforts in Japan even now to obscure or obliterate aspects of Japan's history from 1931 to 1945—speaks volumes about the power of language to corrupt and confuse reality, ultimately to construct new ones. "'When a new history is created, the old history is totally thrown out,'" Tengo tells her, "'and when history is changed too often, gradually no one knows anymore what the truth was. . . . Our memories are made up of individual memories and collective memories. . . . History is our collective memories. When those are threatened—even rewritten—we lose the ability to maintain our true selves'" (1:459–60). This process can be applied to the individual as well, and in fact it is precisely what is happening to Aomame, who begins to doubt her memory and her identity as she realizes that the world of "1Q84" is altered from "1984" in minute but noticeable ways. Her first inkling is when she notices the Tokyo Metropolitan Police carrying automatic weapons rather than the revolvers to which she is accustomed. Asking someone when this change occurred, she is told it was following the shoot-out at Lake Motosu—an incident she does not remember despite being an avid newspaper reader. Exploring the incident through newspaper archives, she begins to wonder how she could have missed this major event that led to the shootings of several police officers and a major change in their sidearm policy.

In time, Tengo finds himself enveloped by the world of "1Q84" as well, a fact as difficult for him to accept as it was for Aomame. He is particularly troubled by the fact that this new world is virtually identical to the setting of the story he has created with Fukaeri. "Am I in the world of the novel?" he asks himself when, looking up, he sees two moons hanging in the sky, precisely as he described them in the final manuscript (2:425–26). In time Tengo realizes, as does the reader, that he has internalized that world, so that when he writes—and later, even when he is not writing—he has difficulty keeping track of the various realities that swirl in and out of his mind, until the external, "objective" world has all but ceased to exist, or more accurately, has joined together with all other language-based worlds:

> He wrote a story in which there were two moons. A world that contained the Little People and the air cocoon. These were things he had borrowed from Fukaeri's *Kūki sanagi,* but by now they had become wholly his own. While he faced his manuscript, his consciousness lived in that world. Even when he had put his pen down and left his desk, his consciousness sometimes remained there. At such times he had the peculiar feeling his flesh and consciousness were separated, and he could no longer distinguish where the real world ended and the imaginary world began. (3:57–58)

In a sense, Tengo expresses many of Murakami's own statements on the act of writing, the dilemmas faced by the imaginative novelist who grapples with a vast array of worlds, all fictitious, but none necessarily more so than the "actual" world. One hears in the passage above echoes of the author's metaphor of descending into the depths of the cellar beneath the "two-story house" of the imagination.

Through the simple fact of being *declared,* then, both in the spoken and written word, the world of "1Q84," with its two moons, Little People, and automatic weapon–carrying police officers, has come into actual existence; it is unquestionably constructed from words, from language, yet it has also taken on actual, concrete existence—others inhabit it, and those who are capable of doing so remark on its peculiarity.

Interestingly, though privileging neither, Murakami makes a clear distinction in this text between spoken and written language, with Fukaeri and Tengo representing each of these respectively. The new world initially comes into being when Fukaeri *speaks* it to her adoptive sister, but its potential is not fully realized until Tengo has interpreted it and (re)produced it through the simultaneous act of reading and writing, lending it coherence and order. There is an underlying sense of the *sacred* in this joint act of creation, for Tengo and Fukaeri have assumed the roles and responsibilities of creator deities, and yet, as even the gods eventually discover, no reality lasts forever; whether grounded in the spoken or the written word, every reality is ultimately revealed to be shifty and impermanent.

And so, we might ask, is there a moral to this story? What can we learn from these texts? First and foremost, we may conclude that words are fallible, not to be trusted, but in the end *words are all we have,* and it is with words that we must construct and interact with the world's various realities. For Murakami, these realities are best understood as "narratives," but we might as easily call them ideologies; and like most human-made constructs—insofar as all ideologies are ultimately revealed to be constructs—such "narratives" prove vexingly unstable entities, despite their apparent solidity as they grow more widespread through the groups, cults, or even societies that generate them, and despite the evident determination of those societies to uphold and protect those narratives (think, for instance, of America and "democracy"). Furthermore, Murakami's mistrust of language-bound narratives is not a new or recent development; indeed, it has been more than half a century since Roland Barthes constructed his theory of what he called "myth," describing essentially the same thing as we mean here by "narrative." Barthes argues that modern, industrialized societies are governed in large part by such myths, constructed by each society's political arm and disseminated via the mass media (the political arm's propaganda machine) as commonsensical, therefore as absolutely real. For Barthes, myth is always political, always constructed, and at the same time always constitutive of our view of the world, and yet myth nearly always seeks to masquerade as something timeless, eternal, and "natural." He says:

> Semiology has taught us that myth has the task of giving a historical intention a natural justification, and making contingency appear eternal. . . . The world enters language as a dialectical relation between activities, between human actions; it comes out of myth as a harmonious display of essences. A conjuring trick has taken place; it has turned reality inside out, it has emptied it of history and has filled it with Nature, it has removed from things their human meaning so as to make them signify a human insignificance. The function of myth is to empty reality: it is, literally, a ceaseless flowing out, a hemorrhage, or perhaps an evaporation, in short, a perceptible absence.[42]

What this finally comes to mean, in slightly less elaborate terms, is (a) that historical discourse, like political discourse (and, as we shall see, journalistic discourse) is a series of decisions, of revisions, many or most of which are calculated to certain ends, while others are accidental; and (b) that myth treats these choices as inevitable, presents such discourses as faits accompli, thereby lending an apparently—

but falsely—*natural* (predestined) grounding to choices that, ultimately, could have turned out otherwise. In a sense, this is also what Jacques Derrida sought to do through deconstruction: to challenge the center, or the grounding, of those "truths that we hold to be self-evident," as the expression goes, to expose human constructs *as* constructs, and to "de-*con*struct" (emphasis on the first syllable of *construct*, as a noun) ourselves, that is, rid ourselves of the burden of such assumptions. In exposing those "self-evident" groundings as fallacies, we encounter both the curse and the blessing of the shifting center: on the one hand we realize that all reality becomes somehow less reliable in the process, mutable as the center shifts, now this way, now that; on the other, we are liberated from constructs masquerading as absolute truths. Thus is all language politicized.[43]

Tamura Kafka's friend and protector Ōshima recognizes the risks of such constructs-turned-absolutes in *Kafka on the Shore* when dealing with activists who spout slogans of which they have no clear understanding, noting that "'theses that take on lives of their own, empty slogans, usurped ideals, inflexible systems, these are what I fear most. . . . Narrow-mindedness and intolerance born of lack of imagination are like parasites; they change hosts and forms, but they go on living'" (1:314). Inevitably the question arises as to *how* this process occurs, *who* is empowered to transform these essentially *subjective* matters—insofar as all linguistic decisions are ultimately subjective—into *apparently* objective, "natural," inevitable, commonsensical reality. This only becomes a major dilemma, presumably, when the inner narrative of the individual is threatened or replaced by that of the group, as noted in the introduction; at such times, individual subjectivity is compromised in favor of social homogenization.

The tension between individual subjectivity and the group has been a central conflict in Murakami's fiction from early on. Certainly from *A Wild Sheep Chase* the subversion or appropriation of the individual subject and his/her internal narrative has been a prominent theme. Initially this appropriation was attributed to the postwar Japanese State, which offered in return a comfortable life of affluence and a state-sponsored ideology of economic participation. The State, represented in highly concentrated, yet thoroughly abstract images and characters (the semimythical sheep in *A Wild Sheep Chase,* the System in *Hard-Boiled Wonderland and the End of the World,* Wataya Noboru in *The Wind-Up Bird Chronicle,* and so on), appeared to hold insurmountable power, a mixture of political, commercial, and media muscle, and yet, somehow, Murakami's loner protagonists, representing the voice of the nonconformist, the determined individualist, battled with considerable success against these superpowers. This is what Murakami meant when he spoke in Jerusalem about eggs hitting a great and powerful wall. His protagonists have always been the eggs, and somehow or other, even after shattering, they show that the egg can and does continue its struggle. Indeed, some of them, as will be seen, grow even stronger once having broken out of their shells. . . .

All of this serves to remind us that if language is indeed the progenitor of reality, then he who speaks becomes ultimately powerful—like a god, as Murakami once put it—and so the stakes are rather high in the question of "who speaks." If, as I contend, our internal "narrative" is constituted by language, and if our identity is grounded in that narrative, then the power to speak amounts to the power to construct (or, more importantly, to *re*construct) identity itself, the very right to exist. And if we expand this argument to include the collective narrative to which all humanity connects, from which all humanity derives its understanding of what it actually means to exist as an individual and a human being (our place determined in the context of all others), then the stakes are even more awesome.

Such questions continue to be played out in more recent works, like *Kafka on the Shore* and *1Q84,* as well, and yet in these more recent works a new model emerges, a more aggressive strategy of resistance to the encroachment of ready-made group narratives that seek to destroy and replace the individual narrative. Not surprisingly, this signals the advent of a new and improved Murakami protagonist. Whereas characters like Rat and Naoko would simply lie down and die, and the old "Boku" characters would leave the field of conflict depressed and apathetic, the new Murakami hero will not go quietly, nor will he or she accept defeat. Tamura Kafka's reconstruction of his identity is undertaken through the confrontation with and proactive manipulation of his internal narrative, rather than through the denial or erasure of it. Aomame, allied with Tengo and Fukaeri, will battle fiercely to resist the efforts of the Little People to control the narrative world Tengo and Fukaeri have created, and as the parodic nature of the work's title suggests, at stake is the past, present, and future "history" of humanity itself.

If it is true, as I have argued in this chapter, that all reality is perception and that all perception is based upon language, culture, and experience—individual and collective—then we are naturally led to consider how language and culture play a role in other aspects of human development and social structure. The chapters that follow will explore the nature, structure, and actual landscape of what I shall term the *metaphysical realm*, an admittedly general and unsatisfying term, but used because that realm seems to embody so many things at once: the individual unconscious, the collective unconscious, the mystical "world soul," and even the mythological land of the dead.

TWO

Into the Mad, Metaphysical Realm

> I went into the bedroom to check the time on the watch I had left by the bed. But the watch had stopped.
>
> —Murakami Haruki, *Umibe no Kafka*

SUPERNATURAL OR METAPHYSICAL ELEMENTS have been an integral part of Murakami Haruki's fiction from the beginning of his career. In those early days, however, those elements, which are widely understood to be associated with that type of writing known as magical realist, presented themselves as peripheral to the principal narratives being told. They were, rather, a means or a tool by which the Murakami hero gained access to his inner mind, the metaphysical realm. It is even possible that the author himself, as he learned through practice the craft of writing in these early works, was not wholly aware of the centrality of that "other world" to his narratives. As a tool that world was functional, to be sure, but we see little urge in Murakami's first few works to explore it in any great detail.

Near the end of *Hear the Wind Sing,* for instance, when a boy throws himself into a seemingly bottomless well on Mars, emerging more than a billion years later to have a chat with the wind, the well and its adjacent tunnels receive no more than a few lines. When the boy realizes he is really talking to himself, he ends his life. In *Pinball, 1973* the "other world" is presented as a cavernous cold-storage facility filled with pinball machines, but still, in the end it is just a warehouse. Readers may even have missed the growing sense of unreality that unnerves the protagonist as he makes his journey to the warehouse by taxi, a point I make in greater detail below.

This idea of the journey to the "other world" as a process of moving from "this side" to "over there" gains ground and detail in *A Wild Sheep Chase* when the protagonist moves from Tokyo to Hokkaido and gradually to more and more remote places, until he finally penetrates the core of the metaphysical realm in the form of his friend Rat's mountain villa. Not until *Hard-Boiled Wonderland and the End of the World* does Murakami attempt a detailed and focused examination of the "other world," yet even in this instance he shies away from description of the actual inner mind; rather, "the Town," as we saw in the previous chapter, is an artificially constructed approximation of the inner world. Nonetheless, this novel gives our first hint of the growing importance of the inner world in Murakami's mind.

Perhaps this is why, even in works like *Norwegian Wood* and *South of the Border, West of the Sun*—by the author's own estimation written in a quasi-realist mode—the "other world" continues to make its presence known. *Norwegian Wood* concerns the relationship between a college student named Watanabe Tōru and Naoko, a young woman suffering from a serious psychological condition that, in all likelihood, resulted from the suicide of her boyfriend Kizuki some years previously. Watanabe, who loves Naoko himself, tries desperately to keep her in this world, on "this side," but to no avail; for Naoko, the voices she hears calling her from "over there"—the land of the dead—are too attractive to ignore. *South of the Border, West of the Sun* is the tale of a middle-aged husband and father named Hajime, who suddenly runs across a woman he knew in childhood. He makes up his mind to run away with her, but in the end she disappears—again, very likely into the "other world"—before he gets the chance. In both of these so-called realist narratives the metaphysical realm always lurks just beside these characters, calling to them, inviting them to cross over to the other side. It is a motif that returns with great prominence in the most recent work, *Colorless Tsukuru Tazaki and His Years of Pilgrimage,* as well.

We see the trend away from the individual model of the "this side-over there" dichotomy toward a more collective one beginning with *The Wind-Up Bird Chronicle,* a signal that Murakami was beginning to recognize more clearly that the metaphysical realm is more than simply a means of reconnecting with the individual past; rather, from this point it begins to take shape as a venue in its own right, the very point of creation and continuation of what might be called the human experience. Marked by its transcendence of the human construct of time, preserving simultaneously *all* human consciousness and memory, past and future, the metaphysical realm now grows into a timeless Time and a spaceless Space wherein characters are connected yet at the same time absorbed, dissolved into the totality and wholeness of the realm, merging with all humanity, living, dead, and yet to be born.

Mapping "Over There"

Before getting into a detailed consideration of how the "other world" functions in Murakami fiction, we need to examine some of the important characteristics of this realm. There is, of course, no one simple way of describing the "other world," given the guises it takes across the broad spectrum of the author's repertoire, a fact that has contributed, no doubt, to the variety of labels that have been applied to it. I have generally preferred terms such as *metaphysical realm* and *other world,* but many Japanese critics opt for the even less specific *achiragawa*, or "over there." Part of our challenge lies in the fact that this *achiragawa* is many things at once: a metaphysical zone, freed from the constraints of time and space; a wormhole, or conduit into other physical worlds; an unconscious shared space, similar to Jung's collective unconscious; a repository for memories, dreams, and visions; the land of the dead; the "world soul" of mysticism; heaven or hell; eternity. With respect to Murakami's fictional landscape, it is most effective to imagine this realm alternately as psychological or spiritual, though at times these clearly overlap. This is because the characteristics that mark the unconscious as envisioned by psychoanalysis, for instance, are frequently similar or identical to those that mark traditional visions of the underworld, of the mystical "world soul," and the spirit world. As we shall see, most of Murakami's stories shift back and forth between these two conceptualizations of "over there."

Murakami's metaphysical other world stands outside the boundaries of what we think of as reality, can (usually) be reached only unconsciously, by accident or chance (much, in fact, like entering the state of sleep); it contains no actual fixed boundaries (though this is not always evident to visitors); it is seldom found the same way twice; and when "time" exists there at all, it seems to run unpredictably, in all directions, quite unlike the linear, mono-directional tool we have constructed in the conscious, physical world. The reason for this, ironically, is most simply and clearly stated by the celebrated theoretical physicist and mathematician Stephen Hawking, who writes in *A Brief History of Time* that "[t]he increase of disorder or entropy with time is one example of what is called an arrow of time, something that distinguishes the past from the future, giving a direction to time."[1] This, however, cannot occur in the metaphysical world, because, transcending the physical as its name implies, neither entropy, nor indeed change of any kind, can affect what is stored there. Psychologist Iwamiya Keiko, writing on *Kafka on the Shore,* notes similarly that "on the other side of the 'gateway stone,' the everyday flow of time is transcended, we are separated from the world grounded in cause and effect, and another, different sort of reality comes into being."[2] This is paralleled in our conceptions of the psyche, for, as Freud notes in his introductory lectures on psychoanalysis, "[i]n the id there is nothing corresponding to the idea of time, no recognition of the passage of time, and . . . no alteration of mental processes by the passage of time."[3]

The key phrase in Freud's statement is the "*passage* of time," for time does not "pass"—does not *move*—in the other world. It would be a mistake to imagine, however, that no form of time exists there; rather, that realm is bound up in a transcendent form of what I will call "Time" (with a capital *T*), something like Plato's ideal. This Time exists in the "other world" as a totality, a unity that precludes any distinction between past and future, functioning solely as an endless "present." This is why we often have the illusion of timelessness in the metaphysical realm, and why those who enter it can never gain their temporal bearings, for the meaning in any specific time in the physical world is grounded in its distinction from all other times that it is *not*. Because Time exists as a solitary unity in the "other world," these distinctions, by definition, cannot exist.

Freud's dictum on time is useful here, for we may understand the metaphysical realm in early Murakami fiction to correspond, roughly, at least, to Freud's concept of the "id," the reasons for which are not necessarily capricious. Beyond the happy pun on the terminology—the Japanese pronunciation of "id" is *ido,* a homonym in Japanese for "well"[4]—the well turns out to be an ideal sort of image for Murakami's purposes, as it both physically and figuratively leads from the world

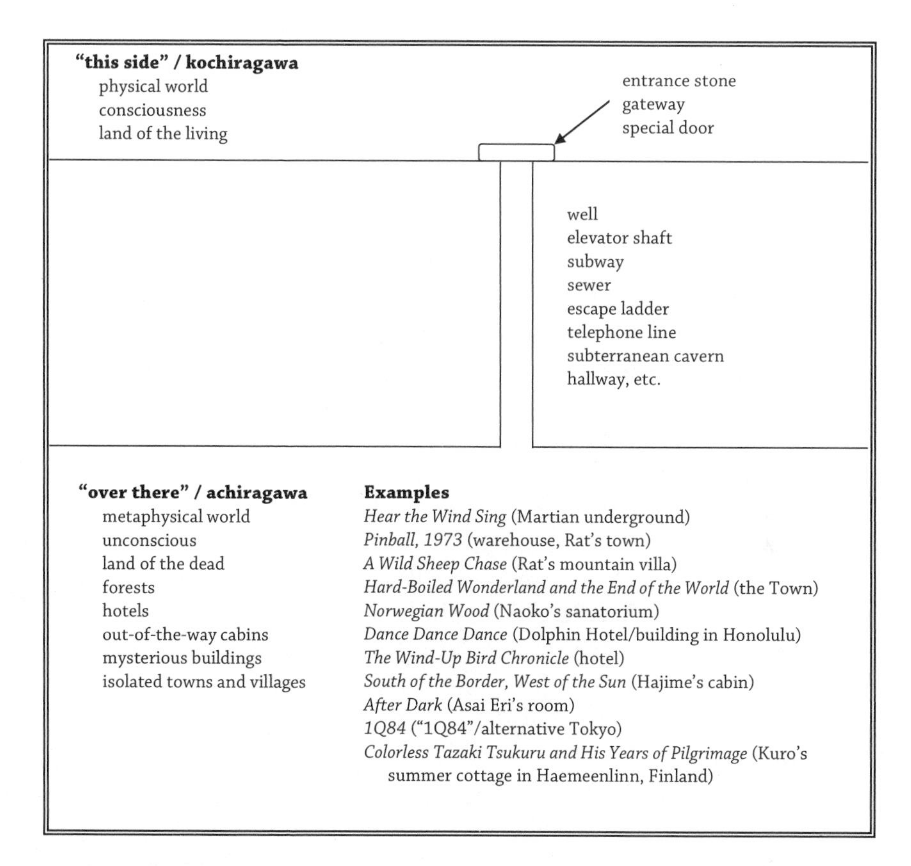

Physical and metaphysical realms

"up here"—that is, the world of light and life, of the everyday—down through a mysterious, often perilous shaft into the underworld, where darkness, cold, and, of course, death lie in wait. Over time Murakami has expanded his repertoire of such passageways to include elevator shafts, telephone lines, hallways, subway tunnels, ladders, sewers, and subterranean caves, among other things. Sometimes the conduits are blocked off, as indeed the metaphysical world is sometimes blocked off as well, while other times it stands open.

Suspension of physical time and space are not the only aspects of Murakami's model of the metaphysical world that stand out or remain constant in the author's work today. He commonly characterizes the place as dark, dank, and cold (though this has changed slightly in degree in recent years) with a persistent sense of dread or foreboding. In later works—most notably from *The Wind-Up Bird Chronicle* in the mid-1990s—the area has become a labyrinth, but even this was hinted at a decade earlier in *Hard-Boiled Wonderland and the End of the World* when Murakami added a surrounding forest to the unconscious Town in which his protagonist was trapped; the forest is an obvious image for the maze or labyrinth because the trees all tend to look the same, and one easily becomes lost. The forest, as Joseph Campbell notes, is also a common setting not only for magical unions that occur between lovers in ancient legends (Tristan and Isolde, Lancelot and Guinevere) but for the mystical trials that befall mythological heroes, the destination for "the questing individual who, alone, would seek beyond the tumult of the state, in the silences of earth and sea and the silence of his heart, the Word beyond words of the mystery of nature and his own potentiality as man—like the knight errant riding forth into the forest 'there where he saw it to be the thickest.'"[5] Campbell's understanding of the forest as a departure from the impositions of the State is both appropriate and yet ironic in the context of *Hard-Boiled Wonderland and the End of the World,* whose hero is essentially banished to the "forest" *by* the State itself, yet finds in the metaphysical forest a place that appears to lie beyond the reach of the forces that seek to control him.

Yet another aspect of the metaphysical realm is its surrealist atmosphere, accompanied by the gradual loss of memory and will. This, too, is prominent from *The Wind-Up Bird Chronicle,* essentially a psychological thriller wherein Okada Kumiko gradually loses her sense of identity in the other world, but once more has its roots in *Hard-Boiled Wonderland and the End of the World,* in which the inhabitants of the Town, once their shadows have died, lose all sense of who they are, or were, as well as their relationship to others in the physical/conscious world. This is likely what Murakami means when, in his two-story house metaphor, he says that one ought not spend too much time in the subbasement, for the longer one spends down there ("over there"), the less likely one is to return to "this side" with any concrete sense of who one is. From Kumiko and Lt. Mamiya in *The Wind-Up Bird Chronicle* to Nakata in *Kafka on the Shore,* Murakami fiction is littered with the shattered empty shells of characters whose shadows have been left behind in—dissolved into—that daunting realm.

Of Psyche and Soul

Before exploring the manner in which the physical and metaphysical worlds function in the various texts to be examined in this and later chapters, I will briefly describe how these worlds connect with one another and how each is accessed by the various characters who populate Murakami fiction. And while it would be overly simplistic to characterize these realms purely and simply in the psychological terms of *conscious* and *unconscious*, certain aspects of the Freudian and Jungian models of the psyche will prove useful in showing the true nature of the "other world," even in its more mystical/spiritual aspects. Indeed, one recalls that Jung himself, from his early writings, acknowledges a close connection between the human psyche and the human soul, lamenting that the price of our modernity has been the loss of our spiritual awareness:

> We moderns are faced with the necessity of rediscovering the life of the spirit; we must experience it anew for ourselves. It is the only way in which we can break the spell that binds us to the cycle of biological events. My position on this question is the third point of difference between Freud's views and my own. Because of it I am accused of mysticism.[6]

Later in life, in a series of informal reminiscences (many of which, incidentally, describe visions that are unquestionably mystic in nature), Jung notes that "the soul, the anima, establishes the relationship to the unconscious. In a certain sense this is also a relationship to the collectivity of the dead; for the unconscious corresponds to the mythic land of the dead, the land of the ancestors."[7] For Jung—and for Murakami—the inner psyche and the "other world" share certain characteristics and might even be conflated into a single entity.

Murakami's early works, on the one hand, show greater similarity to a Freudian model of the mind, in which the individual psyche exists autonomously, disconnected from other minds except in the conscious realm. In these works—up to (but not including) *The Wind-Up Bird Chronicle*—the protagonist gains access to his own individual inner mind, a metaphysical realm that is entirely his own, and the memories he meets there are equally connected to himself alone.[8] When Boku enters Rat's mountain villa at the end of *A Wild Sheep Chase*, for instance, and has a long conversation with the dead Rat, he has entered a space that cannot be accessed by anyone else. This, more than any other reason, is why his ear model girlfriend must be sent away shortly after their arrival at Rat's mountain villa near the end of the novel.

From *The Wind-Up Bird Chronicle* onward, on the other hand, the metaphysical world is thrown wide open, depicted as a kind of "shared space" to which all characters appear to have access, wherein they meet, engage one another, and return to "this side." In psychological terms this may be viewed as a shift from the Freudian model to the Jungian one; in metaphysical terms, it permits Murakami a considerably wider range of imaginative depiction for the "other world," for what was personal, individual memory is now a collective one—*the* Narrative—that grounds all humanity from the beginning of time. In Jungian terms this is the "collective unconscious"; a mystic would call it the *anima mundi,* or "world soul."

Having reached this point in our general description of the "other world," we can now usefully examine some of the specific depictions of that world in Murakami's fiction, from early to recent. These examinations will reveal the gradual but noticeable development of both the "other world" to which the Murakami hero gains access, and the hero himself, whose ability to recognize, access, and manipulate the "other world" grows proportionally with Murakami's ability to write it.

Martian Winds and Wells: *Hear the Wind Sing*

Our first glimpse of the metaphysical realm comes rather tentatively in *Hear the Wind Sing,* which follows "Boku" through a period of eighteen days in late summer of 1970. Boku's summer is spent drinking beer at J's Bar and attempting to make friends with a rather difficult young woman who has only nine fingers. The woman—barely more than a girl, really—has some cause to be difficult with Boku, who has a significant advantage when they first meet: he is wide awake, having brought the woman home after she had too much to drink the previous night. She awakens to find herself in her bed, naked, with Boku watching her, and is thus understandably mistrustful of his intentions.

In numerous ways the nine-fingered girl serves as a prelude to Naoko, the tragic heroine of *Norwegian Wood.* Like Naoko, whose first and only experience with intercourse is followed by a rapid decline in mental health, the nine-fingered girl has been injured sexually—in fact, she is pregnant but has no idea when this happened or with whom. Also like Naoko, the nine-fingered girl hears voices from "over there" urging her to die. "'When I'm all on my own and it's quiet, I can hear people talking to me. . . . people I know, and people I don't. My father and mother, my teachers in school, all sorts of people. . . . It's usually horrible stuff—like that I ought to get on with it and die—and then they say dirty things, too.'"[9] What these "dirty things" are is not made clear, but it is quite obvious that these messages of death and (presumably) sexuality represent the uninhibited voices of her id.

Further, the nine-fingered girl is not the only character in this novel to hear the spectral voices emerging from the metaphysical realm. The work takes its title from a scene (in an embedded narrative by the fictitious writer "Derek Hartfield") wherein a boy jumps into a seemingly bottomless well on Mars, seeking the ultimate abyss. As he falls deeper and deeper, he begins to feel a sense of benevolence from the well, his body gently enveloped in its peculiar strength. At last he enters a side tunnel and walks along it for an indeterminate period; it may be hours or even days, but he cannot judge, because his watch has stopped and he feels neither the hunger nor the fatigue that would indicate the passage of time. Eventually the boy locates an adjacent tunnel and climbs back to the surface, where the wind whispers to him that he has been in the well for more than 1.5 billion years. "'That tunnel you came out of was dug out by a time warp,'" the wind goes on. "'So we're wandering around in between time. From the Big Bang to the Big Crunch. For us there is no life or death. We are the wind'" (1:97). The boy then asks the wind what it has learned in this endless wandering but receives only a sardonic laugh in return, whereupon he puts a gun barrel into his mouth and pulls the trigger.

This, then, is our first glimpse of the Murakami metaphysical world, which we might not recognize as the unconscious, however, until the boy expresses wonder that the wind can talk, and the wind replies, "'Me? You're the one talking. I'm just giving hints to your inner self'" (1:97).[10] Tsuge Teruhiko, who points out the homonymic relationship between "id" and *ido*, identifies the wind as the boy's own unconscious voice:

> The "wind" that emerges here is the narrative of the youth's inner self, which has escaped from the "id" *(ido)*. . . . If we take this "wind" as a metaphor for Jung's "collective unconscious," the meaning of the work's title becomes quite clear. . . . The wind's message to the boy is to "listen to the voice of the collective unconscious that has arisen through your individual unconscious."[11]

Invocation of the voice of the "individual unconscious" connects effectively with the notion of the "inner narrative" noted in the previous chapter, but what is the boy to have learned from the wind? Murakami once described his earliest works as expressions of the confusion experienced by his generation in the aftermath of the 1960s.[12] That confusion is clearly evident in this novel, whose nihilistic message seems to be that life is meaningless, a realization that leads the boy to despair, and death.

Into the Chilly Gloom: *Pinball, 1973*

The "other world" receives a more concrete description in *Pinball, 1973*, a work structured through parallel narratives that depict, alternately, the movements of Boku in Tokyo (now running a small public relations firm with a friend) and Rat, from whom he is now permanently separated. It is through the Rat sequences that we find the "other world" emerging.

Many commentators on the Rat trilogy have argued that Rat is a doppelganger figure to Boku, his dark, brooding, yet outspoken inner self. He is best thought of as a kind of inner voice, a companion for Boku, who is almost pathologically withdrawn from the world around him. The extent of his interiority is hinted early in *Hear the Wind Sing* when we learn that Boku as a child was so quiet as to be virtually mute. Then, quite suddenly at the age of fourteen, "I suddenly started talking, like a dam had burst. I don't remember what I talked about, but I talked nonstop for three months, like I was filling in fourteen years' worth of blank space. Then, in mid-July, I developed a 104° fever and took three days off from school. After that I became your average fourteen year-old boy, neither mute nor chatterbox" (1:26). We see here the buildup of internal, psychic pressure, a "venting" of sorts, followed by the restoration of a sense of balance between the two worlds. And yet, throughout the Rat trilogy we see that Boku maintains the habit of saying no more than necessary. And most of what he really needs to say is addressed to Rat and "J," the Chinese owner of the bar where he and Rat drink. This is slightly misleading, however, because neither of these two characters actually exists in the world outside of Boku's mind.

It is highly tempting when reading nearly all of Murakami's works to overschematize the events and relationships that emerge in those narratives. This is particularly true of the relationship that forms between Rat and Boku, whose parallel narratives seem to point us toward some symbolic or thematic revelation about them. One celebrated attempt at such schematization was performed by Katō Norihiro, one of the more prolific Murakami scholars, who attempts to chart out the movements and events that befall each of these characters.[13] Such exercises are unfailingly entertaining and all but irresistible, but in this case pointless because Rat is never actually alive, in the physical sense of the word, within the pages of any of the novels that form the Rat trilogy. Rather, Rat exists—and has always done—as part of "the town" *(machi)*, presented to us as Boku's hometown but in fact nothing more than his memory of the place where he passed his youth.

There is considerable evidence to support this argument. Early in *Hear the Wind Sing* Boku describes his first meeting with Rat. The year is 1967, the same year Boku begins university in Tokyo. Boku has no recollection of how he and Rat were introduced but recalls being in Rat's Fiat 600 sports car, blind drunk, tearing down a rural road at more than fifty miles per hour, when they went through a fence and slammed—still at full speed—into a stone pillar at a park. Although the Fiat is completely destroyed, neither man has a mark on him. After Boku pulls Rat out of the wreckage, the two buy more beer, then drink it by the seashore, possessed by an uncanny sense of strength.

So how did they even survive this crash, let alone emerge without a scratch?

The answer is, of course, that the "crash" took place in the "other world," where neither alteration nor death can occur. It is something like having an accident in a dream; eventually one awakens. Boku eventually wakes up in the physical world; Rat remains where he belongs and has always been: "over there."

Whether Rat *ever* existed outside of Boku's mind is another matter, and one for which no definitive answer is possible. There is a flashback in *Pinball, 1973* in which Rat thinks back to the spring of 1970. "For Rat, the flow of time had gradually begun to lose its consistency three years earlier. It was the spring he had dropped out of college,"[14] we are told, but are we truly reading the narrative of Rat here, or is this the story of Boku himself? The corruption of time may as easily signal the moment at which Boku's (outer) world begins to close itself off from Rat's (inner) world, leaving the latter trapped and isolated. This puts into clearer perspective the "final" meeting between Rat and Boku, at Rat's mountain villa in Hokkaido at the end of *A Wild Sheep Chase,* as well. Rat begins their meeting by announcing that he is already dead, having hanged himself a week earlier, but the mountain villa is merely one more manifestation of the "other world," and to hang oneself in that realm carries no more meaning than to crash one's Fiat into a stone pillar there. It is, finally, just one more death in the dreamscape, nothing more.

If the Rat sequences, as I have contended, take place solely in the "other world," then what sort of a place is it? On this point we have considerably more detail. The "town" from which Boku comes, and to which he returns periodically, is dominated by an atmosphere of gloom and stagnation, and other characters who turn up there—including Rat—are part of that atmosphere. This includes J, the bartender who looks after Boku and Rat in all three novels. Interestingly, J confides to Boku in *Hear the Wind Sing* that he has not set foot outside the town "'since the year of the Tokyo Olympics'" (1:115), suggesting for us that the year of his death (or at any rate Boku's last time to meet him) was 1964. In a similar fashion "the woman," with whom Rat carries on a rather melancholy relationship, reminds us of a lost soul, crushed by a sense of loss and desolation. As they take a "romantic" stroll one evening near a seriously depressing cemetery, she leans heavily on Rat, barely moving, somewhere between sleep and death. The cemetery itself forms an effective microcosmic depiction of the "town" itself:

> The cemetery looked less like a collection of graves than a town that had been cast aside. More than half the plots were empty. Those for whom this ground was reserved were still living. . . . The cemetery was a place that had had special meaning for Rat when he was young: back before he could drive a car, he

> had brought girls up the river path to this place on his 250cc motorcycle any number of times. . . . So many scents had come to him, then disappeared. So many dreams, so much sadness, so many promises. *Now they were all gone.*[15]

Scenes such as this, as well as the ever-present images of the harbor lighthouse at dusk—a place Rat (Boku) used to play as a boy—and the dim glow of the streetlights, lend the text a sense of nostalgia and of decay, leaving us in little doubt that Rat, from the very start, has existed in the realm of memories, the land of the dead.

At the same time, this metaphysical realm is always connected to Boku's waking world as well, for it remains a part of Boku's overall psyche. That Boku's present girlfriend (the "nine-fingered girl") in *Hear the Wind Sing* is narratologically linked to the girl Rat carries around with him on the other side is strongly suggested from the respective scenes in which two women are initially encountered. In each scene we notice that both women are physically appraised while sleeping, defenseless, and in both cases we are given the impression of a healthy facade masking inner fragility, physical and mental. Here is the introduction of the "nine-fingered girl" in *Hear the Wind Sing*:

> I leaned against the headboard, naked, and after lighting a cigarette took a good look at the woman sleeping next to me. She was bathed in sunlight shining through the south-facing windows, sleeping soundly with the towel that had covered her pushed down to her feet. Occasionally she'd breathe hard, and her nicely shaped breasts rose and fell. She was well tanned, but it had been a while, so the color was starting to turn a bit drab, and the part normally covered by her swimsuit stood out in white, and looked like rotting flesh. (1:27)

And now Rat's girlfriend:

> She had small breasts, and her body, devoid of excess flesh, was nicely tanned, but it was a tan that looked somehow like she hadn't meant to get a tan. Her sharp cheek bones and thin mouth gave the impression of a good upbringing and inner strength, but the slight changes in expression that flitted through her body betrayed a defenseless naïveté deep inside.[16]

The initial description of Boku's "nine-fingered girl," in fact, with its mixture of good health ("nicely shaped breasts") and of death ("rotting flesh"), intimates her simultaneous existence in both worlds—that of the living and of the dead; Rat's girl, with her ambivalent combination of "inner strength" and "defenseless naïveté," signals a similarly dual existence. Are they the same woman? Has the "nine-fingered girl," by the time of *Pinball, 1973,* finally listened to the voices from the "other world" and joined them? If only Rat had taken the trouble to examine her hands instead of her breasts!

Passages to the World of the Dead

These depictions of the "other world" continue to develop in *A Wild Sheep Chase,* the third work in the Rat trilogy. As noted earlier, *A Wild Sheep Chase* is an adventure tale in which the protagonist embarks on a quest for a semimythical, all-powerful Sheep. Boku's quest for the Sheep is, of course, really only symbolic, for the true object of his search is Rat himself, and so when at last he discovers the one, he also finds the other, at Rat's mountain villa in the wilds of Hokkaido. This villa we may view as the "core" of Boku's inner mind.

Two separate descriptions of a journey highlight the descent into this metaphysical realm: first is a history of the town of "Jūnitakichō" and its settlement in the nineteenth century by farmers on the run from their creditors; the second is the trek carried out by Boku and his ear model girlfriend, which takes them first to Sapporo, then to Jūnitakichō, and finally to the villa. Both of these journeys are marked by fear and hardship. For the nineteenth-century farmers, it means months of hiking, led by an Ainu youth, across mountains and tundra, and the farther they move into the wilderness, the less fertile and hospitable they find the land, until they reach the site of present-day Jūnitakichō, little more than an infertile swamp filled with mosquitoes, plagued by swarms of locusts. It might as well be the end of the world, which suits the fugitives fine.[17]

The journey undertaken by Boku and his girlfriend is less arduous, to be sure, but also contains its moments of danger, for theirs is both real and symbolic, a journey of passage from the world of the living to that of the dead, what Japanese literary convention terms the *michiyuki.* This "passage"—an essential part of classical Japanese theater, particularly in love suicide plays—is undertaken to prepare the travelers for death. For Boku and his girlfriend, it amounts to a long walk along a perilous road, complete with howling winds and the fear that the ground itself might crumble away and swallow them up. This is not lost on Boku, who reflects that "it was like we had been deserted at the very edge of the world."[18] As they begin their hike through this mountain pass, Boku considers further that the mountain scenery in the distance "was certainly splendid, but looking at it brought no pleasure; it was too cold and distant, and somehow wild" (2:292). Moving forward along the road to a tight curve famous for being treacherous after the rain, Boku senses its malevolence:

> As the caretaker had said, there was definitely something ominous about the place. I had a vague sensation of its ill will in my body, and soon that indistinct bad feeling was setting off alarms in my head. It was like crossing a river, and suddenly stepping into a much colder bit of water. (2:293)

His instincts are quite correct, as each step takes him farther into the forbidden land of the "other world," closer to the very center of his inner mind, the land of dreams, memories, and even death. As they move beyond the treacherous "dead man's curve," they find themselves in a vast plain, at the center of which rests Rat's villa. (With a little imagination Boku's "river" above might be named "Styx," and this plain "Elysium.") Although the villa looks impressive from a distance, its age becomes more visible as they approach. "It looked a lot bigger than it had from a distance, and a lot older" (2:297), and the door opens with "an old-fashioned brass key that had turned white where hands had touched it" (2:298). Inside the villa, the furnishings are a monument to a bygone era. "By the window were a desk and chair of a simple design you wouldn't often see these days," and in the drawers, "a cheap fountain pen, three spare boxes of ink, and a letter set" (2:301). The bookcases are lined with "basic reading matter for an intellectual forty years ago" (2:302). Simply put, this is a place forgotten by time, a time capsule from the early 1940s.

Not long after their arrival at the villa, Boku's girlfriend disappears without a trace, and in her place appears the Sheepman, a bizarre, filthy little man in an even filthier sheep suit who speaks rapidly and irritably (the English translation cleverly removes the spaces between words, lending him a comic air that almost outdoes the original). The Sheepman explains to Boku that his girlfriend needed to leave because "'she shouldn't have come in the first place,'" adding that "'you aren't thinking about anyone but yourself'" (2:316). But what does this mean? One senses that more than telling Boku he is selfish, the Sheepman is reminding him that this is his own mind, and that only *he* is entitled to the thoughts and memories that exist here. In other words, insofar as the core of one's consciousness is the most intensely personal place that can exist, to bring another into it is by definition inappropriate. This is why the ear model is "confused," as the Sheepman puts it.

The Sheepman himself, on the other hand, is constructed from a variety of memories in Boku's mind, principally Rat and the Sheep, but also the information he has gleaned from his conversations with the Man in Black, the Sheep Professor (who was once possessed by the Sheep), and from his readings on the history of Jūnitakichō, including the story of the Ainu youth, who surfaces briefly in the Sheepman's comments against war.[19] In the main, however, the Sheepman is comprised of Rat and the Sheep, and it is through him that Boku communicates his desire to meet Rat as soon as possible.

When he finally does meet Rat *as* Rat, their meeting takes place at night in the villa, now perfectly dark and freezing cold, much like the warehouse in which Boku found the Spaceship in *Pinball, 1973*, but thanks to the darkness, Rat is able to emerge as himself rather than as the Sheepman. He explains himself as well as he can, including the fact that he is already dead, but as noted earlier, this does not matter, since death holds no lasting meaning in the "other world." This is hinted at the end of their conversation, in fact, when Rat tells Boku, "'I'm sure we'll meet again'" (2:259), and in truth, there is no reason why this should not be so, for death is clearly not the end of the road in this realm of timeless Time.

Metaphysical Realism: *Norwegian Wood*

If *A Wild Sheep Chase* ranks among the most heavily metaphysical of Murakami's novels, his 1987 best-selling *Norwegian Wood* is among the most realistic, and indeed the author has stated on many occasions that he intended all along to write a "realist" work.[20] Part of this realist approach lies in his style, which, at least in its dialogue, is largely devoid of the lyrical, almost fantasy-like speech used by inhabitants of "the Town" in *Hard-Boiled Wonderland and the End of the World,* or some of the absurdist conversations that occur between Boku and the Twins in *Pinball, 1973*. Yet even in the "straightforward" writing style of *Norwegian Wood,* according to some, the realism is lost. Odaka Shūya, for one, notes that the "straightforward" discussion of sexuality, particularly by a nineteen-year-old protagonist like Watanabe Tōru, is anything but realistic, and "quite the reverse, that characteristic of conceptualized frankness obscures what the author terms a 'realistic novel' as a whole."[21]

But style alone does not determine whether a work should be characterized as "realistic" in any case, and much in *Norwegian Wood* precludes such a claim. It is true that Murakami, in this instance, abandons the dualistic narrative structure of many of his earlier works, in which "this world" and the "other world" are clearly separated, each portrayed separately; it is equally true that we find none of the bizarre, otherworldly characters in it—no Sheepman, no Twins, no talking pinball machines. Everything that occurs in this novel *can* be explained in terms of physics and (aberrant) psychology, if this is what one chooses to do; in fact, *any* of Murakami's novels could be read in this way, simply as hallucinations, intense psychotic episodes on the part of their protagonists. But where would be the fun in that?

Much may be gained from the reading experience, on the other hand, if we admit that the constant presence of the metaphysical world in this work, thinly disguised as dreams, hallucinations, schizophrenia, and what appears to be madness on the part of the novel's heroine, may, in fact, be read just as effectively as the same awareness of that presence shown by every other Murakami hero. We do see, however, a new phase in the construction of the "other world," one in which the metaphysical world lurks beneath the surface of the text, at key moments subtly but inexorably drawing nearer the physical one, exerting its influence, drawing those in the physical world into itself.

The plot of *Norwegian Wood* is straightforward enough: Kizuki is a close friend of Watanabe Tōru, and Naoko is Kizuki's lover—his soul mate, in fact. Their relationship is physical, but it does not include actual intercourse, the reasons for which are never stated in the novel. Without warning, Kizuki commits suicide, leaving Naoko alone with Watanabe Tōru, who cares for her the best he can, but the death of Kizuki has left her, like so many Murakami characters, feeling as though she has lost half of her self.[22]

Both Naoko and Tōru attend university in Tokyo—she at a college for well-bred young women, Tōru at a more general university—and when Naoko is emotionally stable, they spend their Sundays together, saying little, but taking comfort in one another's presence, quietly mourning the absence of Kizuki. Finally, on her twentieth birthday, the physical gateway to Naoko's metaphysical world—here represented through her sexual organs—opens up, and she engages in intercourse with Tōru. It is her first and last time. Not long after this she is sent to a remote sanatorium in the mountains, where Tōru visits her twice. Just as it seems she may be on the mend, however, Tōru receives word that Naoko has committed suicide, hanging herself from a tree in the woods adjacent to her sanatorium.

Tōru's journeys to this location should interest us here, for they bear many of the same markings as previous forays into the metaphysical realm we have already seen. Starting from the northern part of Kyoto, he rides a bus, which carries takes him farther and farther away from inhabited areas, until they enter a valley—just one more well, elevator shaft, telephone line—where the bus driver must tack the bus back and forth along a twisty, uncomfortable road. At length they enter a wood of cedars, where the chill uneasiness of the "other world" becomes noticeable: "the wind that came through the windows of the bus suddenly became cold, its dampness painful on my skin. We ran along the river in that cedar wood for a long time, and just when I was starting to think the world had been buried in an endless expanse of cedar woods, we came out of it."[23] This description is strongly reminiscent of the *michiyuki* we saw in *A Wild Sheep Chase* and suggests that Tōru has now traveled to the world of the dead (or at least its antechamber) to find his beloved. The gate to the sanatorium is protected by a guard, yet another common feature of the entrance to "over there."[24]

Naoko herself is by this time already perched precariously between the worlds of life and death. This is strongly hinted at two points: first, when Tōru awakens from a peculiar dream to find her seated at the foot of his bed; and second, when Naoko admits to hearing Kizuki calling her from "over there," inviting her to join him. In the first scene, each detail suggests Tōru's absorption into the world Naoko inhabits: he gropes for his watch but cannot find it (human-made time does not exist here); the moonlight is bright, but its light cannot penetrate every corner, causing a strong contrast between shadow and light; and Naoko herself is clearly not the Naoko he is used to seeing. "With a faint rustling of her nightgown she knelt beside my pillow and stared into my eyes. I looked at her eyes too, but they said nothing to me. They were unnaturally clear, as if you could see right through them into the world *over there,* but no matter how far I looked, I couldn't see all the way to the bottom."[25]

But her eyes are not the only things Tōru finds unusual about Naoko; her body, too, is unnaturally perfect, as though she were a kind of idealized copy of the real Naoko.[26] He tries to reach out and touch her, but she moves away from him, as though fearing the touch of the physical world, for this is her metaphysical self revealing itself to him. Tōru is literally seeing Naoko's spirit, her very soul, freed from her body by the night and by her proximity to the world of the dead. Her spirit is strong here because she has already completed her own *michiyuki* and now stands (or at least sits) at the gateway to the underworld. Her efforts to explain this to Tōru would seem to confirm this:

> "If I'm so twisted up like this that I can never get back, I'm afraid I'll just stay like this, growing old here and rotting away. When I think about that, I feel like I'll freeze right to the core. It's horrible. Painful, freezing. . . . I'd swear I can feel Kizuki reaching his hand out of the darkness to me. 'Hey, Naoko, we can't be apart,' he says. I never know what to do when I'm told such things."[27]

When Naoko says she can "never get back" *(modorenai),* she means not the everyday world of Tokyo but returning to the world of the living from that of the dead. It is only a matter of time before Naoko takes heed of Kizuki's call, takes that one final step, and joins him fully in death, as indeed she does near the end of the novel.

We see, then, that even within this so-called realistic novel, Murakami employs many of the same markers he uses in his magical realist fiction to indicate the borders between the physical and metaphysical worlds; perhaps even he cannot prevent the intrusion of the metaphysical realm on what we might concede to be a *comparatively* realistic narrative. Possibly the author meant this to be a more psychological penetration, a look into the mind of the schizophrenic, but in the end he proves something rather less empirical, namely, that behind our scientific approach to the mind lies the primordial memory of something less subtle but no less real: our awareness and dread of the mouth of the cave that leads beneath the earth, where the souls of the dead await our arrival. We recognize yet again that for Murakami, wittingly or not, the world of the unconscious and the metaphysical land of the dead are finally inseparable.

The Unconscious "Shared Space": *The Wind-Up Bird Chronicle*

Because Murakami aimed at a quasi-realism in *Norwegian Wood,* we find none of the peculiar transformations that mark passage between the physical and metaphysical realms—Naoko turning into a pinball machine, Rat and Sheep combined into Sheepman, and so forth—in that novel. Naoko, whether in Tokyo or her mountain sanatorium, remains Naoko throughout. By exposing the metaphysical aspects of *Norwegian Wood,* however, we have also revealed its positioning as a transitional novel between the two models of the inner and outer minds—individual and collective—that have marked Murakami fiction. That is to say, in constructing a metaphysical space in the form of the sanatorium, the author actually develops a prototype for what becomes the norm in his depiction of the "other world," namely, a realm in which a variety of characters meet one another, interact, and return (or fail to return, as the case may be) to the real, physical world.

This (for Murakami) novel approach to the "other world" is a useful prelude for what he achieves in *The Wind-Up Bird Chronicle,* in which the unconscious hotel wherein Okada Tōru's wife, Kumiko, is held captive is presented as a sort of hub for all human consciousness, a dimension that not only transcends the limitations of physical time and space (as previous manifestations have done) but now allows access to all characters, who are free to cross the boundaries of history, even of life and death itself, interact, and even interchange with one another, in the metaphysical maze. It is within this unconscious hotel, this metaphysical shared space, that the final conflict between Okada Tōru and his archenemy/doppelganger Wataya Noboru will be played out for the sake of Kumiko's inner self.

Our first view of the hotel from Tōru's point of view comes shortly after his first meeting with Kanō Creta, who has just finished telling him about her early life, marked by constant, unendurable pain, her attempted suicide—like Rat, she drove a car at full speed into a solid object—and the beginning of a new life afterwards, including her time as a prostitute. This last presumably plays a role in what happens in the chapter that follows, when Tōru dreams of being in the hotel for the first time. At a bar where he has just ordered a Cutty Sark, he is accosted by a man with no face, who leads him to Room 208 of the hotel. His impressions of the room are reminiscent of Boku's description of the anachronistic fixtures of Rat's villa: "a spacious room. It looked like a suite in an old hotel. It had a high ceiling, with an old-fashioned chandelier hanging from it. But the lights in the chandelier were not on. Only the small wall lamps gave any light to the room. The window curtains were tightly shut."[28] Tōru's drink at the bar having been interrupted, the faceless man invites him to have one out of the liquor cabinet by the door, but when Tōru attempts to open the cabinet, he discovers that "what had looked like doors were all skillfully made false doors" (1:187). Following this, he realizes Kanō Creta is in the room with him. Without hesitation she strips off her clothes and fellates him with consummate, professional skill.

This description contains numerous points of interest, among them the identity of the "faceless man," a character who will return in the novel *After Dark*. What is the role of this peculiar character in this narrative? Jungians no doubt begin to salivate, Pavlovian-style, at the appearance of the faceless man, and would link him to Jung's anima/animus, and one suspects that such an analysis would bear considerable fruit.[29] In certain ways he resembles a trickster spirit: he promises to guide Tōru to the room he seeks, but then hands him a pen light, tells him to mix himself a drink, only the cupboard doors are only painted on, not real. My own approach, related to this role, suggests that he be read as a mischievous, almost comic keeper/guide to the "other world," not unlike the Sheepman, but here presented faceless because he must stand in for the unknown inner selves of *all* people. As such, he must be a neutral character, and while he guides Tōru to the mysterious Room 208, in which Kumiko languishes, he does not go so far as to solve the mystery for him but merely warns him when there is danger. The faceless man's role is to maintain a sense of balance between the various dichotomies at work here: consciousness versus unconsciousness, physical versus metaphysical, evil versus good, male versus female, passive versus aggressive, asexual versus sexual, order versus chaos. Maintaining balance in all these things, as will be seen shortly, is key to the orderly movement of time and space in the physical world and one of the major functions of the metaphysical one.

This helps us to understand more clearly what Kanō Creta means when she warns Okada Tōru that he and Wataya Noboru cannot live simultaneously; she does not mean necessarily that one of them must die, but rather that *they cannot occupy the same world.* Tōru and Wataya Noboru represent these various oppositions, and if one of them lives in the physical world, then the other will have no choice but to occupy the "other world." This also helps us to understand the importance of the motif of war in this text; when Okada Tōru lives in the physical world, "order" prevails, but when Wataya Noboru is turned loose, the result is "chaos"—violence and destruction. This idea will be explored at greater length later in this chapter.

The Body as Vessel

We have already noted that *The Wind-Up Bird Chronicle* is the first place wherein we see the *collective* nature of the other world portrayed in Murakami fiction. Why is this so important? Simply stated, it is because a whole new range of movement opens up to Murakami and his characters as a result. No longer confined to the limitations of the individual, seeking in vain to protect a lone identity connected with that individual, in *The Wind-Up Bird Chronicle* Murakami begins to play with the notion of detaching mind from body, to view the body as an interchangeable vessel containing a more permanent—but, in the physical world, invisible and intangible—self.

This idea seems to be on the minds of all the characters in one form or another. Lt. Mamiya, describing himself after the incident in Outer Mongolia, uses the expression "empty vessel," and in fact his experience in the well could be read as a metaphor for this same idea: he is placed into the earth—the "body" of all living things—and then removed from it, a "core" with no body. In the same manner, somehow Lt. Mamiya's "core" has been removed from his body, leaving him empty. Kanō Creta, similarly, explains to Tōru the odd sensation of having somehow separated her mind from her body following her unsuccessful suicide:

> "My body felt terribly light. I felt as if I were floating, like this wasn't my own body. It was as though my soul had inhabited a body that didn't belong to me, something like that. . . . a gap had opened up someplace. I was confused. I felt as though I were completely disconnected from this world." (1:183)

A similar message is passed along to Tōru by an old family friend, yet another clairvoyant, called "Mr. Honda," but in a rather more cryptic fashion: it is an empty gift box for Cutty Sark whiskey. The box is ornately gift wrapped, but the bottle of whiskey that ought to be inside—the "core" of the gift—is missing. In this gesture Honda suggests the tenuous nature of the connection between mind and body, the impermanence of the flesh that houses the core spirit within, and the ease with which flesh and spirit may separate.

And in the second half of the novel, this is precisely what Tōru aims to do. Seated at the bottom of his own well, he attempts to separate his body and his "core" from one another. "Just as I do when I am with 'those women,' I try to separate from myself. Crouched in the darkness, I try to escape from this awkward body of mine. I am nothing but an empty house now, nothing more than a cast off well. I am trying to transfer to a reality that runs at a different speed" (3:100). That "different speed" is, of course, a dead halt in time, during which time not only Tōru but others slip into something more astral and gather for a game of "musical bodies" in the unconscious hotel. This is more or less what occurs when Tōru dreams once again that he is making love to Kanō Creta in Room 208 later in the novel. She still wears a dress belonging to Kumiko, but as she writhes atop him, the room goes dark, and Tōru hears her speaking to him in the voice of the "telephone woman." And although this is a dream, we begin to have an inkling of what is really happening: in this dream world, people can and do borrow one another's forms, quite as if the outer body were really nothing more than a hollow shell, a suit of armor hiding the "true" self within.

That motif is given considerably more disturbing expression at the end of book 1, when Lt. Mamiya tells a story about his days in Manchuria during World War II. Mamiya is part of a reconnaissance team infiltrating enemy territory across the Mongolian border. Their team is captured by Mongolian troops, led by a sadistic Russian. In the course of interrogation, Mamiya's team leader, an intelligence officer known only as "Yamamoto," is staked to the ground by his captors and slowly skinned alive. It is a singularly gruesome scene and at the time seemed rather out of place in Murakami's ordinarily easygoing narrative world. Why, of all things, would he have chosen skinning as the method of death? The answer, of course, is that this merely takes to a more physical level the notion of gaining access to the "core" identity. In their efforts to reach the truth—in effect, Yamamoto's "true" self—his captors literally remove his outer skin to reveal the genuine core lurking inside. A different, but related, sort of mutilation occurs in book 3 when the father of "Cinnamon," son of "Nutmeg," is murdered, his body discovered in a hotel room with all its internal organs removed. This is more than gratuitous mutilation; the removal of his organs indicates an attempt to remove his "core," while the outer shell of his body was cast aside.

This, then, presents to us an interesting progression in Murakami fiction: whereas in works like *A Wild Sheep Chase, Hard-Boiled Wonderland and the End of the World,* and *Dance Dance Dance* the Murakami hero struggles to protect his core identity from internal, metaphysical attack, later works reveal their equally desperate struggles to defend the physical shell that houses that core, against enemies whose methods have grown more extreme.

Against these acts of violence, these aggressive attacks on the physical manifestation of the human soul, there is finally no defense; the only salvation for victims of such violence is the recovery of their "core" in the "other world," and it is to this end that Tōru and his fellow cast members slip in and out of the various physical vessels that house them. This is why Tōru keeps climbing down into his dry well, attempting to cast off his "awkward body." Iwamiya argues that Tōru's attempt to change himself into what she calls his "invisible" form is an indispensable step in his quest to rescue Kumiko, for it is her inner self, rather than her body, that must be saved:

> Even in the improbable event that the two were able to meet, there would likely be nothing [Tōru] could do to rescue her. Without rescuing Kumiko's "invisible form" from the world of darkness, her spirit will not return to this world. To this end, Tōru himself must assume the "invisible form" in order to resist Wataya Noboru's power.[30]

One reason for this lies in the essential nature of the inner self, which possesses no tangible form in the physical world; how is one to grasp a spirit, the wind? One must first *be* a spirit. At the same time, Tōru's evident dissatisfaction with his body—"this clumsy flesh of mine"—as well as his urge to "change vehicles," signals his realization that the metaphysical state permits him to cover distances not possible in the physical state. Like Wataya Noboru, Tōru has found the secret to astral transmigration and uses this to gain access to his elusive enemy and destroy him.

Not surprisingly, given the newly collective nature of the "other world," events that occur "over there" have actual consequences in the physical realm. At the very moment when Tōru beats Noboru to death with his baseball bat in the metaphysical realm, the physical Noboru, many miles away, collapses of a fatal brain hemorrhage. Exactly how this happens was not evident at the time *The Wind-Up Bird Chronicle* was written, but we gain some insight, in retrospect, from the events that transpire in *Kafka on the Shore* and *1Q84*.

Into the Forbidding Forest

Having considered in some detail the functioning of the metaphysical hotel as unconscious "shared space" in *The Wind-Up Bird Chronicle,* it is time to explore the other recurring representation of this realm in Murakami fiction, the labyrinth of the forest. Indeed, among the various metaphorical expressions of the "other world" in the author's fictional universe, none appears more commonly than the forest. This begins, if we read carefully, from *Hear the Wind Sing,* with the death of Boku's "third girlfriend," who "hanged herself in a wild little stand of trees by the tennis courts one spring break" (1:60). In fact, most of our early encounters with the forest in Murakami fiction are associated with unhappy or unsettling events. In *Pinball, 1973,* the cemetery to which Rat brings his girlfriend for a walk is laid out at the edge of a wooded area, and after their walk, "the two of them *returned to the woods* and embraced tightly."[31] Rat's villa in the mountains of Hokkaido is also surrounded by white birches, which have "continued to grow ceaselessly, in contrast to the aging house."[32] The forest plays an important role in *Norwegian Wood,* as we have seen, forming the boundaries of Naoko's sanatorium, a buffer between her world and that of Watanabe Tōru; it is also the setting of her suicide. In *South of the Border, West of the Sun,* the protagonist, Hajime, reencountering his childhood sweetheart, Shimamoto, accompanies her through forested mountains to pour her deceased child's ashes into a river. Along the way, Hajime takes note of the crows that seem to be everywhere, their sharp cries unsettling.[33]

But the forest first becomes a serious part of the setting in *Hard-Boiled Wonderland and the End of the World,* where it forms a kind of buffer zone between "the Town" in which Boku and his fellow dwellers live, and the high wall that holds them all virtual prisoners. The forest, according to Boku's friend and advisor, "the Colonel," is a place to be avoided. "'Once winter begins, don't go near the wall. The forest, too. They gain great power in the winter.'"[34] He goes on to say that although there are certainly people living in the forest, "'they are different from us in just about every way you can imagine. But listen, I don't want you getting interested in them. They're dangerous'" (4:198). Exactly what makes them so dangerous remains unclear, but eventually we learn that the forest people are those whose shadows were imperfectly removed when they entered the Town, and so they retain traces of memory from the conscious world.

For Boku, on the other hand, his initial, tentative forays into the forest give him a sense of tranquility: "as I moved away from the wall and pressed on deeper into the forest, a strangely quiet and peaceful world spread out before me" (4:199). Still, he recognizes the dangers of venturing too far from the wall, for "the forest was deep, and if once I became lost it would be impossible to find my way again. There were no roads, no landmarks" (4:200). While on one of his excursions, he happens to fall asleep in a forest clearing, and when he awakens, looking up at the wall, "I could feel them looking down at me" (4:203). To whom "them" refers is not clarified in the novel, but we might plausibly surmise that "they" are the other souls who live in this collective repository of memory. In the end Boku helps his shadow—who still clings to life—to escape into a pool believed to lead back to the freedom of the outside/conscious world, but at the last moment Boku himself decides to remain in the woods, to continue searching for traces of his mind. It is an apocalyptic ending, for we have no reason to believe that Boku will ever be reunited with his shadow; at best we may say he has finally made a choice.

In *Kafka on the Shore,* the forest plays an even more central role as a narrative setting, not only in terms of the detailed description it receives but also for its function as a repository of the collective memories of humanity and a meeting place for those memories. In its role as the "other world," reprising the metaphysical hotel in *The Wind-Up Bird Chronicle,* the forest also serves as a conduit between worlds and as a sort of "changing room" wherein the inner self may leap from one physical vessel to another. Access to this forest, as always, requires a journey, yet the "other world" of the forest also seems to lurk always just beside us, waiting for us to take that one step farther across its boundary, into oblivion.

This journey, in the case of *Kafka on the Shore,* is made by the title character, Kafka himself. As will be recalled from the previous chapter, having fled from his father's prophesy to Takamatsu City in Shikoku, Kafka lays low at the Kōmori Memorial Library, where the cross-dressing Ōshima provides him company, counsel, and, when necessary, an escape route. As detectives hunt for Kafka as a "person of interest" following the murder of his father, however, they track him to Takamatsu, eventually coming across the library, and Ōshima, fearing that Kafka may be implicated, takes him deep into the forested mountains of Shikoku outside of Takamatsu City. There, at a tiny, secluded cabin owned by Ōshima's easygoing surfer brother, Kafka spends a few days in seclusion, warned by Ōshima not to wander too far into the forest, as he might never find his way back. As a cautionary tale, Ōshima tells him about two deserters from the Imperial Army during World War II who escaped into the forest, never to be seen again.

In time, of course, Kafka *does* enter the forest, marking trees with spray paint as he goes, like Hansel and Gretel dropping bits of bread. During his initial stay at the cabin he explores slowly and methodically, venturing slightly farther each day into its murky depths. Even here, at the edge of the metaphysical world, he senses something powerful and mysterious. The description is remarkably like that of the protagonist in *Hard-Boiled Wonderland and the End of the World:*

> Like yesterday, the forest is dark and deep. The towering trees surround me like a wall. In the gloomy hues, something hidden among the trees, like in an optical illusion picture, is observing my movements.[35]

Not until the end of the novel, however, does Kafka finally penetrate deeply enough to discover those who actually reside in the metaphysical realm of the forest. Initially, he meets up with two soldiers—the same two who disappeared during World War II, and although the war has been over for decades, both appear exactly as they were the day they deserted from the Imperial Army. They lead Kafka into a dense part of the forest, eventually coming upon a small cluster of cabins deep in the woods. One clever narratological detail worth noting here is that although the soldiers speak to Kafka and he asks them questions, Kafka's utterances are not set off by quotation marks; we may conclude from this that Kafka's utterances are really thoughts, for his mind is directly hardwired into the collective unconscious represented by this forest. Much as we see in the latter pages of *Hear the Wind Sing,* as Kafka converses with others, he is also conversing always with himself.

When Kafka finally does reach the village, he is mildly surprised to find that it has electricity supplied by wind power, and even electrical appliances, though they are uniformly fifteen to twenty years out of date and look as though they had been taken out of trash dumps. This suggests that the metaphysical world—or at least this little part of it—has been closed off since the 1960s, presumably when Saeki and her boyfriend opened and closed the "Gateway Stone." Since that time, the village has remained isolated, blocked from receiving fresh input. (The repetitive showing of *The Sound of Music* on the television Kafka discovers would seem to suggest the year 1965.) That fresh, current input (memories) from the physical world is supplied by Kafka himself, and thus the "Saeki" whom Kafka meets there is, simultaneously, the middle-aged woman he fantasizes to be his mother (and with whom he has by now had sexual intercourse) and also the fifteen-year-old girl who first entered that world more than twenty years earlier. The forest will preserve both versions of Saeki forever.

Exploiting the Mind-Body Split

In addition to its function as a repository for memory, the "other world" in *Kafka on the Shore* serves as a conduit by which characters may cross vast physical distances in this world without ever leaving. This is accomplished through exploitation of the mind-body separation we have already seen in *The Wind-Up Bird Chronicle.* In this later work, however, the phenomenon is used to open up the narrative structure to virtually endless possibilities as each character's true identity grows less and less clear. This is, on the one hand, liberating, as our potential readings of the text increase exponentially depending on how we choose to confront each character; at the same time, much of the complexity—and confusion—in this novel arises from its use of a kind of latticed structure, in which characters with intact inner selves are juxtaposed with those who have no inner self, as well as some who appear to have *multiple* inner selves. When this inherent confusion of character identity is combined with the overlay—like transparency films placed atop one another—of multiple historical eras in physical time, the tangle grows still worse.

Among the trickier characters in this text is Tamura Kafka's father, Tamura Kōji, a sculptor who is, for at least part of the narrative, possessed by the spirit taking the form of "Johnny Walker." But is Johnny Walker actually Kafka's father, or has he joined the party, so to speak, at some later point? Kafka's loathing of his father brings this dilemma into sharper relief; is the man Kafka detests Tamura Kōji himself, or is he the spirit we know as Johnny Walker? Kawai Hayao is also drawn to this slippage between identities within these father figures:

> Kafka's real father, Johnny Walker, Colonel Sanders, Nakata—they are all father images. This novel is full of fathers. So it is not so simple as just killing the father and having done with it; no matter how many times the father is killed, he just keeps reemerging in different guises.[36]

Further, Kafka's father is not the only tricky issue in this story. Whether Kawai means to argue for shifting core identities, this is precisely what leaves us in so much doubt about who is really who.

One approach to this dilemma is to explore the historical layering of the novel. Each of the three principal characters we meet—Nakata, Saeki, and Tamura Kafka—represents a distinct generation, a discreet historical era, and each at some point in his or her youth, for various reasons, enters the metaphysical world. Beginning chronologically, Nakata first enters this world as a child in 1944, the closing days of World War II, whereupon he loses his "shadow," in effect, his mind. Saeki, a musician who shared a relationship with a young man very similar to that of Naoko and Kizuki, entered the "other world" during the turbulent 1960s, seeking a place where the chaos of the outer, physical world could not threaten the perfect enclosure in which she and her boyfriend lived; she, too, emerged from this world without her other half—her boyfriend. Kafka, finally, goes "over there" near the end of the novel's present (concurrent with the novel's writing), but, unlike the others, escapes with more than he possessed when he entered. The one thing each character's foray into the "other world" has in common with the others is that it occurs at a moment of chaos and fear: Nakata's during the conclusion of a disastrous war, Saeki's during the rising tide of violence attending the antigovernment student movements in the 1960s, and Kafka's in the face of a more personal crisis, namely, his association by blood with a man he considers to be evil.

Despite their distinct historical epochs, however, these three cases are also linked obliquely by a voice in Kafka's head, whom he knows as "the Boy Called Crow" *(karasu to yobareru shōnen),* who guides Kafka in nearly all of his movements away from his father and the prophesy he has received from him. For purposes of this discussion, it is useful to state at the outset that this "voice" very likely represents the shadow lost by Nakata as a child. As such, we will focus our attention chiefly on what actually happened to Nakata on that day in 1944.

Nakata's entry into the "other world" takes place during something that comes to be known as the "rice bowl hill" incident. Although this incident is narrated through chapters that occur far apart from one another in the text, the narrative may be reconstructed as follows: Nakata's teacher, a woman whose husband has been killed fighting in the Pacific theater, has a vividly erotic dream about her husband one night. The following day, as she leads her class—Nakata's class—into the mountains to hunt for wild mushrooms, her menstruation suddenly begins, her blood flow unusually heavy. After cleaning herself as best she can, she buries the bloody towel far from the group, yet not long thereafter finds Nakata standing before her, presenting her bloody towel to her in silence. Possessed by a sudden, uncontrollable rage, she beats him savagely about the face. Shortly after this, a silvery glint is seen in the sky—the teacher assumes it is a lone B-29 bomber, perhaps on reconnaissance. Suddenly all the children collapse in a collective faint. All awaken some hours later, with no apparent ill effects, save Nakata, who remains in his coma for several weeks. When at last he awakens, he has not only lost his memory but the ability to construct *new* memories as well. He has, however, acquired the ability to speak the language of cats. He spends the rest of his days a ward of his family, and later the state, unable to read or write but useful to the families in his neighborhood in locating lost pets.

If previous Murakami fiction is any guide, we may conclude that like the protagonist of *Hard Boiled Wonderland and the End of the World* and Kumiko in *The Wind-Up Bird Chronicle,* he simply remained for too long in the "other world," to the point that he could no longer maintain connection with his shadow. In fact, more than once Nakata explains to other characters that he is without a shadow, and so we may view in him an idea of what might have happened to the protagonist of that earlier work if, rather than remaining in the forest that stands between the physical and metaphysical worlds, he had instead managed to escape the Town and return to the physical world without his shadow—one of four possible scenarios Murakami identifies for the earlier novel.[37]

But what actually happened to Nakata's shadow after its separation from him in 1944? Did it die? Did it remain in the "other world"? Or did it perhaps find other hosts—other physical beings—with which to join when they happened to wander too far into the forbidden forest and found themselves in the metaphysical world? This appears to be what has happened with Nakata's shadow, not just once but several times.

If the inner mind or spirit is indeed capable of moving from one body to another, as previous Murakami texts have clearly suggested to be the case, it is not implausible to suppose that Nakata's shadow has had not one but many lives. How, for instance, might our reading of the novel change if we could imagine that Nakata's shadow originated with the husband of his childhood teacher (which is why he so unerringly located her menses, a silent communication to her from the dead), and later inhabited not only Saeki's boyfriend at one time (which would go far in explaining the question of why Saeki tells Nakata that "'I have known you from a long time past'" [2:293]) but also Kafka himself in the form of "the Boy Called Crow"? Having taken our (admittedly speculative) reading this far, why not suppose that Nakata's shadow at one time inhabited Kafka's real father, Tamura Kōji, as well? If Saeki actually were Kafka's mother, this would help us to understand why she was drawn to him in the first place.

The final piece of the puzzle is, of course, the trickster spirit now calling himself Johnny Walker, for if Nakata's shadow can move from body to body, so too can Johnny Walker. If we imagine in this work a sort of pursuit, in which the Johnny Walker spirit and Nakata's shadow chase one another through time, across generations, driving each other from one body to another, we might gain insights into several of the riddles Murakami sets up in this story, among them (a) why Saeki's boyfriend was killed in Tokyo, and (b) why Saeki left Kafka and his father behind, if indeed she is his real mother.

It may also mean, of course, that Kafka is his own father . . .

This reading is but one of many, intended not to offer a definitive explication of *Kafka on the Shore* but rather to highlight the extraordinarily open-ended text that results when the fixed nature of the "self"—combining flesh and spirit—is disrupted and the two become separable. But what is the role of the "other world" in this instance? To answer this, we need to look at the moments at which flesh and spirit break apart. This occurs most notably in the chapters in which Nakata, led to the home of Tamura Kōji and Kafka in Tokyo by a large black dog, is confronted with the horror of Johnny Walker's harvest of cat's souls.

The sequence, which stretches across three chapters, begins in a vacant lot where Nakata has been waiting patiently, seeking information about a missing cat named "Goma." While he waits, an enormous black dog approaches him and, without actually speaking, communicates to him that he must follow it. This he does and soon arrives at the home recently abandoned by Kafka. The house itself is protected by an "old fashioned gate," and upon being led into what appears to be the study, Nakata finds it quite dark (1:214). In the dim light admitted through the closed curtains, he can see only that there is a desk in the room and the silhouette of someone seated beside it. The atmosphere of the room, reminiscent once again of Room 208 in *The Wind-Up Bird Chronicle* and the living room of Rat's villa in *A Wild Sheep Chase,* marks it as a part of the "other world."

There he meets Johnny Walker (but not being a drinker, does not recognize his iconic costume), whose description is equally otherworldly, a mass of negatives: "His face had no distinguishing characteristics. He was neither young nor old. He was neither handsome nor ugly" (1:216). He is, rather, just "in-between" all descriptors, marking his place as something belonging neither to "this side" nor to "over there" but to both. He is, however, at present located in the "other world," and it would seem that the only way he can break free of the metaphysical realm and emerge into the physical is through his own death. This is why he has summoned Nakata.

His choice is an apt one, for mild-mannered though Nakata appears, his self-description as a "man without a shadow," an "empty shell," makes him the ideal tool for the job. Nakata's physical self is, finally, a mere portal, a conduit between the physical and metaphysical worlds, and into his body virtually any force of Will may lodge.

However, he must be brought to the proper "temperature" before this may occur. Johnny Walker brings Nakata to his boiling point by committing acts of brutality—of war, as he himself terms it—against the very cats who form Nakata's circle of attachment. He urges Nakata, likewise, to do his duty as a soldier:

> "You have never killed anyone, nor have you ever wished to kill anyone. You don't have that tendency. But listen here, Mr. Nakata, there are places in our world where that kind of logic doesn't work. There are times when no one cares much about your tendencies. You need to understand that. Like in war. . . . When war starts, you get taken to be a soldier. When you're taken as a soldier, you sling your rifle and head off to the battlefield, and you have to kill enemy soldiers. You have to kill a lot of them. No one cares whether you like it or not. It's what you have to do, and if you don't, you get killed instead." (1:246)

In this statement, Johnny Walker reveals his true character as a spirit: he is a force of chaos, of bloodlust, the madness that possesses ordinary people in times of war. If we consider his function in terms of history, we recognize that the moments of chaos and struggle in our world are precisely those in which he has been released from the "other world" to play his role on "this side." Within this context we may understand better why Nakata's shadow chose to remain in the "other world" in 1944; like Kizuki and Naoko in *Norwegian Wood,* and indeed like Saeki and her lover (who, I maintain, actually *was* Nakata's shadow) in this novel, he sought to escape the ravages of violence that had gripped the physical world, to find a place of perfect, utopian peace. Herein we discover the cause of the inherent, incessant conflict that exists and will always exist between this spirit and Nakata's shadow, the former seeking to foment chaos and destruction, the latter to stamp it out. This is why, in the face of Johnny Walker's acts of brutality—indeed, witnessing any acts of brutality—Nakata's "empty vessel" connects with its inner core and is overcome by the urge to return violence for violence. "Something was definitely beginning to happen inside him. A violent confusion was attempting to change the constitution of his flesh" (1:252). And at last, unable to bear any more, "Nakata stood up from his seat without a word. No one—not even Nakata himself—could have stopped him. He advanced with great strides, and without hesitation snatched up one of the knives on the desk" (1:257). He then plunges the knife into the breast of Johnny Walker, right up to the handle. Johnny Walker laughs hysterically throughout his own murder, for he knows that this killing is the key to his release into the physical world.

This explication of the role of the spirit taking the form of Johnny Walker gives us insight into the nature and role of the other important spirit in this novel, that taking the form of Colonel Sanders. Moving beyond the obvious dichotomy their forms represent as "spirit" and "flesh" (whiskey and meat), we note that Colonel Sanders's character is, on the whole, marked by the pleasures of the flesh, not only of eating but of sex. When Nakata and his young sidekick Hoshino reach Takamatsu, the latter takes a stroll around town and meets up with Colonel Sanders, who, in addition to promising to help him locate the Gateway Stone that blocks the portal between the physical and metaphysical worlds, procures for him a stunning prostitute—significantly, a university student majoring in philosophy, thus representing the rational, ordered nature of the universe. From this we conclude that where Johnny Walker is a force of destruction and death, Colonel Sanders is a force of life, plenty, fertility, and pleasure.

It would, however, be a mistake to assign value judgments to these two sides of the dichotomy, for the two spirits transcend such human considerations. Rather, both are necessary, both forces of nature, each defining the other. Johnny Walker's behavior is undoubtedly disturbing, disruptive, but he is not evil; rather, he serves to awaken a destructive impulse that lurks beneath the surface, both for Nakata and for Kafka. Jung's model would suggest that both Johnny Walker and Colonel Sanders represent "archetypes" of the inner mind, each with an equal capacity either to guide or to deceive. Both transcend human emotions, and this is why neither of the two spirits betrays what Colonel Sanders (somewhat disdainfully) terms "feelings," and yet each is indelibly linked to our human minds as well. When Colonel Sanders dominates, we behave in a manner that leads to order and tranquility; when Johnny Walker takes over, we lose our cool and act as beasts. For Jung, the latter would be considered the darker, more primitive side of the inner shadow, emotional and unpredictable. "Closer examination of the dark characteristics—that is, the inferiorities constituting the shadow—reveals that they have an *emotional* nature, a kind of autonomy, and accordingly an obsessive or, better, possessive quality," writes Jung. "On this lower level with its uncontrolled or scarcely controlled emotions one behaves more or less like a primitive, who is not only the passive victim of his affects but also singularly incapable of moral judgment."[38] This is essentially the transformation that overcomes Nakata when he witnesses brutal acts: his darker inner self rises to the surface, forcing his surface persona into a subordinate position, and lets loose its destructive urges. The question, as always, is one of balance between our own inner forces of nature, between the inner and outer minds, the flesh and the spirit, the physical and the metaphysical aspects of our selves. This balance is achieved through control (or, at times, the lack of control) over the flow of psychic energy between the two realms. Nakata's role, as Iwamiya also notes, is to facilitate the movements of these elemental forces from one realm to the other, keeping them balanced in their respective realms. "When overwhelmed by the power of the other side, life in this world loses its weight and becomes distorted. When the distortions of the world are corrected, these distortions are also corrected. The burden of correcting these distortions falls to Nakata."[39] He does this, as we have seen, through the violence that is released when his own psychic energy is "brought to a boil," so to speak, but also by opening the Gateway Stone, permitting the necessary flow and equalization of energy between the physical and metaphysical worlds.

Balance and Flow

Just as in the human psyche it is important to maintain a healthy contact between conscious and unconscious, then, it is important within the Murakami fictional universe to maintain a healthy flow of energy between the physical and metaphysical worlds. These two worlds, both before and following the author's shift to the collective metaphysical model, may be said to complement one another, to feed one another, and at the same time to exert tension or stress on one another. If we think of the two realms, more or less as we did in the two-story house metaphor (see figure in the introduction), as separate modes or realms of consciousness connected by some type of conduit—a passageway, a wormhole—then we see that various forms of "energy" pass bidirectionally between the two worlds. This depends, however, on whether these realms are capable of sending or receiving such energy, and in this instance it is perhaps useful to imagine swinging "doors" that facilitate or prevent movement between the conduit and each respective realm. These doors, which open and close at regular intervals, as between waking and sleeping, also open at other odd moments, producing unexpected interaction between the two systems. This interaction, borrowing Murakami's own terminology, we will call "flow" *(nagare)*. When the two systems are open to one another and psychic energy is flowing between them, then it is logical to imagine that they maintain a sense of balance. In practical terms, this means a symbiotic relationship in which the physical self—consciousness—continually interacts with the outside world, receives external stimuli, processes these data according to information stored in the metaphysical realm—memories stored in the unconscious mind—and acts accordingly. The physical self is thus supported by knowledge stored in the metaphysical realm. The metaphysical realm, for its part, continually receives and stores new information and experiences, processing these according to what is already there, including collective memory, and in this way simultaneously feeds the physical self and adds its input to the collective memory.

The flow of energy is bidirectional, and generally the system functions most effectively when there is equilibrium between the volume of energy flowing in each direction. It is also essentially true, in Murakami fiction, at least, that when the two realms are cut off from one another, that is, when the doors to the conduit are closed, the other realm will react negatively. Left to its own, the physical self will lose track of who it is, growing stupid and lethargic, uncertain of what to do; the metaphysical self, on the other hand, with no outlet for its energy, will develop a dangerous level of psychic pressure, which ultimately must escape somewhere. Venting of this type tends to be dramatic and is especially noticeable in characters who normally keep themselves under tight control. We see it, for instance, when the mild-mannered Nakata loses control at certain points in *Kafka on the Shore*—the aforementioned hacking to death of Kafka's father a case in point. Murakami's female characters, on the other hand, tend to vent their psychic energy sexually. This occurs in *Norwegian Wood* when Naoko, on her twentieth birthday, suddenly finds the blockage to her sexuality (hitherto locked away in the "other world") removed, and she is able to have intercourse—but only for one night—with

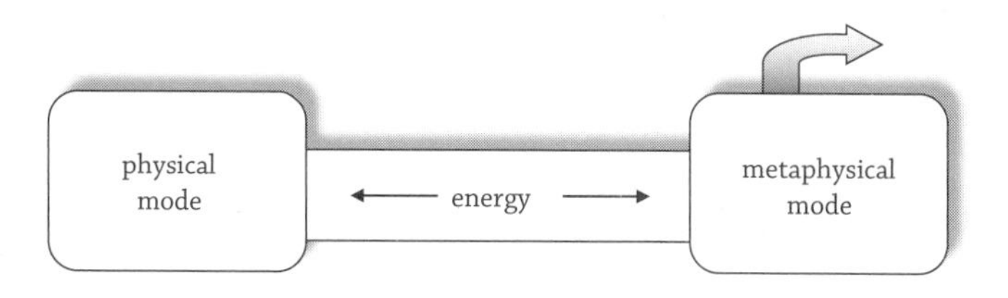

Balancing physical and metaphysical modes

Watanabe Tōru. Such pressure is also the cause of Kumiko's extramarital affair in *The Wind-Up Bird Chronicle,* when, without warning, the membrane closing off the dark sexuality she harbors within her inner self bursts open, leaving her helpless against the waves of sexual desire that attack her. Similarly, in *1Q84* Aomame experiences monthly attacks of uncontrollable sexual desire; these too may be viewed as discharges of psychic energy that her tightly controlled personality normally keeps bottled up.

As this suggests, the connection between the physical and metaphysical worlds in the Murakami universe can be a volatile one in which the balance of dominance can and does shift from one to the other, and when the imbalances are severe, they manifest themselves as peculiar behavior on the part of the individual in question. In *Hear the Wind Sing* Boku talks for three straight months, while in the two works that follow he encounters his "nostalgic images"; Okada Tōru climbs down dry wells and tries to separate his physical and metaphysical selves; Kafka sees apparitions of the fifteen-year-old Saeki, and Nakata causes a rain of leeches; Tengo tries to lose himself in the dry world of mathematics.

Despite these awkward moments, however, there is no doubting that the metaphysical realm is quite as necessary as the physical one to the overall development and well-being of the individual. Perhaps this is why this tension between the two has been such an integral part of the Murakami literary landscape from the very beginning of his career.

An Uncontrolled Substance: *After Dark*

These uncontrollable emotions lie at the heart of the novel *Afutādāku* (2004; translated as *After Dark*) as well. Although this work has drawn little critical attention—and is, in fact, rather forgettable in the overall repertoire of Murakami writing—it does contain some interesting points that are relevant to our discussion of the structure of the metaphysical world, particularly in the context of the buildup of emotional energy or pressure leading to a violent release of some kind.

After Dark is peculiar even among Murakami fiction and seems at times to draw images and elements from a number of previous works. Its plot—a term I use advisedly—takes place over the course of a single night; the time is marked at the top of each chapter so that readers may keep track. Once again Murakami (loosely) constructs alternating narratives, this time between two sisters: Asai Mari and her older sister, Eri. Like other pairs in Murakami fiction, the two girls are quite different from one another; whereas Mari is bookish, intelligent, and slightly antisocial, Eri is pretty and popular, more interested in boys and popular music than in books. It is Eri who receives her parents' love and attention, while Mari is relegated always to second place. Like Boku and Rat in the Rat trilogy, Mari and Eri occupy different "worlds": Mari spends the story moving through the nocturnal but *physical* cityscape, interacting with shady characters from Tokyo's nightlife—prostitutes and mobsters, love hotel managers, and nocturnal musicians; Eri spends her time entrapped in a simple room that represents the metaphysical world. In this one sense the central structure Murakami commonly employs is slightly altered, for Eri's worldliness would ordinarily mark her as part of the physical world, while Mari's preference for the shadowy gloom of night would normally place her into the metaphysical realm. But in this novel Eri has been driven into the "other world," much like Kumiko in *The Wind-Up Bird Chronicle;* it falls to Mari to play the role of Okada Tōru and bring her back.

The work begins with Asai Mari meeting a trombone player named Takahashi Tetsuya at a Denny's late one night. While she does not particularly wish to spend her time talking with him, the acquaintance leads to her meeting "Kaoru," the very tough, bullish lesbian manager of a love hotel called the Alphaville. Kaoru asks Mari's help, adding that her friend Tetsuya recommended her because she could speak Chinese; Kaoru needs an interpreter to help her speak with a Chinese prostitute named Guo Dong-li, who has been savagely beaten and left naked by her Japanese customer. Mari agrees and assists Kaoru in helping the girl to contact her employers—the Chinese mafia.

Meanwhile, Eri sleeps at home in her bed, and what makes this sequence interesting is that the various angles of view are expressed through a camera lens. Murakami's use of the first-person *plural* pronoun "we" *(watashitachi)* is notable here, for it serves to bring the reader explicitly into the narrative process:

> What we see is the city.
>
> We take in the scene from high above, through the eyes of a high-flying night bird. From this wide angle, the city looks like a massive living thing.[40]

> We have a single point of view, and we are watching her. Or maybe we should say we are *spying on* her. Our perspective is that of a camera hanging in midair, and we may move freely throughout the room. At the moment the camera is positioned precisely above the bed, and is pointed at her sleeping face. (35)

The third important character in this novel is "Shirakawa," to all appearances a regular sort of person, a hard-working computer programmer, whose sole flaw appears to be that as a workaholic who spends too many nights at the office, he neglects his wife. However, it becomes clear before long that Shirakawa is the man who attacked the Chinese prostitute because her menstruation began suddenly and she was unable to have sex with him. Shirakawa makes ironic reference to this instance when his wife asks him what he had for his supper, and he responds, "'Just some Chinese'" (119). But there are two Shirakawas: one a model of self-control, reminding us of Kumiko, the other a violent, dangerous man. The difference between Shirakawa and Kumiko is that Shirakawa not only appears to be aware of this "other self," but seems even to welcome its arrival. Standing before the bathroom mirror,

> Shirakawa studies the reflection of his face in the mirror. Keeping the muscles of his face still, he observes his face

critically for a long time. Both hands are on the sink. He does not breathe, nor does he blink. If he keeps this up, he feels certain in his heart that some kind of *other thing* will appear. He objectifies his senses, flattens his consciousness, temporarily suspends logic, and to some extent halts the progress of time. This is what he is trying to do. He hopes, as far as possible, to melt this "self" into the background. (191; emphasis in the original)

Following this scene, the "camera view" that combines narrator and reader remains fixed on the mirror long after Shirakawa has left the room, while his reflection in the mirror also remains. "In the mirror, Shirakawa's image is still reflected. Shirakawa—or should we say, his image—is looking this way through the mirror. He does not change his expression, nor does he move. . . . Finally, though, as if he were tired of this, he relaxes the muscles in his body, takes a deep breath, turns his head. Then he puts his hand to his face, strokes his cheek several times, as if to make certain his flesh has feeling" (192).

Clearly it is this "other Shirakawa" who attacked Guo Dong-li and who represents the dark "shadow" of the physical Shirakawa, Jung's "emotional" side of the inner self. Here, too, we see a parallel between the Shirakawa who works all night (or at least pretends to work), building up a tremendous head of sexual/emotional steam that *must* be released upon someone, and the "other" Shirakawa who carries out that release. His choice of a prostitute is logical, because the energy he vents is grounded in the shadow, the primitive self, and must take the form of something socially unacceptable. Indeed, we have already seen this in the "telephone woman" who talks dirty to Okada Tōru in *The Wind-Up Bird Chronicle.* This is pure libido, pure sexual charge, rough and liberating. That is what Shirakawa is after as well. The fact that the prostitute is an illegal immigrant from China, enslaved by the local Chinese mafia, is also appropriate, for it links Shirakawa's violence and aggression to the same stability-chaos dichotomy we have already observed in *The Wind-Up Bird Chronicle* and *Kafka on the Shore,* in which normally controlled and orderly people are transformed by war into beasts. The violence enacted against Guo Dong-li is connected allegorically to the history of Japan's aggression in China, the brutality enacted against the Chinese by men who, in peacetime, were farmers, businessmen, and teachers but in the uncontrollable violence of war became monsters. Once again the "balance" has tipped in favor of our "Johnny Walker" tendencies.

Finally, we note with interest the return of the "faceless man," who spends the whole novel watching Asai Eri. Once again his identity is difficult to pin down, but as with the faceless man who guarded the metaphysical hotel in *The Wind-Up Bird Chronicle,* we suspect he is a guardian of the "other world," neither wholly benevolent nor malevolent. He does not molest the sleeping Asai Eri in any way but merely watches over her, receding into the background when she "awakens" within the metaphysical room that imprisons her. Here the faceless man represents Asai Mari, observing her sister in sleep, but also Eri herself, for the two are closely linked to one another, once again two sides of the same coin. The faceless man serves as a mediator between the two girls—and the two disparate worlds they inhabit—and maintains a sense of balance between them.

We learn quite late in the novel that Asai Eri has been asleep for two months, and that although there appears to be nothing wrong with her physically, no one has been able to awaken her. Perhaps what is most revealing about the passages involving Eri is how little anyone understands the sense of total emptiness and isolation she feels. This emptiness is not solely emotional but carries with it a physical sensation for her as well:

> The inside of her body has lost its necessary heaviness, transformed into an empty vessel. All the organs, sensations, muscles and memories that have made her up until now have been, one by one, neatly stripped away. As a result, she knows she is now nothing, just a convenient object through which external things are passed. Her whole flesh crawls as she is assailed by a violent sense of isolation. (162–63)

Despite being universally admired and fairly successful—she has modeled for magazines and even appeared in television commercials—we come to recognize that Eri, like Kumiko in *The Wind-Up Bird Chronicle,* like Matsunaka Yūko in "A Shinagawa Monkey," even like "the Boss" in *A Wild Sheep Chase,* has everything on the outside but nothing on the inside, and this is why she must fall into a deep and lengthy sleep: within the womb-like enclosure of this metaphysical room, she must re-create her inner self and become a whole person. At present she is nothing more than an attractive, but empty, shell of a person, but as she sleeps, she progresses through the various stages of development signifying the rebirth of her consciousness: sleep (gestation), awakening (birth), and finally standing, walking, and exploration of the room (development of consciousness/self).

Precisely how Eri happened to lose her inner self in the first place is never made clear in the narrative, but we may surmise with reasonable confidence that it is connected to her gradual separation from her sister, Mari, a process that seems to have begun early, as we learn from the sudden recovery by Mari of a traumatic memory she has suppressed since early childhood. As children, she and Eri were on an elevator that stopped because of an earthquake. Eri, who was only in the second grade at the time, continues to call out to Mari, but in the pitch darkness of the elevator car, Mari is too terrified to move. Finally, Eri comes to her and holds her tightly, "'as if our two bodies would melt together into one. She never loosened her grip for a second,'" Mari says, "'as if, should we be separated even for a second, we would never again meet in this world'" (273). But the two *are* separated over time, estranged in part by a clear partiality on their parents' part for Eri. This separation is catastrophic for Eri, for, in the absence of another (an Other) person, no one can be fully "concretized" but remains instead a virtual reality. When Mari ceases to show interest in Eri, her older sister begins to lose her sense of self. Mari, however, having recovered this childhood memory, hits upon the idea of holding her sleeping sister, rejoining with her as they once did as children, and thus bringing her back into the conscious, physical world. It is uncertain, however, whether this will mean the relegation of Mari into the "other world" to take Eri's place.

In this novel, then, it is safe to say that the metaphysical world, sterile though it may seem in the guise of a simple room, has become symbolic of the womb, wherein life originates and where—for Murakami's characters—recovery and rebirth become possible. It is an idea that forms a central motif in *1Q84* and, somewhat less prominently, in *Colorless Tsukuru Tazaki and His Years of Pilgrimage* as well.

Once More into the Wormhole

As noted in the previous chapter, *1Q84* is a relatively simple narrative, particularly when compared to *Kafka on the Shore*. Its plot is relatively explicit, though like most Murakami works, it contains certain puzzles that remain unsolved to the end (the "Little People," to name one), intentionally left for readers to decipher on their own. *1Q84* also contains a quasi-sacred subnarrative, which will be explored in detail in the next chapter, that deals with mythological aspects of the "other world," so here we will confine ourselves to the metaphysical qualities of this novel as a prelude to that discussion.

We have already seen that *1Q84* is centered on the gradual convergence of its two lead characters, Tengo and Aomame. The work's title is derived from the name Aomame assigns to the "other world," the *Q* standing for "question mark." However, use of the expression "other world" in this particular work is somewhat unsatisfying; in fact, it is more like a time slip or, as the Leader describes it to Aomame shortly before she ends his life, like a train switching tracks. "'This is not a parallel world. . . . Here the problem is one of time . . . the point where the track switched, and the world became 1Q84.'"[41] It would be most accurate, then, to envision "1Q84" as a side step for time, not unlike opening one new circuit while closing off another. Murakami himself may have been concerned that his readers would misunderstand this point, for more than one character remarks that there can only be *one* reality at any given time.

Structurally, too, the world of "1Q84" represents a significant departure in how Murakami handles the idea of other worlds. Aside from certain bizarre details—the existence of the Little People, a second moon hanging in the sky, police who carry automatic weapons rather than revolvers—this new dimension is virtually indistinguishable from the old, and while Aomame unmistakably enters "1Q84" in the characteristic Murakami way, that is, via an escape ladder from an elevated highway, even she does not initially notice anything different. The eerie, gloomy, atmosphere that normally marks the metaphysical realm is nowhere to be found.

Or rather, it is to be found in the "1Q84" world's own "other world," the characterization of which, however, is strictly imaginary: for Tengo, it takes the form of a "forest" in his mind, which he associates with the unfettered imagination of Dickens, and of Chekhov, who wrote of the primitive "Gilyaks," aboriginal people who once inhabited the primeval forests of the Kurile Islands north of Hokkaido. For Fukaeri, this links them with the "Little People"—earth spirits or deities similar to "Johnny Walker" and "Colonel Sanders"—who rule the forests with absolute supremacy and, when released into the physical world, bring with them a kind of elemental violence, expressed as torrential rainstorms and violent thunder.

In the actual, physical world this realm comes to be known to Tengo as "Catsville" *(Neko no machi),* named for a short story he has read about a man who gets off a train at a lonely stop along the line and finds himself in a deserted town inhabited solely by invisible cats whose language he can understand. Eventually the man realizes that this town is the land of the dead and that the cats are the souls of the departed. By then, however, it is too late; the tracks have switched, and the train will no longer stop here to pick the man up. For Tengo, this name takes on a natural connection to the rural seaside geriatric center where his father lies dying, and as his father progresses through the final stages of life—from consciousness to coma, coma to death—the geriatric center and its surrounding town also "switch tracks," from a place of dying to the actual land of the dead. Two scenes particularly stand out as significant in this regard, both occurring in book 3. The first comes early in the volume, while Tengo's father still lives and Tengo spends the night with a woman named Adachi Kumi, one of the nurses who is caring for his father. Their night is potentially sexual—Adachi Kumi lies in bed with Tengo, rubbing her lush pubic hair against his thigh—and yet they do not have sex; instead, they smoke hashish (a first for Murakami characters), and Kumi, after confiding to Tengo that she can remember dying once before, urges him, in all seriousness, to "'get out of this place while the exit is still unblocked'" (3:184). Much later in the work, after Tengo's father has died, Kumi clarifies that she was strangled to death on a chilly, rainy, lonely night (3:484–85). This, we have since learned through another character, is precisely how Tengo's mother died,[42] and we can hardly be blamed for wondering whether Adachi Kumi, now existing in the land of the dead, looking after Tengo's father until his death, is not actually the spirit of Tengo's mother.

In the physical world of "1Q84," on the other hand, we find that the same kinds of mysterious conduits—what I term *wormholes*—that functioned so cleverly in *Kafka on the Shore* are even more explicitly depicted in this later work. We never quite see how Kafka's inner shadow makes the metaphysical journey between Shikoku and Tokyo to emerge in Nakata's physical self; we know only that it has happened, resulting in the death of Tamura Kōji/"Johnny Walker." By comparison, in *1Q84* Murakami selects his symbolic imagery more carefully, turning the process into a highly sterile, ritualistic act of reproduction.

The most critical part of Fukaeri's narrative concerns the *kūki sanagi,* or "air chrysalis," as the English translation has it, referring to a kind of cocoon. According to her story, the heroine (presumably Fukaeri herself) is punished for failing to look after a dying goat by being placed, along with the goat's corpse, into an underground room. As she languishes there, the "Little People" emerge from the mouth of the goat's corpse and teach the girl how to spin a cocoon out of the air. Upon completion of the cocoon, it is opened, and out comes a perfect copy of the heroine. Similar to the room in which Asai Eri is trapped in *After Dark,* this "cocoon" may be viewed as a real and metaphorical image of the womb, though this process of procreation is unnatural indeed, for it is sterile, involving no intercourse, an "immaculate" conception in every sense.

If the purpose of the air chrysalis is to create human replicas, for what purpose is this done? We receive one clue near the end of book 1, in a rather unsettling scene involving a little girl named Tsubasa, allegedly one of the Leader's rape victims, now under the care of the old woman who directs Aomame's activities as an assassin. Tsubasa's case is unusual even in the old woman's experience, for her reproductive organs—particularly her uterus—have been damaged virtually beyond repair. The reasons for this are revealed only when Tsubasa is unwatched:

> At length, her mouth opens slowly, and the Little People emerge one after the other. They appear, one by one, looking cautiously around themselves. If the old woman had awakened she would probably have been able to see them, but she was deeply asleep. . . . When they came out of Tsubasa's mouth, they were no larger than her little finger, but once they have fully emerged they expand, like pieces of inflatable furniture, until they are about thirty centimeters tall. All wear the same unremarkable clothing, and their faces are without any distinguishing characteristics, so one cannot tell them apart. (1:446–47)

Like the goat in Fukaeri's narrative, Tsubasa is a replica of an original, and her function is to transport the Little People from one place to another. As it turns out, however, the Little People are not the only ones who have access to this means of transport. On the night of the Leader's death at the hands of Aomame, Fukaeri herself becomes the conduit by which Tengo and Aomame are joined. In an atmosphere rich with metaphysical markers, Tengo senses that something is different on this night; "the air was dripping with moisture, and he felt that the world was marching steadily toward a dark end" (2:295). In this perfect mixture of fertility (moisture) and death (the dark end of the world), Fukaeri enters his bedroom, and Tengo experiences an erection like no other he has ever known. Not wishing to commit an act of immorality with Fukaeri, who is only seventeen and under his protection, he "switches tracks" in his mind, taking refuge in the sterile world of mathematics, eventually falling asleep. Upon awakening, he finds himself naked and unable to move, his erection unchanged. A now naked Fukaeri climbs atop him, and he is struck by how artificial her sexual organs look. "Where her pubic hair should have been there was only a mound of smooth white skin. The whiteness of the flesh emphasized too much how defenseless she was down there. Her legs were spread, so he could see her vagina. Like her ears, it looked like something that had just been constructed. And maybe it *really had* just been constructed" (2:301; emphasis in the original). Using this newly formed canal to "envaginate" Tengo's penis, Fukaeri gyrates upon him until he ejaculates, sending forth his semen into the wormhole. As we later realize, it is at precisely this same moment that Aomame, on the other side of Tokyo, is using *her* weapon—a homemade, needle-sharp ice-pick tool—to pierce the Leader's neck, pricking him at the base of the brain and ending his life. We presume that this forms the other side of the wormhole and that Tengo's seed has passed through the needlelike end of Aomame's tool into her hand and thus to her womb. Both Fukaeri and the Leader, then, have functioned as gateways to the wormhole, perceiver and receiver.

Interestingly, Fukaeri's manipulation of Tengo's penis—note that he is entirely in the passive position—is a verbatim reenactment of the Leader's ritualistic manipulation by members of his cult using their own daughters. Whether these girls are their actual daughters or merely replicas of them, created in cocoons similar to the *kūki sanagi* Fukaeri describes, is never made clear, but in the end this is less important than the fact that the female sexual organs and womb serve explicitly as passageways to the "other world," either as wormholes that connect people in disparate locations (as in Fukaeri's case) or as *living* cocoons, human hothouses in which to grow new life. What they seek to grow, presumably, is a new "chosen one," a sacred being who will take the Leader's place as the "one who hears the voices" of the Little People. In this sense, when Aomame's classmates teased her as a child, calling her "the One," they were unwittingly hitting the nail squarely on the head, for Aomame *is* "the One," possessing the sacred Womb that will produce an heir to the Leader, the next generation of divinely connected beings. And it has all been accomplished through the immaculate remote control of the metaphysical wormhole.

What we have seen in this chapter, above all, is that the metaphysical world as it is conceived in Murakami Haruki's fiction has developed quite significantly since its inception in *Hear the Wind Sing,* and yet in other ways it has remained very much as it ever was. Certainly this realm has lost none of its underlying tension since *Pinball, 1973,* wherein Boku enters the freezing darkness of a chicken warehouse, wondering whether he will remain trapped there forever. From the terror of "dead man's curve" near the end of *A Wild Sheep Chase,* to the seemingly endless forest road to Naoko's sanatorium in *Norwegian Wood,* to the gloomy corridors of the unconscious hotel in *The Wind-Up Bird Chronicle,* to the bedroom Tamura Kafka occupies at the back of the Kōmori Memorial Library in *Kafka on the Shore,* or the darkened hotel room wherein Aomame cuts the power to the Leader's brain, these places are never insignificant, never innocent. No one ever "simply exists" in Murakami's metaphysical realm; even Okada Tōru, sitting for days at the bottom of his dry well in the heart of Tokyo (a real and figurative conduit through the very center of Japanese society), experiences visions, considers major life problems, confronts his instinctive, primordial fear of darkness, loneliness, and death.

And yet, as we have seen, the metaphysical world has also developed considerably since those early novels; what was a dark and lonely place reserved for the protagonist alone, a simple binary opposition of conscious and unconscious, has developed into something that accounts for a spirituality always present in the "other world" (even in *Hear the Wind Sing*), yet never fully understood or explicated as such until the individual dark place became a gathering ground for all the souls of the world, past, present, and future. Above all, we have seen the metaphysical realm grow in prominence within the

Murakami literary landscape, from merely a means of accessing individual memories and dreams to a central structuring element of the narrative in its own right, grounding all characters' interactions, along with the formation of their selves. It has also been revealed, by its nature, to be a realm in which the individual inevitably surrenders his or her individuality, where the many must finally dissolve into the Oneness of Time and Space that unifies the metaphysical realm, a seemingly paradoxical zone into which fresh data are constantly, ceaselessly entered, yet that never expands; it is a land of the dead in which death can never occur.

And in this last sentence we realize, I think, that the underlying theme of Murakami fiction has not changed all that much even after more than thirty years of writing. If *A Wild Sheep Chase* and *Hard-Boiled Wonderland and the End of the World* depict a desperate effort to maintain a conscious, and above all distinct, individual sense of identity, then surely works like *Kafka on the Shore* and *1Q84* depict no less the desire of the individual to grasp his or her uniqueness and preserve it not so much in spite of the collective identity that lurks in the metaphysical realm but through (necessarily brief) interaction with it, for therein is housed a collective narrative—*the* Narrative—that bears all the markings of all the human lives of all epochs, one whose natural function is to absorb all memory and diffuse it throughout itself. This is not to be confused with "group narratives," as noted earlier, which frequently masquerade as *the* Narrative but are in fact merely individual narratives (political ideologies, religious awakenings, and so on) borrowed, enhanced, and finally adopted by those with insufficient connectivity to their own inner selves.

In the chapter that follows, we will revisit the metaphysical, but this time in terms of its connection to collective (or world) mythologies. In particular, we will explore the nexus between classical Western and ancient Japanese mythological depictions of the underworld and the borders that lie (increasingly blurrily) between the realms of "life" and "death."

THREE

Gods and Oracles, Fate and Mythology

> I'm not just some passive creature caught up in someone else's plans, brought here regardless of my own mind . . . being here is something I chose myself. *My presence here is an act of my subjective will.*
>
> —Murakami Haruki, *1Q84,* book 3

IN CHAPTER 1 WE EXPLORED how language constitutes realities, as well as the rather vexing question of "who speaks," that is, who rightfully wields the power of creation through language. Murakami once said that he feels "like a god" when he writes, and the comparison is an apt one, for the creation of worlds is often regarded as the work of divinity. It is time, therefore, that we confront the appearance of the gods in Murakami's fictional universe, why they have appeared, and what they mean to his overall agenda as a writer.

We might begin by imagining how early humans perceived their environment. It would not be unreasonable to suppose, for instance, that early humans would have looked upon awesome natural phenomena with a certain wonder. They may have wondered why the sun rose and set, why the moon went through phases, why the sky rumbled and flashed in a storm, why the tides came in and went out, why the seasons changed, why earthquakes and typhoons occurred, and so on.

"Man is always found in company with some god," writes Thomas Bulfinch in the opening lines to his seminal nineteenth-century description of myth, and "left to himself, he constructs one of his own."[1]

Let us, then, consider the following scenario. In response to natural phenomena, perhaps to render them comprehensible to our children, we created stories—myths—to explain them. As characters for those myths, we created gods, spirits, fairies, supernatural beings who could take responsibility for what happened in nature. In this manner, we created the gods.

Over time the gods grew to be more than mere embodiments of natural events as they occurred; they were also given the power to determine future events. We hungered for some clearer sense of why we were here, of what the gods had in store for us, so we began to seek them out in an effort to divine their will. Through incantations, divination, prayer, fortune-telling, "prophetic" dreams, and oracles, the gods "spoke" to us, and in so doing, created for us not only what *is* but what *shall be*. Thus fate was born.

But somewhere along the way, we forgot that it was *we* who had created the gods, not the other way around. In our desire to understand and explain the world around us, we relinquished the power to speak in our own right and became prisoners of fate.

The ways of the gods we created are strange, mysterious, and their communications with us are just as mysterious. How can we understand their riddles? We seek the help of wise persons, skilled in interpreting (writing) the messages of the gods in ways that the rest of us can understand. In this manner we recovered some small part of our power to speak, but only some of us—our priests, shamans, vestal virgins, priestesses of Isis—received, interpreted, and codified the messages of the gods, working them into narratives by which we all were governed, passing them on from one generation to the next. Thus the words of the gods became part of a tradition, and the gods gained even more prestige.

And we can no longer recall that we created the gods. We "remember," instead, that *they* created *us*.

From this point forward we lost much, if not all, of our power to determine our own future, to create our own world. More accurately, the worlds we spoke and created through our words were required to agree with those of our codified divine messages, or they had to be declared false. But still we maintained—and maintain now—vestigial ties with that earlier, more basic sensation felt by the first person, who looked out of the first cave, saw the first sunrise, and called it "god." And from this we understand more than we realize.

In the previous chapter we examined this sensation, this initial act of creation and all acts of creation since, in terms of what Jung called the collective unconscious, mystics call the world soul, and I have been calling "the Narrative." As we move further into our discussion of this realm, particularly as it relates to Murakami's more recent works, we find two interesting things taking place: first, that the gods have been allowed back into the game; and second, that a new struggle has developed as a result, one between the traditional (collective) narratives of our fathers and the (individual) narratives of their children. This is the true advent of the mythological in Murakami Haruki fiction.

This is not to suggest that mythological motifs have been absent in Murakami's writing until now. What was the Sheep in *A Wild Sheep Chase,* after all, if not a figure of mythology, yet one more attempt to explain the unexplainable? One might even argue that the nostalgic images I have posited have quasi-mythological overtones.

But these stop at the water's edge, at the "quasi-" stage, for mythology, in my view, requires more than for something simply to be metaphysical; it must tap into something more common to all humanity, must be connected, on some level, to our hopes, our desires, and of course our dreads. Perhaps most important of all, mythology begins and ends with our need to explain the world, how it came to be as it is, and what our own role ought to be vis-à-vis those who made it and us (even if that creator happens to *be* us). Mythology is an expression of our will to find and commune with the gods themselves.

To speak of gods and their will is to enter deep waters. Every culture has created its own gods, and they vary widely. What do our gods want from us and for us? Is it enough to say that the Greco-Roman gods wanted the love and respect of their people, that Aztec gods required blood sacrifice, that the god of Moses demanded total obedience and an exclusivity clause? There is little point in such wild overgeneralizations, because most gods are a lot like humans: they want something different and have a way of changing their minds without warning. This is because the will/desire of the gods reflects the culture that created them, and as cultures change, so does the divine "agenda." Just look at what happened to the god of Moses when Jesus came along. . . .

And what of the Japanese gods? Can the native spirits of the Shintō tradition, commonly called *kami,* be termed gods at all? This depends on our definition of "god," of course, but we generally envision an immortal being with considerable power. Amaterasu, the sun goddess, and her brother Susano-ō, god of the moon and sea, would certainly qualify, but does one apply the same measuring stick to the *inari* spirits who look after rice harvests, or local village shrine deities, or even the spirits who belong to shrines no larger than birdhouses? Approaching the question from this angle is likely to result only in our becoming bogged down in hopeless (and pointless) speculation about how Japanese deities compare, both to one another and to other deities from mythologies around the world. Let us instead simply note that like the human communities they represent, Japanese deities vary widely in size, power, and prestige, as well as the kinds of human affairs in which they interest themselves.

For purposes of the discussion that follows, we will find it more useful to examine Japanese deities in terms of how they function within the human communities to which they are connected, from which, after all, they sprang in the first place. This connection is often a highly proprietary one, for local communities and groups in Japan—even some families—have their own related deities, which are supposed to look after them, and vice versa. A spirit who belongs to a particular village is considered a member of the community and will be honored as such. What Japanese gods want, seen from this point of view, is simply to be included, honored, and welcomed into all aspects of community life. This is the purpose of the *matsuri,* festivals that are held regularly in every community, no matter how small; *matsuri* comes from an old word meaning "to worship," and the deafening, joyous music and copious consumption of *saké* at these events are intended to bring participants and their local deities together in one riotous celebration of life. Traditionally, indigenous Japanese religious practices centered upon fertility and its requirements (much as those of the ancient Hebrews did), and the favor of the gods was—and still is—thus sought for bountiful harvests, healthy birthrates, and, more recently, financial prosperity.[2]

It is just these sorts of deities—let us term them spirits—who now make an appearance in the literary landscape of Murakami. Their infiltration begins subtly, with a "son of the gods" dancing in tune with the universe in "Kami no kodomotachi wa mina odoru" (2000; All children of the gods dance), develops into the slightly absurd characters of Johnny Walker and Colonel Sanders in *Kafka on the Shore,* and finally into the Little People in *1Q84*. In each of these works the reader is compelled to wonder, what do these spirits really want? And so, like the various heroes and heroines who seek to enact the will of the gods, the reader, too, must listen to the voices, hear the wind sing, in hopes of deciphering the oracle. At the same time, however, like these heroes, we must protect ourselves against being consumed by those oracles, the narratives of the gods—and their interpretations by humans—lest we lose our grasp on the right to tell our own stories.

Mythology's Greatest Hits

To say that an author's works contain mythological elements is, in most cases, no great statement at all, since nearly every work of fiction, drama, or poetry—including the most elementally formulaic types—echo our mythological past. Myth is, after all, an expression of our deepest instinctive fears—cold, loneliness, hunger and thirst, disease, darkness, death—and our desires—warmth, brightness, satisfaction, good health, fertility, immortality. Our myths put us in touch with these basic instincts, show us how to avoid (or at least put off) the former and accomplish the latter. Our greatest fear is, perhaps, death, which we associate with what is dark and unknown, and so we construct myths in which we travel into the darkness and mystery of the world of the dead, to Hades, Hell, Yomi-no-kuni, where death is either confronted and reversed (Jesus, Persephone) or accepted and understood as irreversible (Orpheus, Izanagi). Such narratives frequently take their heroes underground, where reign darkness and cold, contrasted with the warm sunlight of the world above. Fear of disease, starvation, and underpopulation have led to myths that enforced taboos against "unclean" foods (Judaism, Hinduism), against contact with putrefied matter and blood (Shintō), against nonprocreational forms of sex (homosexuality, masturbation, bestiality), against incestuous relationships—though chiefly those involving intergenerational partners. The need for obedience to authority has spawned tales of vengeful, jealous deities. We seek our place in the world and universe, and as a result construct and hand down narratives that pit individual desires against the demands of our gods and our society. We seek out a relationship with the gods and create their voices and images, drawing them in our image or from natural places that inspire awe—the horrific bowels of the earth, the stormy depths of its oceans, the freezing peaks of its great mountains.

Of course, every work of fiction that contains a hero, a protagonist who confronts a dilemma, task, or quest, is to a greater or lesser extent grounded in mythological archetypes, and this is naturally true of the works of Murakami as well. But Murakami's exploitation of the quest structure goes considerably beyond generalizations concerning protagonists who overcome problems to resolve the central conflict in the narrative; they follow, rather, a more recognizable pattern or progression commonly seen in myths and legends from around the world. Joseph Campbell postulates these patterns as specific phases to the archetypal mythological quest, which include the call of the hero to the quest (and his initial reluctance to undertake it), the supernatural assistance he is granted, his journey belowground to battle dark forces (or encounter benevolent ones), his defeat of the enemy, and his restoration of some essential need to his community, whereby, in Campbell's words, he "brings back from his adventure the means for the regeneration of his society as a whole. . . . Tribal or local heroes . . . commit their boons to a single folk; universal heroes—Mohammed, Jesus, Gautama Buddha—bring a message for the entire world."[3]

The purpose of this chapter, then, is to explore some of the specific mythical antecedents to Murakami's texts, for by expressing his mythological underpinnings explicitly, Murakami does comment, wittingly or not, on the role of myth in the grand human narrative, what we have been calling *the* Narrative, that grounds and informs all meaningful human experience. Perhaps because of this, his use of the structures and tropes of myth reveals something about the connectivity of all myth, for Murakami creates in his fictional universe a nexus of mythological expression that both celebrates and obliterates regional distinctions and cultural specificities, mingling in particular elements from classical Greek and ancient Japanese mythology so seamlessly that it becomes at times difficult to see where one tradition ends and another begins. Perhaps it is an inevitable result of our greater global awareness in the face of communications technology that seems constantly to shrink the distances and gaps between geographically separated regions and cultures, but as we grow less culturally distinct, emerging as so-called global citizens in a shrinking world, our mythological roots appear to grow together, intertwined, until we have finally gained access to a global mythological narrative that is capable, simultaneously, of expressing national origins (i.e., Japanese myth) while acknowledging a connection with the rest of the world that begins to reflect "the Narrative" in earnest.[4]

In addition to its revelations about cultural aspects of myth, however, Murakami's fiction, almost from the beginning, can and should be read with an eye toward the political underpinnings of mythology, particularly with regard to religion and its role in satisfying the human need for the inner narrative, that is, an ideology or belief system on which to order our individual lives. We note, for instance, that even as we explore the metaphysical realm as a manifestation of the human psyche, the collective unconscious, as we did in the previous chapter, we find also an essentially mystical quality to that realm, one that lies within the purview of spiritualism, if not always religion proper.[5] It should come as no surprise that religion—or at least spirituality—has grown considerably more prominent in Murakami's fiction during the past fifteen years or so, given the greater prominence of organized religion in the public mind-set following the Aum Shinrikyō incident of 1995, and the simultaneous attacks against multiple targets in the United States on September 11, 2001. This is not to suggest that Murakami has jumped onto the bandwagon of demonizing religion in general—particularly Islam—in the wake of the 9/11 attacks, however; quite the contrary, the author has shown restraint and sensitivity in handling religious groups, both in his fiction and nonfiction.

One aspect of this restraint is the lack of specificity that marks his portrayal of religious groups. This presented no particular difficulty when Murakami's manifestations of the "spiritual" amounted to fantastical elements like magical sheep, talking pinball machines, and clairvoyance. It became trickier in works like "All children of the gods dance," in which a young man named Yoshiya is told he is the son of God or the gods (the Japanese word *kamisama* does not distinguish), and in *Kafka on the Shore,* whose spirits/deities, as we have seen, take the forms of iconic consumer goods. Neither of these last claims to be a god, but in their ability to take on any form they resemble trickster spirits with extraordinary powers and are thus potentially associated with Japan's native animist tradition of Shintō. "'I'm currently appearing to you in this temporary human form, but I'm neither a god *(kami)* nor a buddha,'" the spirit taking the form of

Colonel Sanders explains to Hoshino, the young man who looks after Nakata. "'I've never had feelings, so my mind works differently from that of a human.'"[6] As beings grounded in the metaphysical, spirits like these transcend both human emotions and also such human constructs as "good" and "evil," "right" and "wrong." What does concern them, as we saw in the previous chapter, is maintaining a sense of balance in the universe.

Most recently, the religious cult to which Aomame belongs in *1Q84* is recognizably similar to the Jehovah's Witnesses, as Jay Rubin has noted,[7] and the cult "Sakigake" is strongly reminiscent of the Aum Shinrikyō, one of the so-called new religions, but in neither case does the author come straight out and identify the religious tradition he depicts. One reason for this, I suspect, is that Murakami seeks to portray something more or less universal to *all* spiritual belief systems, something that reveals, as do myths, that beyond the cultural specificities of each mythological or religious tradition lie commonalities that mark all believers as connected to a universal (metaphysical) whole.

In the pages that follow we will explore some of the mythological aspects of Murakami's fiction, paying particular attention to the author's use of recognizable elements from classical Greek mythology but also exploring how he fuses these Western elements—which might be called elemental to the very fabric of Western culture itself—to those of ancient Japanese mythology. The result is a kind of hybrid mythology that contains elements of Eastern and Western spiritual and religious thinking, a nexus of two worlds in which new ideas are hatched concerning traditional taboos and the role of the sacred or spiritual world in everyday life. What emerges from his experiments in this regard is a new model by which the contemporary subject might develop the spiritual resources to encounter, interpret, and develop his or her own inner narrative, one grounded in the realm of the eternal and sacred, capable of responding to the collective human Narrative, and yet able to free the individual from the traditional snares of fate and social convention.

The Mythological Murakami

While the Murakami protagonist's ongoing battle with an evil presence has been widely noted, it is somewhat surprising that more has not been written on the deeply mythological underpinnings of the author's work, especially the peculiar affinity he shows for classical Greek mythology. Among those who have taken notice of this aspect of Murakami fiction is Uchida Tatsuru, who discerns "a mythological narrative structure in the Murakami world in which the Murakami heroes, acting as sentinels, do battle against some sort of 'cosmological evil' that invades their world."[8] Uchida goes on to note that this structure is present in virtually every Murakami work yet written. Both Rubin and Susan Napier note an Orphean reference; Rubin, writing on *The Wind-Up Bird Chronicle,* notes the similarity of Okada Tōru's forays into the unconscious "other world" to a variety of mythological tales:

> He becomes a modern-day Theseus, advancing into the dark convoluted labyrinth of linked computers, guarded by the half-human, half-bull Minotaur named Ushikawa (Bull River). Or he is Orpheus or Japan's earth-creating god Izanagi, pursuing his dead wife into the depths of the underworld, where she forbids him to gaze upon her physical decay.[9]

As we have seen in our discussions of the metaphysical realm in the previous chapter, the "underworld" aspects in Murakami's fictional landscape have been around more or less since the beginning of his career. The image of the well in particular, already discussed as a passageway linking physical and metaphysical worlds, conscious and unconscious, while suspending the temporal and spatial constraints of the physical realm, may be likened to the Delphian oracle, a fissure in the earth through which the gods—Hermes, Apollo—speak to mortal humans, foretelling the future, (partially) revealing the course of fate, guiding and instructing, though always in riddles that require interpretation, a point that will be important to my discussion of *1Q84* below.

Whether Murakami had Greek antiquity consciously in mind when he constructed his dichotomy of "this side" and "over there," some of his portrayals do bring to mind what we find in those ancient works. Kawai Hayao notes a similarity between Johnny Walker's jovial slaughter of cats in the scene leading up to his death and the treatment of the tortoise by Hermes, messenger of the gods, in the Homeric hymn.[10] Asked by Nakata why he kills cats and removes their internal organs, Johnny Walker replies that he is "constructing a flute." "'I'm killing cats in order to collect their souls,'" he explains cheerfully to a horrified Nakata. "'Then I use the souls I've collected to construct a special flute. When I play that flute, I can collect larger souls.'"[11] Johnny Walker's immunity to such human constructs as pity and remorse reminds us of the young Hermes's laughing speech to the tortoise prior to bringing it into his home, scooping out its insides, and stringing it with a cow's intestines to make a lute.

> "Hail, comrade of the feast, lovely in shape, sounding at the dance! With joy I meet you! Where got you that rich gaud for covering, that spangled shell—a tortoise living in the mountains? But I will take and carry you within: you shall help me and I will do you no disgrace, though first of all you must profit me. It is better to be at home: harm may come out of doors. Living, you shall be a spell against mischievous witchcraft; but if you die, then you shall make sweetest song."[12]

Kawai finds something unsettling in the way Hermes can look at the living turtle yet see only a musical instrument. Johnny Walker is cut from the same cloth. "This is how the gods are," writes Kawai. "Words like 'treacherous' and 'heartless' belong to the human realm, but a god spots a tortoise and instantly sees a lute. To carry on with such treachery in order to construct a lute is the god's task. Johnny Walker is like a god. Coming across a cat, he sees the flute therein."[13]

Murakami is not rewriting the myths of ancient Greece (or for that matter, of ancient Japan), but we sense these tales always lurking behind his texts, particularly in how spirits and deities populate his metaphysical realm, how ordinary mortals confront that metaphysical realm as the domain not only of those spirits and deities but of the "invisible" form, as Kamata Tōji terms it, of the physical self.[14] There is no denying that Murakami's characters, as they drive ever deeper into the metaphysical landscape, confronting eternity itself in the dark and forbidding underworld, seem to relive some of the more widely disseminated events both from classical Greek myth and from ancient Japanese mythology.

Most prominent among these would likely be the tale of Orpheus and Eurydice and the early sequences of the *Kojiki* (ca. 712; Record of ancient matters), Japan's creation myth. In the former, Orpheus, a surpassingly skilled musician, loses his beloved wife to the bite of a venomous snake, and travels into the underworld in hopes of persuading its ruler, Hades, to allow her to return. Hades initially refuses but, wooed by Orpheus's sweet song, at length relents, allowing him to lead his wife back up to the surface on condition that he not look back at her while they make their journey out. Because Eurydice makes no sound as she walks behind him, however, Orpheus doubts that she is there, and turns around to look. At this moment she is whisked away back into the underworld, there to remain forever.

The *Kojiki* myth, while quite different in many respects, contains certain common elements. In it, two gods—the brother-sister/husband-wife team of Izanagi and Izanami—create the earth by dipping a spear into the ocean, churning it around, and pulling it out, allowing the muck from the ocean floor to drip off the end of the spear, forming the islands of Japan. This obviously sexual metaphor is followed by more conventional copulation, resulting in the birth of the various elements that make up the earth, including water and fire. In giving birth to the element of fire, however, Izanami suffers severe burns to her genitals and eventually dies of her injuries. She then descends (or perhaps is placed) into Yomi-no-kuni, the land of the dead. Yomi-no-kuni, at this point, is still accessible to the living, and the grieving Izanagi has no difficulty entering the underworld in search of his wife. Locating Izanami, he invites her to return to the land of the living. Izanami agrees to do so, but because she has already eaten the food of the dead, she warns her husband not to look upon her.[15] When he does, he is repulsed by the sight of maggots consuming his wife's face, and cries out. Greatly shamed, Izanami flies into a rage and chases Izanagi out of Yomi. Upon his escape, he rolls a boulder across the entryway to Yomi, dividing forever the worlds of living and dead, reminiscent of the stones used to close ancient *kofun* tombs in the third and fourth centuries.[16]

Myths of this type are, of course, meant to demonstrate behavioral proscriptions (such as contact with the dead) and at the same time to explain how the world came to be as it is. The tale just related no doubt reflected ancient burial practices during the period in which it was written down, but the deeper lesson given is that the worlds of the living and the dead are divided by an insurmountable barrier, just as life and death, while separated by only a moment, are nonetheless divided irrevocably, for death is not reversible.

Journeys into the underworld, visitations to the dead, Orphean quests to recover those who have been lost, do indeed run throughout the full body of Murakami fiction. A sampling would include the following: Boku's quests for Naoko in *Pinball, 1973*, Rat in *A Wild Sheep Chase*, and "Kiki" (the ear model who goes missing at the end of *A Wild Sheep Chase*) in *Dance Dance Dance;* add to this Watanabe Tōru's attempts to bring Naoko back from the precipice of death in *Norwegian Wood*, Okada Tōru's rescue of Kumiko in *The Wind-Up Bird Chronicle*, K.'s search for Sumire in *The Sputnik Sweetheart*, Mari's attempts to reawaken her sister Eri in *After Dark*, and Tengo's visits with Adachi Kumi in *1Q84*, and we begin to see something of a pattern developing. Not all of these involve the underworld per se (those in *The Sputnik Sweetheart* and *After Dark*, notably, do not include an actual journey by the hero into the metaphysical realm), but others bear a striking resemblance to the very kinds of mythological quests from antiquity just described.

The Early Underworld: Cold Storage

The most obvious of these quests is in *Pinball, 1973*, in which Boku goes hunting for a pinball machine that, in his imagination at least, comforted him around the time Naoko died. His obsession with pinball begins when he hears the pinball machine calling to him. "The 3-flippered Spaceship . . . she kept calling to me from somewhere. This went on for several days."[17] Near the end of the work he receives a tip from a friend about a collector of pinball machines and makes a journey to the warehouse in which it is stored. Boku's journey to find the "Spaceship" contains numerous similarities with his later journey to find Rat, most notably, a *michiyuki* marked by a sense of uneasiness; looking out of the window, he sees a darkness that is "no longer just dark, but as if someone had plastered it on like butter with heavy paint" (1:230), and Boku cannot help but ask his friend whether they are even still in Tokyo. "'Of course,'" replies the other man. "'Does it seem like we're not?'" "'It's like the end of the world,'" replies Boku (1:232). He is correct, in a sense: it is the end of the world of the living. Boku's friend also carries out a recognized mythological role, as a guide to the underworld, while the unseen collector of pinball machines could, with a little imagination, be read as a Hades-like character. As the taxi approaches the warehouse, "the 3-flippered Spaceship continued to call out to me" (1:232).

Upon entering the warehouse, Boku's impressions do not dispel the atmosphere of death and burial in the place. The description is that of a well-preserved crypt, with heavy metal doors that open noiselessly, thick walls, pitch-dark and freezing cold.[18] Boku is assailed by a fear that "I might be stuck in here forever," and describes the place as looking like an "elephant graveyard" (1:235). The pinball machines are lined up, row upon row, in perfect order, all facing the same direction, not one of them even a centimeter out of place, giving the impression of a vast cemetery, with row upon row of perfectly equidistant headstones, identical but for the names carved on them. At length, Boku makes his way down five steps to the level of the pinball machines—a symbolic and actual descent into the underworld—and wanders among the machines "as if I were inspecting troops," (1:238) he says, but in fact more like a man seeking the grave of a loved one. The machines themselves are varied, familiar and unfamiliar. "Some were vintage machines I had seen only in photographs; others called back fond memories of when I had seen them in arcades. And some had simply been lost to time, remembered by no one" (1:238). Is this not an apt description of the land of the dead and the souls who inhabit it?

Not surprisingly, although Boku locates his beloved pinball machine, he cannot restore Naoko to life, nor can he bring her out of the storehouse with him. There can be no return from the world of the dead, and even visits to that place by the living must be kept brief lest, as Boku worries, we might never get back. What Boku *can* do is to find a sense of closure with Naoko, to offer her words of comfort—and apology—and receive her forgiveness in return.[19]

One final point needs to be made concerning Boku's communion with Naoko's soul in this novel, and that is the role played by sound. Boku's quest begins, as we have seen, with Naoko's cries from the "other world." His closure occurs through the "sound"—albeit only in his head—of her words of forgiveness. This use of sound is prominent in *Hear the Wind Sing* as well, in the wind to which the boy listens, and the voices of the dead that call out for the nine-fingered girl. Boku's quest for "Kiki" in *Dance Dance Dance* begins with Kiki's cries for him; Naoko responds to Kizuki's voice in *Norwegian Wood;* Okada Tōru catches the tune of the "wind-up bird" in the novel of that name, along with his wife's (distorted) voice over the telephone; Sumire calls out for K. in *The Sputnik Sweetheart;* the "Boy Called Crow" offers advice and encouragement in Kafka's moments of doubt or confusion; and the Leader listens to "the voices" of the Little People in *1Q84*.

There can be no doubt that sound plays a central role in the process by which the "other world" communicates with "this world" and vice versa. As we will now see, however, its significance in mythological terms goes considerably beyond that.

Thunder of the Gods

Sound—both human-made and the sounds we find in nature—is a key element in a great many world mythologies, beginning with music. We must not forget that the Muses were closely affiliated with Apollo, god of music, and like him, connected to music and poetry; or that Orpheus's principal tool in dealing with the hostile spirits of the underworld was his own singing voice. In the Old Testament, Psalm 100 reminds us to "make a joyful noise unto the Lord . . . come before his presence with singing," Job 38:7 tells of how "morning stars sang together and all the angels shouted for joy" when the god created the universe, and Genesis 4:20 tells of Jubal's amazing skill on the lute. Most religions contain some form of singing or chanting in prayer, the simplest of these being perhaps the sacred *aum,* a sound that connects us with all the cosmos, combining the beginning and end, alpha and omega, of all things. Uttering this sacred word, according to the Upanishads, can allow us to grasp everything in the universe, not merely those things that exist but also those that do not. In Japanese culture, too, this syllable contains all, the first and last sounds in the Japanese syllabary, beginning and end.

To these various sounds of worship and meditation, the gods respond through the myriad sounds in nature. The hissing of the steam at the oracle in Delphi was said to be the dying breath of the great serpent slain by Apollo there, but through its sound came the messages from the gods. Ancient Norse mythology claimed that thunder came from the sound of Thor hurling his massive hammer across the sky, while in Greek lore it was Zeus flinging his lightning bolts like javelins. Other sounds harm or warn of danger: Odysseus and his crew are tormented by the lovely voices of the Sirens, mermaids who lure sailors to their doom, while Celtic and Welsh mythology tells of the banshee, a fairy whose cry can harbinger death for those who hear it, or in some traditions, may actually cause death itself. These are, of course, but a handful of examples, but they illustrate the importance of sound in our connectivity with the supernatural.

Japanese mythology and traditional religious practice also place great significance in sound. We have already noted that the *matsuri* tends to include music—particularly the flutes and drums that once kept time during the planting of rice seedlings—and worship at Shintō shrines begins with loud clapping of the hands, intended to make the gods aware of our presence and to show respect, and also with the ringing of bells, calling the gods to join us in celebration.

And when the Japanese gods seek to make themselves known to us? Naturally, their presence is announced by thunder.

In this regard, mythologist Kamata Tōji has carried out useful analyses of the various terms that inform traditional Japanese religious and supernatural concepts, arguing for the typically aural, rather than visual, manifestations of Japanese *kami*. This is seen easily enough in the term *kaminari* ("thunder"), which is homonymous with words meaning "be/become a deity" (神成り) and "cry/call of a deity" (神鳴り). Perhaps less widely known is the origin of the word *kami* itself, which Kamata argues comes from a contraction of *kakurimi* (隠身), or "hidden body/hidden self." His point is that Japanese deities have always been aural first, a fact that highlights the importance of ears in Japanese folklore and mythology:[20]

> It is highly doubtful whether humans, had they lacked ears, would ever have discovered the gods. The term *kami* has its origins in a contraction of the word *kakurimi*, and if the gods are invisible, they would likely never have been "discovered" or "invented" by humanity. To play on the words, the "birth" (*hassei* 発生) of the gods occurred simultaneously with the vocalization (*hassei* 発声) of the gods. . . . The gods visit humans first through their ears.[21]

As we have already noted, however, while hearing the gods "speak" through the thunder of the heavens may be common to all, catching their meaning—grasping what the gods are trying to say—is another matter entirely, and this becomes the role of the priest, shaman, the "hearer of the voices." In ancient times, he (or, more likely, *she*) who possessed the knack would have taken up the role of shaman, of priestess, as indeed prehistoric Japanese chieftains were said to be. And this is where Murakami reenters the discussion.

The gift of hearing and comprehending divine voices is given only to a chosen few, as we have already seen in a great deal of Murakami fiction. This is surely what the Leader refers to in *1Q84,* as well, when he points out to Aomame that ancient kings were religious rulers first and thus very clearly sacred beings, for as Kamata reasonably points out, "if the gods do indeed show themselves through sound and voice, then the ear that catches these sounds may be called a divine vessel *(yorishiro).*"[22]

This may aid us in understanding to some extent Murakami's fixation on ears, particularly in his early fiction. As Rubin notes, "Murakami's characters take extraordinarily good care of their ears. They clean them almost obsessively so as to keep in tune with the unpredictable, shifting music of life."[23] The ability to hear things that others cannot is most obviously portrayed in the character of Boku's ear model girlfriend in *A Wild Sheep Chase,* whose ears are in fact revealed to be more or less directly connected to the metaphysical world, marking her as the possessor of the very sort of "divine vessel" to which Kamata refers. Yet even as early as *Pinball, 1973* we find references to the importance of ears and hearing. In a hilarious scene near the end of that novel, Boku has his ears—his direct "conduit" to the other world—cleaned by the Twins, who stand on either side of him, patiently working away with cotton swabs. Just then, disaster strikes: Boku sneezes, causing the Twins to jam their cotton swabs into his ears, leading to temporary deafness—closing off the "other world" to him. Interestingly, the physician who treats Boku informs him that his ear canal is "'much more twisted than most people's'" (1:252). Is this a sign that his ears are special, or a hindrance that leads to his chronic inability to catch the messages being passed along to him from the "other side"?[24] Finally, it is both.

Twisted or not, Boku spends the better part of this novel attempting to do what its predecessor commands in its title, to "hear the wind sing," that is, to hear the "other world," and it is his inability to catch more than fragments of that tune, or to make sense of what he does hear, that causes Rat, throughout *Pinball, 1973,* to grow increasingly despondent, cut off as he is from Boku, his other self. This connects to our earlier discussion of "flow" between the two worlds, a point highlighted in one of Naoko's stories, in which she describes the exceptionally tasty water people enjoyed in her town.

Their supply of this excellent water was interrupted, however, when the diviner who located the right spots to dig their wells was killed in a train accident. The connection between "this side" and "over there" is thus neatly metaphorized as the flow of water from underground to the surface. If we understand the diviner here to perform the role of the priest, the one who establishes contact with the gods, however, then we quickly recognize that water is a metaphor for the divine voices themselves, whose communication must be unobstructed in order for the world to function in proper balance. Beyond an obvious psychological significance, this lends a new dimension to the fact that Boku has always found water wells to be a source of comfort. "I've always liked wells," he relates immediately following Naoko's tale. "It's my habit to toss a stone into any well I happen to see. There may be no more comforting sound than that of a small stone hitting the surface of the water in a deep well" (1:133). By converse logic, there may be no more despondent sound than that same stone striking hard, dry earth at the bottom of a dry well.

It is not only sounds themselves but changes in sound that mark the approach of the metaphysical world or, in later works, the arrival of the gods. As Boku and his ear model girlfriend make their away around the treacherous "dead-man's curve" en route to Rat's villa in *A Wild Sheep Chase,* "the sound of our boots on the ground continually changed,"[25] and the hero of *Hard-Boiled Wonderland and the End of the World,* when he first descends into the subterranean caverns of the old scientist in that work, is unnerved by the completely silent environment (owing to the fact that the scientist he is going to meet has "removed the sound" from the surrounding area).[26] Naoko's mountain sanatorium in *Norwegian Wood* is similarly marked by the peculiar way that sound absents itself there: "What an incredibly quiet place," Tōru muses as he enters the grounds. "There wasn't a sound anywhere. I wondered if it was siesta time or something. It was a quiet afternoon on which every person, animal, insect and plant was sound asleep."[27] Sometimes those who can hear the voices themselves have their external sound turned off; early in *The Wind-Up Bird Chronicle,* Okada Tōru and his wife, Kumiko, are reminded by the deaf clairvoyant, Mr. Honda, to "listen to the flow," the subtle changes in sound that occur as the energy between worlds ebbs and flows.

But this is easier said than done. It is precisely his catastrophic inability to perceive the correct frequency of psychic energy as it passes from one world to the other that lies at the heart of the Murakami hero's inability to reconnect with Rat, to "save" Naoko, to find Sumire before she goes "over there," to discover the identity of the "telephone woman." This is the true significance of the ubiquitous embedded narratives that litter the Murakami literary structure as well; each time a character relates a story to the protagonist, they are revealing something essential—an "oracle" of sorts—to him. And when he listens to these voices with his ears fully opened, the Murakami hero draws just a little closer to hearing them meaningfully. The problem, of course, is that Murakami's heroes seldom do listen with their ears "fully opened," and when they do, they show spectacularly poor ability in unscrambling the coded messages contained in what they hear. And so their friends die or simply disappear, and the hero has no clue as to why.

This, at any rate, was the case up to—and possibly including—*The Wind-Up Bird Chronicle,* when, after three agonizing volumes and more than 1,200 pages, Okada Tōru finally riddles out who the "telephone woman" is, and what she is trying to tell him. But was he in time? The novel ends inconclusively, and we are left wondering, along with Tōru, whether Kumiko will ever actually be restored to a life with him in the physical world. It is not until *Kafka on the Shore* and, later, *1Q84* that the Murakami hero at last catches the messages being delivered to him and acts upon them in such a way as to lead to positive results.

Interestingly, Murakami uses thunder as a metaphysical marker in both of these novels with considerable effect. In *Kafka on the Shore,* on the evening that Kafka confronts Saeki with her past and discusses the "other world" with her, a tremendous thunderstorm occurs, and we later realize that this is the very same moment that Nakata and Hoshino are lifting the Gateway Stone that blocks the passage between the physical and metaphysical worlds. Here, opening the passageway between "this side" and "over there" means suspending not only the laws of time and space but of social and moral code, right and wrong, good and evil, and it is at precisely such moments that our thoughts and dreams of forbidden things that normally remain "over there"—sexual liaisons, violent acts—are free to manifest themselves with impunity on "this side." Furthermore, Murakami's choice of a stone for his gateway is not accidental; in mythological terms it hearkens back to the stone that protected Izanagi from his wife's wrath when he fled the underworld, the stone that covered Jesus's tomb prior to his resurrection, a physical, yet also symbolic, barrier that guards the passage between life and death. To move it is to release the awesome power of the metaphysical into our world, to tamper with the natural order of the universe itself; seen from the opposite angle, it also signals the infiltration of the metaphysical realm (the realm of deities) by mortals. It is little wonder, then, that the gods roar with thunder.

This sacred thunder returns in *1Q84* on the night that Aomame kills the Leader, but in this case both rain and lightning are conspicuously absent, leaving only the "voice" of the thunder itself. This, as noted earlier, is also the precise moment that Tengo and Aomame achieve their metaphysical connection through Fukaeri (yet another kind of "Gateway Stone") and conceive a sacred child through what can only be termed an "intensely sexual immaculate conception," one in which penetration and ejaculation occur, yet the two parties never come within five miles of one another. This is only possible because Tengo and Aomame are sacred beings themselves.

It's Not Easy Being Divine

Only recently has Murakami begun writing about the "sacred," and the author might even be a little uncomfortable with such a term, but it is the right one, for ever since the short story "All children of the gods dance," he has been inching his way toward the production of divinely inspired—indeed, immaculately conceived—heroes and heroines.

This began, as noted near the beginning of this chapter, with the character Yoshiya, whose name means "goodness," and whose mother, according to the narrative, took every possible precaution against getting pregnant yet still conceived Yoshiya. If the story related to Yoshiya can be believed, she had a physical affair with a man, was careful to use a condom, yet still conceived. The doctor, believing that she used the condom incorrectly, demonstrates its use to her himself—in bed. Again she conceives, and this child is Yoshiya. The doctor denies responsibility, and Yoshiya is determined to find this mysterious doctor and confront him with his patrimony. His mother, however, has a rather different interpretation of the story. She tells Yoshiya:

> Your father is "the One" (this was what members of her religion called their god), his mother kept repeating to him from the time he was small. And because He is "the One," He can only exist in the sky. He cannot live with us. But he who is your father will always care about you and watch over you.[28]

Yoshiya, refusing to believe this story, persists in seeking out the doctor, in effect denying both his heritage as a child of heaven and whatever adventure or responsibility might accompany such an acknowledgment (insofar as divine sons are rarely sent into the world just for fun). In the end he discovers, however, that he cannot simply walk away from his divinity. Riding a train one evening, Yoshiya spots a man who meets the description of the doctor he believes to be his biological father (among other things, he is missing part of one ear). He follows the man off the train, chases him by taxi, and is led to a baseball stadium—judging from the area they exit the train, it is most likely to be Jingū Stadium,[29] near the Meiji Shrine—where he follows "the doctor" onto the playing field, only to find the man has vanished. Thereupon Yoshiya makes his way to the top of the pitcher's mound (a symbolic journey up the mountain to meet the gods), stretches his hands toward heaven, gazes at the moon for a moment, and then begins to dance, "one movement calling out for the next and then, all on its own, connecting with the next movement after that" (92). As he does so, he has a vision of a kind of forest opening inside him. "Its interior was filled with terrifying beasts the likes of which he had never seen. Eventually he would have to pass through the forest, but he was not afraid. The forest is inside of me, after all, he thought. I gave shape to this forest myself. The beasts are part of me" (92).

Much as Kafka and Nakata are drawn to Takamatsu, as Boku is guided to Hokkaido, as Tōru is attracted to the well, Aomame to the Leader, Yoshiya has been led by unseen forces to this exact spot to receive some sort of message from the gods. Exactly what Yoshiya's divine mission might be is left out of the narrative, but this could not matter less, for the point of this story is the process by which a young man discovers and acknowledges his proper place in the world. The story illustrates and celebrates spiritual awakening to the internal narrative and to the omnipresent Narrative.

If divine grace plays a central role in this brief tale, then so does the potential for taboo. Yoshiya, in his reminiscences about growing up alone with his mother, recalls that she always looked younger than she was and that she had the peculiar habits of wandering around their home in her underwear and of crawling into bed with him in the middle of the night:

> Wearing next to nothing, she would come into his room and crawl into his *futon* with him. Like he was a dog or cat, she would wrap her arms around him and sleep. Yoshiya knew his mother had no impure intentions, but he was certainly not at ease at such moments. He would have to lie in the most unnatural positions so that his mother would not be aware of his erections in these instances. (71–72)

Titillating as this scene may be for readers in a culture where mother-son incest fantasies are a staple of the pornography industry, there is a deeper significance to this relationship. Late in the story, while on the pitcher's mound, Yoshiya recalls Mr. Tabata, a family friend, who had made a deathbed confession to Yoshiya about having harbored lustful thoughts about Yoshiya's mother. Standing on the pitcher's mound, the young man remembers his urge to confess similar feelings of his own for her. But this causes him to recall the words he would like to have said to Tabata: that our hearts contain both good and evil, but in the end what matters is sharing our souls with one another. This, finally, seems to bring Yoshiya inner peace, and if there is a "quest" in this story, we might conclude that it is not for the absent/invisible father but for self-absolution. In confronting and forgiving himself for his incestuous thoughts, Yoshiya has for the first time truly given himself up to his inner narrative, and in so doing discovered the sacred spark that dwells there. The final lines of the story are singularly beautiful:

> Yoshiya crouched on the pitcher's mound, surrendered his body to the flow of time. He heard the faint sound of an ambulance siren in the distance. The wind blew, making the blades of grass dance, the prayer of the grass song.
>
> God . . . Yoshiya said, aloud. (95)

If Yoshiya is unable to escape the fate of being a child of god, at least he does seem to come to terms with his troubling memories of his mother. Given the peculiar nature of his conception, however, his connectivity to the metaphysical/divine, we might also argue that Yoshiya transcends mundane notions of incest, for in uttering the name of "God" *(kamisama)* at the end, Yoshiya declares himself as well.

If the divine spark, as it were, makes its first appearance in Murakami fiction in the character of Yoshiya, it becomes a central theme for the first time in *1Q84*. In that work, while continuing to pursue the tension between the individual and the forces that surround the individual, Murakami tackles the extremely sensitive issue (particularly in Japan) of religious cults and the role they play in contemporary society. Surprisingly, given the general public rancor and mistrust directed at religious cults since the Aum Shinrikyō incident, Murakami not only portrays aspects of the "Sakigake" cult in *1Q84* in a generous—even positive—light, but within the context of the story actually seems to ground origins of the cult in the sacred.

Of True and False Prophets

If the metaphysical world is as real as the physical one (at least within the context of Murakami's fictional world), so too the "sacred" realm, as part of that metaphysical world, must be regarded as real. Ordinarily such a point would not need to be made with respect to Murakami, except that there is a natural inclination, particularly in "modern" societies, to regard people who hear voices as mad. (It is an interesting point of irony that there is a greater tendency among people—especially those living in advanced industrialized societies—to place their faith in religious leaders whose faith is grounded in sacred writings rather than in direct sacred experience.) Perhaps this is because most organized religions exist at a comfortable distance from the direct experience of the ancient seer on whose teachings their belief system is founded. Then, too, it may be inevitable that industrialized people should be more comfortable with the sense of order that comes with organization and tradition.

But all religions must start somewhere, and if we think about the growth of some of the major ones—Judaism, Buddhism, Christianity, Islam, for instance—we note that they generally begin with a charismatic leader who claims direct experience and contact with a deity or deities. Certainly this was true of Moses, Buddha, Jesus, and Mohammed. Even assuming that their experiences and instructions were preserved for a generation or two by disciples, fellow mystics or seers, eventually those teachings were codified, written down, and maintained by a priesthood whose ordained have little or no direct contact or experience with the deity/deities but whose faith is grounded in the codified teachings themselves. This process is not confined only to ancient religions; new religions and cults spring up regularly even into the present era, many of them offshoots of established religions (many Japanese cults, for instance, are variants of Buddhism, founded by leaders who claim direct mystical experiences). Invariably, tension is born between the established, textually based religions and the "new," experience-based derivatives, and religious history is filled with stories of burning or banishing as madmen or "heretics" those who claim to have had a direct encounter with the deity. Joseph Campbell usefully defines these two phases of religious experience as those of the "shaman" and the "priest":

> The figure now in the primary role is the priest, who is an ordained official of the tribal or village deities; these are not of his personal experience. He is in the service of the society and its deities, for the priestly society. The shaman is an archaic danger. He represents the early mystic, one who has had the individual mystic experience and is supported by his familiars—his own special deities—whereas the priest is supported by and is in turn the supporter of the cultural deities. The two systems are inherently in conflict. The priest is the man of the book; the shaman is the man of the experience.[30]

What Campbell describes can also be expressed as the conflict between collective thought/experience and individual thought/experience. In the case of *1Q84,* we see this best exemplified, sometimes explicitly, other times more subtly, in the conflict that comes to exist between what below we will term *true prophets,* that is, those genuinely touched by the divine spark, and *false prophets,* who champion the sort of "myths" of which Roland Barthes wrote, artificial constructs such as "morality" and "justice," as well as religious and political ideological systems, quite as though they represented absolute truth.

In fact, the structure of *1Q84* sets up these oppositions quite plainly, for divinely inspired characters are clearly marked with exceptional physical or mental qualities. Fukaeri, for instance, is marked physically; she is beautiful yet somehow lacks "balance"; physically she is small, but her breasts are unusually large and draw a great deal of attention. But most of all she seems simply artificial. "Her expression was devoid of the scent of life,"[31] Tengo reflects the first time he sees her. Other areas of her body, as we saw in the previous chapter, actually look as though they are not real. But Fukaeri is also "marked" by her inability to communicate in the ordinary way, speaking in extremely short sentences, with virtually no intonation (difficult words for her are written in the text phonetically in *katakana* as a signal to the reader that they are more sounds to her than pictorial images or concepts). It is a point of humor that she always asks questions of Tengo "without the question mark" *(gimonfu o tsukezu ni)* (1:86).

In the context of our mythological analysis, we may associate Fukaeri's difficulty in communicating through normal human channels as a sign that she is a direct receiver—the mouthpiece—of oracles, the first to hear the "voices" of the gods (or of the Little People, in this case) and to pass along what they have said. As with many oracles, however, those messages arrive in jumbled form—as riddles, as parables, in code—and are not intelligible to the uninitiated. Thus, the messages that emerge from Fukaeri must be interpreted by those with the gift for transposing the sublime into the everyday. Initially, Fukaeri's "oracle" is interpreted and transmitted in a primitive form by the teenage daughter of Professor Ebisuno, who provides refuge to Fukaeri after she has run away from the cult. The real task of interpreting and transmitting the contents of the oracle to the masses, however, falls to the Leader and, later, *to his son Tengo.*

Both Tengo and the Leader (who certainly is Tengo's *spiritual* father, if not his actual, biological one) are marked as divine by their extraordinary physical size and strength, as well as their more intellectual gifts in language and reasoning. We recall that Tengo, upon reading Fukaeri's story (as transposed by Ebisuno's daughter), is taken by it in a way that he cannot ignore; the narrative has awakened something inside him, and when directed to rework the piece for publication, despite strong ethical misgivings, he finds that he cannot resist. Like Yoshiya, Tengo cannot deny the divine spark that he carries, nor can he escape his sacred task as prophet, intermediary between humans and the gods. His editor Komatsu says much the same thing when he tells Tengo, "'You'll be the mediator, you'll connect Fukaeri's world with the real world'" (1:101). From the start, then, Tengo has been marked to replace the Leader, whose ability to interpret the words—the Will—of the gods (the Little People) through Fukaeri wanes as his physical body deteriorates. In the tradition of ancient animistic religions—including Shintō—the Leader performs the function of shaman, his experiences with the spirit world immediate and personal. As a holy man he intercedes between the earthly masses and the spirit world, interpreting the raw data transmitted through Fukaeri and transposing it into intelligible Law. And Tengo, in rewriting Fukaeri's narrative for wider dissemination, has unwittingly already begun to take over the family business.

In mythological terms, if Tengo and the Leader are prophets and Fukaeri functions as oracular messenger of the gods, then Aomame fulfills the dual role of bringer and taker of life. Aomame at times strikes us as a series of paradoxes: she can be friendly and appealing, yet her grimace can cause children to soil themselves; she is a fitness instructor and nutrition expert who moonlights as a serial killer and whose best friend is a police officer; she detests the religion in which she was raised yet unconsciously appeals to that very same god when faced with sudden uncertainty. Aomame's lack of consistency is physically marked by her breasts, which are of different size, symbolizing the two sides to her personality and her dual roles. She is a force of nature itself, monster and angel, bringer of death and (as mother to Tengo's unborn child) giver of life. Even as Aomame uses her ice pick–like instrument to turn off the "life switch" at the base of her victims' brains, she zealously nurtures and protects the fragile and defenseless life that grows inside her. In fact, it is precisely for control of her womb—and thus control of her body itself—that the final conflict in this story will be fought out.

This leaves Ushikawa, the last of the characters I would identify as divinely marked, though readers may wish it were not so. Ushikawa, whose name means "bull river," is actually more of a doglike character, marked physically by his small stature and misshapen head. His appearance is particularly striking given that he comes from a family of tall, well-proportioned, good-looking people. He alone is hideous, but this is our best indication that he has been marked by the gods. Blessed with extraordinary instincts, a keen intellect, and a talent for finding things that are unfindable, Ushikawa enters the narrative as a temporary retainer for the Sakigake cult, which sends him to approach Tengo in order to rediscover the whereabouts of Fukaeri; later, in book 3, he is sent out to locate Aomame following the death of the Leader. However, while Ushikawa works for Sakigake, from a narratological point of view his role more closely resembles that of Nakata, whose task is to open the Gateway Stone and restore a sense of balance between the two sides. Despite his unpleasant appearance, Ushikawa's position is neither benevolent nor malevolent. This, however, is also why he must die; the balance must, temporarily at least, be upset in order to break the stalemate and bring the conflict to a resolution. Like the Leader, Ushikawa is a necessary sacrifice.

The stakes in bringing about this reunification are considerable: they involve the establishment of the next generation of divinely sparked humans—beginning with Aomame and Tengo's child—who will be free from the false narratives with which these two characters have struggled their whole lives. Their task, which they must perform together or not at all, is to show the way by breaking free of the various ready-made narratives that have bound them until now.

As we have already seen, both Aomame and Tengo spent their childhoods under the care of parents who zealously adhered to rigid belief systems. In Aomame's case this took the form of evangelical Christianity, and she, too, was forced to follow these customs and rituals without question. Tengo was left in the hands of an equally zealous worshipper of the Japanese State—represented through NHK. His father's loyalty to NHK is understandable; having returned to Japan from mainland Asia following World War II, with neither education nor family, Tengo's father survived because he found employment—an actual home—with NHK.

Sincere as their parents may have been in their devotion to these belief systems, however, those systems ultimately prove unsuited to Aomame's and Tengo's needs, precisely because even as children their inner selves were intact; ready-made narratives such as organized religion and State ideology can only stunt their spiritual and emotional development. Their only hope of meaningful existence is thus to break free and continue to develop their own inner voices. As children, both Tengo and Aomame were pawns for their parents; as adults, it is imperative that they live for themselves.

But do they? Herein, I think, Murakami sets a subtle trap for his readers, for while Aomame and Tengo may appear to have shaken off the shackles of their childhood restrictions and come into their own as adults, I would argue that, quite the contrary, in the process of escaping the evangelical roots in which they were brought up, both have run directly into the arms of a new manifestation of the same sort of ready-made narratives, in the form of the zealotry represented in the old woman and Komatsu. Aomame is still a pawn, an enforcer of the old woman's campaign of vengeance against abusive men, meting out justice, to be sure, but whose justice and on whose terms? Tengo, similarly, is drawn into Komatsu's game of revenge and humiliation against the pretensions of the literary and artistic community. Like Aomame, he got into the game for compelling reasons of his own, but in the end he serves as a mere tool advancing the agenda of Komatsu himself. Komatsu and the old woman, then, within the quasi-religious context of this discussion, represent merely one more pair of "false prophets," exploiting the gifts Tengo and Aomame possess to further their own schemes. Neither Komatsu nor the old woman are presented as evil per se; they are simply a new variation on an old theme.

In time, both protagonists come to recognize this reality. Aomame has no difficulty in accepting the need to stop abusive men from harming their wives and children but is troubled by a vague sense of guilt. "She had just sent someone 'over there,'" she reflects after one kill. "He may have been a useless little rat bastard who had no business complaining even if he *was* killed, but he had been, after all, a human being. The sensation of extinguishing a life still remained in her hand" (1:102). In other words, justified or not, Aomame understands that her actions are murder. This differs significantly from her first kill, an act of revenge against the man who drove her best friend to suicide, for these later kills have nothing directly to do with her; she has no personal connection with either her targets or their victims. The old woman, seeking to alleviate Aomame's sense of responsibility for these actions, attempts to pay her for her services. "'Because you are neither an angel nor a god,'" she tells Aomame. "'I know perfectly well that your actions sprang from pure feeling . . . But pure, genuine feelings can be dangerous, too'" (1:330). At length Aomame accepts this explanation and allows the old woman to set aside money for her, but this, finally, only proves the point that Aomame is caught up in a narrative not of her own making; in fact, the only possible means for establishing the purity of Aomame's actions is to commit them solely out of "pure feeling," as she did in her first kill. This point is driven unerringly home immediately following this scene, when Aomame receives a telephone call from her friend Ayumi, who has been accepting gifts of money from the various men she sleeps with. The parallel between "money for sex" (prostitute) and "money for murder" (assassin) is bluntly made, but it serves a secondary purpose, both for Aomame and the reader: to highlight the fact that Aomame's sexual activities, which have always had the purpose of relieving her sexual stress in order to keep her love for Tengo "pure," are now at risk of being deflected down a more mercenary path through the influences of her more depraved friend Ayumi. Perhaps only in Murakami fiction could we thus find ourselves drawing the following conclusion: that for Aomame, acts of meaningless sex and ruthless killing are losing their "purity."

Tengo's side of the narrative fares little better. A pure wordsmith, Tengo's job until the start of this novel has been to lend stylistic flair to texts produced by writers who have interesting stories to tell but who lack his genius with language. Like any good ghostwriter, Tengo has been content to remain anonymous, placing his technical skill at the service of others. When presented with Komatsu's scheme to rewrite Fukaeri's manuscript into something worthy of the Akutagawa Prize, on the other hand, he is deeply troubled by the ethical questions involved. Komatsu attempts to put him off by paraphrasing Aristotle's *Nicomachean Ethics:* "'The end is good in itself. Good is an end in itself. Doubts should be left for tomorrow,'" to which Tengo aptly responds, "'What does Aristotle have to say about the Holocaust?'" (1:307). A young man who seriously values his integrity, Tengo is uncomfortably aware that he is being used by Komatsu to perpetrate fraud.

What, then, are Tengo and Aomame to do? How can they escape, once again, the forces that bind and control them? The answer is that they must break faith with the belief systems of Komatsu and the old woman, much as they once broke with their parents, and reconnect with the internal narrative that binds them together, a narrative that originated at the precise moment that Aomame first took Tengo's hand in that empty classroom some twenty-five years earlier. At that moment the two exchanged something—the seeds of a narrative that connects their souls and, like the novel written by Tengo and Fukaeri, must be written to the end by *both* of them or not at all. From that moment in the classroom there has existed a need to reunite them, to continue *and complete* the story. In this regard, Fukaeri fulfills an additional role in this novel, serving not only as the mythological oracle but also as a symbolic surrogate for Aomame until such time that she can be reunited with Tengo. Just as Fukaeri serves as a sexual connection between Tengo and Aomame on the night the Leader is killed, she also serves as a temporary carrier of the story they shared. This is why so many of Fukaeri's movements echo Aomame's, and why she seems so explicitly to equate the sexual act with that of their collaborative writing, for both are acts of *pro*creation. Fukaeri views this act, rightly, as a sacred one, and her description suggests marriage and its consummation when she tells Tengo that "'We have become one. . . . We wrote a book together'" (1:426).

In carrying out this act, however, Fukaeri proves herself to be a rogue oracle, for in exposing the story of the Little People through her story *Kūki sanagi,* she has in fact revealed forbidden knowledge to the uninitiated. Her role in this novel is thus ambiguous, not unlike that of Ushikawa: as a conduit by which the new "hearer of voices" is conceived she performs the will of the gods (the Little People), who require a prophet; in revealing them to a wider audience through her story with Tengo, however, she also undermines their authority over the world, threatening the deterministic fate with which they control events of the present and, more importantly, the future. It will, finally, be up to Aomame to act upon these revelations to shatter the imaginary bonds of "fate" and reassert the "free will" of the individual for the sake of herself, Tengo, and their child to be. This is a central issue not only in this novel but in *Kafka on the Shore* as well.

Fate versus Free Will: *Kafka on the Shore* and *1Q84*

We return, then, full circle to the critical question of how fate and free will are handled in Murakami fiction, and for this, once again, we find important antecedents in the author's early works, for while the question is most prominently explored from *Kafka on the Shore,* it begins with the struggle between Rat and the Sheep in *A Wild Sheep Chase.* What *is* the Sheep, after all, but a "ready-made narrative"? It is a system of thought that offers a kind of crystalline perfection, to be sure, a closed utopian circle not unlike the one sought by Kizuki and Naoko, by Nakata and Saeki, but which, finally, comes at a terrible price. That crystalline perfection, beautiful yet mindless and sterile, is balanced by the imperfection, sometimes termed "mediocrity," of the human soul, with all its weaknesses. Yet it is precisely these flaws in our souls that make us all unique, and this is what is at stake for Rat—and through him, Boku, for Rat is the most unique part of Boku's mind. Asked why he finally rejected the Sheep, Rat answers quite simply: "'Because I like my weakness. I like the pain and hardship, too. I like the light of summer and the smell of the wind. I can't help liking them.'"[32] What Rat really loves are the *human* aspects of his life, for these are what make it real and unique for him. And so, rather than surrender all this in exchange for the Sheep's perfection, Rat chooses to destroy the Sheep, and himself with it.

This is a pattern repeated throughout Murakami's fiction. What is Wataya Noboru really claiming when he removes that "something wet and slippery" from Kanō Creta's body in *The Wind-Up Bird Chronicle*? Finally, it is any and all traces of her individuality, including her pain and confusion, which he will then replace with something of his own making, an ideology that will have the appearance of perfection yet will finally be a sterile, closed system, cut off from the collective Narrative from which we all construct our internal narratives. Why is Wataya Noboru portrayed as a slick politician? He represents, once again, the *illusion of truth* bound up in Roland Barthes's definition of "myth," bound up in all political ideologies. Okada Tōru's Herculean task in that novel is to hurl himself—once again the "egg" metaphor is useful here—against the massive "perfect wall" of Wataya Noboru's artificial narrative. The egg may shatter (at it does in Rat's case), but it mars that perfection and preserves its integrity as an egg, rather than become, as Pink Floyd has it, "just another brick in the wall."

No one is talking about "fate" yet in these novels, and even *Kafka on the Shore* does not make an explicit point of it. Yet herein lies the real point of building this novel around a retelling of the Oedipal myth. Sophocles's message in that tale is, ultimately, that the more we attempt to run from our destiny, the more likely we are to run squarely into it. Fate is inexorable, it cannot be fought. Tamura Kafka, however, has other ideas, his solution to the problem resting on the unlikely combination of fate and genetics.

Yet, if one stops to think about it, fate and genetics are not wholly unrelated concepts; the former is an assumption that certain things are bound to happen (or at least likely to do so) through the will of the gods, the latter an assumption that certain traits will be carried on due to shared genetic material, passed on from parent to child through the blood. But if the blood is changed, might not one's genetic “fate” also be altered? Can we, in other words, “rewrite” our blood just as we can rewrite our own inner narrative?

Blood is a key motif in *Kafka on the Shore* from the start, for Kafka’s “trauma” stems not solely from his father’s bizarre prophesy but from even before that, when he feels himself to be trapped by what he sees as his father’s tainted blood, by the very genetic material that flows through his veins. Moreover, because his father has taken the precaution of having DNA testing performed, Kafka does not even have the comforting possibility that his father might be someone else. Once again we find the dichotomy between flesh (vessel) and spirit playing a key role:

> “Ōshima, in all honesty, I don’t like this container I’m in at all. I haven’t liked it once since the day I was born. In fact, I’ve always despised it. This face, these hands, my blood, my genes. . . . it’s like everything that was passed along to me by my parents is cursed. If I could, I’d escape from them, like someone running away from home.”[33]

Kafka’s entrapment is paralleled by the Oedipal prophesy with which he is saddled; the point of the prophesy is less to raise the specter of sexual taboo (though this is an intriguing by-product) than to bring up the tension between fate and free will, or, put another away, an individual’s control over himself/herself versus the control exerted by an external power, whether divine, social, or political.

Kafka’s challenge, clearly, is of the first type, for (in the very fashion of the Greek hero) he is driven first this way, then that, by the power of his prophesy, the ending that fate has decreed for him. Initially he hopes to escape fulfillment of this prophesy, which is precisely why—echoing Oedipus himself—he must leave his home. There is, however, one vital difference between Kafka and Oedipus, noted also by Kawai Hayao: Kafka is fully aware of his fate from the start. For Kawai this is most unnerving, for “in ancient times only the gods knew [our fates], but what was once enacted according to the will of the gods is now done by humans, and must be done.”[34]

And yet this is precisely Kafka’s advantage, for though he cannot change his fate, he is free to turn it to his own advantage. Hearing of his father’s murder in Tokyo and surmising (correctly) that he is responsible for it, even if only by proxy, Kafka recognizes immediately that further evasion is pointless. Thus, still advised by “the Boy Called

Crow," he turns himself squarely into the path of his prophesy and determinedly sets out to fulfill its remaining conditions. Not so much convinced but *deciding* that Saeki will be his mother, he joins his body with hers—though, significantly, both he and Saeki, in the metaphysical no-man's-land of Kafka's bedroom, seem throughout this scene to shape-shift back and forth between their present selves and those of the fifteen-year-old Saeki and her boyfriend from many years earlier. A few chapters later Kafka has a vivid dream in which he forces himself on Sakura, despite her protest that she thinks of him as her younger brother. In this case Sakura protests not that Kafka *is* her brother, but that she *thinks* of him as a brother, and she also warns him that if he persists, this will be tantamount to rape, but Kafka, having brought his prophesy this far, cannot possibly stop now. By the end of this scene, the quiet and determined Kafka has committed patricide (by proxy), matrilineal incest (in partially metaphysical form), and rape (in a dream).

The superb irony of these acts being carried out as an act of will (albeit in the metaphysical world) is that they allow Kafka to succeed where Oedipus failed: he completes the prophesy placed in his path (reasoning that there was no way to avoid it), and in so doing he turns it to his advantage. That is to say, by intentionally coupling (albeit metaphysically) with two women who *might* be his mother and sister, Kafka effectively *forces* them to *become* his mother and sister, thereby recovering his missing family. Clearly, then, he stands to gain a great deal from these acts, though we must wonder, at least in mythological terms, why Kafka is not damned as a result. If patricide, rape, and incest are among the most severely punished taboos in our world, then why is Kafka not punished for transgressing all three?

One important reason is that these "transgressions" are carried out in the metaphysical world, which we have already established to be a realm that lies beyond time, space, or indeed good and evil, and by acting in (or perhaps "acting through") this realm Kafka is able to subvert even the process by which the most prohibited taboo acts are normally judged and sanctioned. Logically speaking, if Kafka and Saeki exist in the "other world," where time cannot exist, then how can generational distinctions exist? And if generations have been erased through the suspension of time, then is intergenerational incest even possible? Similarly, if a murder is committed in the metaphysical realm, where death cannot exist, then how can it *be* murder? If this is so, then surely Kafka is absolved of the killing of Johnny Walker, which clearly took place while *he,* at any rate, was in a very metaphysical place indeed.

All of this merely reinforces what we have been observing all along, namely, that the infiltration of the "other world" on this one has the power to suspend the artificially constructed divisions that govern this side. The most important of these remains "time," for in conflating past, present, and future, the metaphysical realm excludes all events posited on that structure—decay, aging, death—and thus renders the most serious of human taboos, including murder and incest, largely irrelevant, even impossible. In this manner the "other world" transcends such other human constructs as morality, good and evil, as well.

It also transcends the individual, as suggested in the previous chapter. Near the novel's end, when Kafka again makes his way into the metaphysical forest led by the two deserters from the Imperial Army, he finds Saeki living in a place that is so quiet and peaceful it seems to numb the very mind, and much as Adachi Kumi tells Tengo near the end of *1Q84* to get out of "Catsville" before it is too late, Saeki also warns Kafka at the end of this novel to leave the metaphysical forest and return to his own world while he still can. What will prevent him? Nothing so elegant as rivers or chasms, or even gateway stones; rather, simple lack of self-awareness and individual volition are the bars that keep inmates of the other world where they belong, for as the fifteen-year-old Saeki tells Kafka, "here we are all, every one of us, merging our selves together with this place."[35] As such, no one possesses a fixed identity, and Saeki, too, is wholly a part of this realm, for she is now completely erased from the physical world. It is a predominantly Eastern philosophical message, one central both to Buddhism and to Daoism, the erasure of the individual self, which joins with and dissolves into the cosmos, the mystic One, with nature itself, achieving the blissful state of nothingness.

And yet this lack of fixed identity, too, works to Kafka's advantage in the end. Just before Kafka departs, with the remaining traces of consciousness she possesses, Saeki is finally able to give him the one thing he has wished for his whole life: new blood. Pulling a pin from her hair, she thrusts it into her arm and allows Kafka to suck her blood from the wound:

> I stoop down and put my lips to the small wound. My tongue licks at her blood. I close my eyes and savor its taste. I hold the blood I've sucked in my mouth, and slowly swallow it. I take her blood into the back of my throat. It makes its way very quietly into the dry flesh of my heart. I realize for the first time how much I've wanted this blood.[36]

The significance of this act cannot be overstated: in swallowing Saeki's blood, he replaces (or at least dilutes) the hated blood of his father with that of the woman with whom he most desperately desires a blood relationship and now in actual fact does have such a relationship.

This is the final step in Kafka's manipulation of his prophesy, which has permitted him to regain his lost family members (even if only for a short while) and to loosen the dark hold of his father over him. He has not so much "cheated" fate as he has simply forced it to work in his favor. Following this interesting new twist on the transfer of bodily fluids, Kafka summons the strength of will—the power of the world's strongest fifteen-year-old boy—and forces himself to leave the forest while still in possession of his mind.

Returning now to *1Q84,* we may see that Aomame is in a situation not unlike Kafka's: for all her strength and fortitude through most of the novel, she still feels herself to be a slave to fate. For all her bravado, she remains neurotically attached to the religion of her childhood, and she has left the question of whether she will ever find Tengo, as noted earlier, in the hands of chance. She expresses this sense of helplessness before fate to Ayumi over dinner one night as they ponder their dinner menus:

> "Whether it's menus or men or anything else, we always feel as though we're making choices, but maybe we aren't really choosing anything at all. Maybe everything has already been decided, and we are only pretending to decide. Maybe free will is nothing more than an idea." (1:344)

It is an issue that Aomame must and will address by novel's end, when, feeling a sense of responsibility for the child growing in her womb and for the joint "narrative" with Tengo it represents, she elects to defy the Leader's dying prediction that Tengo's life will require the sacrifice of her own. Here, too, genetics will form a critical relationship with fate, for, as I noted earlier, Tengo and Aomame are given the responsibility of bringing into the world the start of a new generation that will be capable of connecting with its own internal narrative.

The matter of evolution, of improving future generations, is very likely the purpose of the Gilyak story on Tengo's side of the narrative, one that otherwise strikes one as rather gratuitous. The Gilyak people, primitive forest dwellers, are presented to us as hard-working and honest, yet their men are notoriously unkind to their women, whose status in the community is lower than dogs, "'treated as barter goods, or as livestock'" (1:468). Innocuous though it seems, the story is useful in a comparative sense, for despite the fact that humanity has, supposedly, advanced far beyond the "primitive" stage of the Gilyaks, still Aomame must spend her spare time exterminating men who continue to treat their women worse than dogs. Here, too, we see the contrast between our modern, "civilized" humanity and our primitive, "bestial" past. But is our primitive nature truly a thing of the past, or does it always lurk just beneath the surface of our modern veneer? Aomame implicitly ponders the same question:

> Men who get off to raping pre-menstrual girls, muscle-bound gay bodyguards, people so zealous they'd rather die than have a blood transfusion, women who commit suicide with sleeping pills when they're six months pregnant, women who stick needles into the necks of rotten men, men who hate women, women who hate men—with such people existing in the world, what possible good was being passed through our genes? (1:443)

Herein lies the purpose behind the apparent fixation in *1Q84* with genetics and the control of the womb, for the only way of progressing beyond the primitive stage of the Gilyaks, and, indeed, the brutality that continues to haunt our modernity, is evolution. The cause of that brutality, then as now, is the urge to control the destiny of others. "'Human beings, finally, are nothing more than carriers of genetic material'" (1:385), says the old woman, and it is precisely this aspect of womanhood that she is determined to protect at all costs. Recalling the case of little Tsubasa, whose reproductive organs have been severely damaged due to violent and repeated sexual entry, the old woman sees this as nothing more or less than an attack on the girl's reproductive system itself and therefore on the one and only thing that truly sets a female apart from a male. "'When a woman is robbed by force of a right with which nature itself bestows her, well, this is not easy to forgive'" (1:430).

But finally, Tsubasa's reproductive system is just one more metaphor for the inner narrative itself, the "story" now being the (re)production of replicas of ourselves through childbearing and the rearing of those children in such a way that they may be free from the "ready-made" narratives that their society will thrust upon them, including their eventual function within that society; will it be as free individuals or as "barter"? Will they determine their own destiny or be forced into predetermined roles by their society? This is the lofty task with which Aomame, Tengo, Fukaeri, the Leader, and Ushikawa are charged: to expose the artificiality of human constructs like tradition and ideology, thereby beginning an enlightened new era in which we are free to develop our own inner narratives unmolested, and *to pass that enlightenment on to our offspring.* To this end these characters are created with a divine "spark," and they must struggle (without necessarily knowing they are struggling) against the innumerable "false prophets" that surround them. In so doing, they will take up, commit, and dispense with a wide variety of social and mythological taboos, reminding us that those who have been selected for sacred tasks, like the spirits with whom they interact (the gods, the Little People, "Colonel Sanders," and so on), are beyond the concepts of "good" and "evil," for these concepts belong to the realm of the *constructed,* are grounded in culture, history, and finally language, but not in any absolute sense of right and wrong.

If this is true, then I think one of Murakami's major points in these novels that deal with the transgression of taboo (whether by "divine" beings or ordinary people) is that such transgressions are sometimes necessary, and perhaps even permissible, when they restore contact with the inner narrative that connects to *the* Narrative, to the world soul. Perhaps this is what Murakami meant to imply in Jerusalem, when he vowed to stand with the egg (individual) against the wall (the System), even if the egg should be in the wrong.

Under what circumstances is authority to be challenged? At what point and to what extent are we permitted, even compelled, to rebel against the systems that bind us and to break free? In short, when do we shake loose of the destiny plotted for us by others and assert our free will? It is fitting, in concluding this chapter, to return to Aomame and Tengo and their efforts to reach escape velocity and leave the false systems of their childhood and early adulthood behind. This, as we shall now see, will require the destruction of the father.

The Killing of the Father

Throughout most of his career Murakami minimized the presence of father characters in his fiction, and while I cannot entirely agree with Tokō Kōji's assessment that they have been "conspicuous by their absence,"[37] it is true that their role has been limited to that of a negative or neglectful presence in the Murakami text. We *do,* nonetheless, see father characters play a role in many of the earlier works. As early as *Hear the Wind Sing* Rat's own father is presented in absentia as an industrialist who became extremely wealthy selling supplies to the U.S. military during the Korean War, perhaps one of the reasons that Rat despises him. Another father, "Makimura Hiraku" in *Dance Dance Dance,* neglects his daughter to the point that he finds himself compelled to pay Boku to spend time with her. We have seen how things go for Kafka and his father, as well as for the writer Junpei in "The Kidney-Shaped Stone That Moves Every Day." The father of Asai Mari informs her matter-of-factly in *After Dark* that she had better study hard, since she isn't very pretty and has nothing else going for her, and Takahashi Tetsuya, in that same work, worries that he will end up like his father, who was in prison. The NHK dues collector who raised Tengo is actually just the latest in a long line of fathers who cannot relate to their children. In fact, going against the conventional image of the father who dispenses useful lessons to his son about how to live well, Murakami fathers consistently dispense information to their children that is either totally useless or, worse still, totally destructive.

Perhaps this is why the confrontation between the Murakami hero and his father has been so greatly anticipated by readers and critics alike, but it is also true that the enmity between fathers and sons in these works is a necessary construct, for the urge to overcome and replace the father is a crucial step for every man, and every society. As we noted in chapter 1, the replacement of one generation by the next is, in mythological terms, one means of ensuring that time moves in a unidirectional manner and that the human race thus goes forward rather than backward.

This conflict becomes an explicit theme in *1Q84,* wherein fathers are portrayed, as the above analyses clearly show, as keepers of a quasi-sacred tradition, as guides to their children, but also as a singular hindrance to the mental, spiritual, and emotional growth of those same children. Freud's writing on the inherent hostility of sons toward their fathers (the so-called Oedipal complex) is widely known, but we deal here with something else entirely: the absolute *necessity* of killing the father, symbolically if not actually, in order that his children may grow up to take his place. But this is not always necessarily a hostile confrontation; rather, as Tengo himself comes to recognize, it is simply a necessary step in his continued growth as an individual. In terms of our discussion of mythology, however, this confrontation takes on a new, sacred, and ritualistic quality upon which the very survival of the community rests.

In *1Q84* this is expressed through reference to James Frazer's seminal work on mythological and magical customs from around the world,[38] *The Golden Bough,* in which he has the following to say about "killing the divine king":

> The man-god must be killed as soon as he shows symptoms that his powers are beginning to fail, and his soul must be transferred to a vigorous successor before it has been seriously impaired by the threatened decay.[39]

> For they believe, as we have seen, that the king's life or spirit is so sympathetically bound up with the prosperity of the whole country, that if he fell ill or grew senile the cattle would sicken and cease to multiply, the crops would rot in the fields, and men would perish of widespread disease. Hence, in their opinion, the only way of averting these calamities is to put the king to death while he is still hale and hearty, in order that the divine spirit which he has inherited from his predecessors may be transmitted in turn by him to his successor while it is still in full vigour and has not yet been impaired by the weakness of disease and old age.[40]

Frazer's analysis is key here in that it highlights a peculiar fact regarding succession: that the slaughter of the king—frequently in the most bloody and gruesome fashion—was in fact a necessary ritual by which the inner spirit of the king might be liberated *in good condition* from the vessel in which it was only temporarily housed. That "liberation" was carried out, depending on the culture, either by the king's own successor or else by one or more priests charged with the duty of maintaining the connectivity between the tribe and the guardian spirit who animated the king. This, in essence, is what the Leader explains to Aomame in the scene leading to his death:

> "In ancient times there were places where, when the king had finished his term of reign, he was killed. His reign might be ten or twelve years. When his time was up, people would come and butcher him. This was necessary for the community, and the king accepted this. Their killing method had to be cruel and bloody, but this was a great honor to the king. Why did the king have to be killed? Because in those days a king was a representative of his people, 'the one who listened to the voices.' Such people were like circuits who connected 'them' and 'us.' And butchering 'the one who listened to the voices' was an indispensable act for the community after his time had passed. It was to maintain proper balance between the consciousness of the people living on the earth and the power wielded by the Little People. In the ancient world, to reign was the same thing as listening to the voices of the gods." (2:241)

And while the Leader is not a king, his function within his organization as the divinely marked "hearer of the voices" places him into the role of the human carrier of the divine spirit, a sacred protector of his people, and so he urges Aomame to end his life so that a new protector—Tengo—may come to succeed him. His death will be, in effect, a ritual sacrifice, though he assures Aomame, with a certain dark humor, that "'there's no need to hack me to bits or splatter my blood all over the place. This *is* 1984, after all, and we are in the middle of a major city'" (2:242). But the act of sacrifice itself is an essential one, bringing with it the potential for eternal continuity, for each new succession brings fresh blood, youth, vigor, and strength. Such continuity is equally assured by the child Aomame carries within her.

The Leader's willingness to be sacrificed for the greater good contrasts powerfully with Tengo's NHK dues–collecting foster father, who even in a comatose state continues to send his spirit forth to knock on people's doors, demanding that they pay the State its due. Tengo's father represents the System itself, a system of collective ideology, whose time, symbolically speaking, has long since passed, yet it refuses to allow itself to be replaced. This is why it is so important that Tengo confront his father, even though it be on his deathbed, and command him to stop knocking on people's doors. This is the signal to the old man that it is time to give up the ghost. It is also a signal that Tengo has broken loose of his influence and is now prepared to move forth into the world on his own terms, on the merits of his own inner narrative.

This is by no means a trivial matter; rather, the death of Tengo's father mirrors the demise of the Leader, for it represents yet another changing of the guard, and the elimination of one person requires his replacement by another. Late in book 3, Adachi Kumi explains to Tengo that "'whatever the circumstances, it's a big deal when someone dies, because a hole opens up in the world. We have to pay proper respect to that, or else the hole won't be filled in properly'" (3:483). But *1Q84* looks equally at the other side of that statement: that *until* a person dies, a new space cannot open up, and thus nothing can progress forward. What is accomplished by Tengo and Aomame at the end of *1Q84,* then, is the preservation—or perhaps the restoration—of the three distinct time periods of past (the Leader), present (Tengo-Aomame), and future (their child). Their emergence out of "1Q84" back into "1984" represents final victory, for it will be in this wholly physical world that such concepts have meaning.

As with *Kafka on the Shore,* it is the future that concerns this novel most: what sort of a future will Aomame and Tengo construct and leave for their own child? This child is the key, finally, to breaking Aomame's neurotic belief in fate and destiny. While in hiding following the death of the Leader, Aomame chances to read the novel written by Fukaeri and Tengo, and something—her own inner narrative, now intertwined with Tengo's—is awakened inside of her, just as it has been awakened inside Tengo. This realization, her newfound certainty that the child is Tengo's, becomes her greatest source of strength to break free of fate and determine her own destiny. Two material points dawn upon her in quick succession as a result: first, that she must protect this child at all costs, transforming herself from destroyer into nurturer; and second, that her destiny is, and always has been, in her own hands:

> I'm not just some passive creature caught up in someone else's plans, brought here regardless of my own mind . . . being here is something I chose myself. **My presence here is an act of my subjective will.** (3:475–76; emphasis in the original)

This realization parallels Tengo's command to his dying father to cease his spiritual wandering and give up his body, and represents Aomame's symbolic killing of the last vestige of her parents' religion—its belief in a destiny preordained by God. Freed from this constraining influence, Aomame takes matters into her own hands and rescues Tengo from the "1Q84" world, along with their unborn child. Like Tamura Kafka before her, she has confronted her "destiny" and emerged victorious.

What we have seen in this chapter, then, is the systematic employment of a wide variety of mythological tropes on the part of Murakami, some Japanese, others of Western origin, in order to facilitate the infiltration of the divine into a world that had been, prior to "All children of the gods dance," a largely secular, if highly metaphysical, literary landscape. This has facilitated a genuine confrontation between generations, highlighting the necessary replacement of the present system or narrative by that which is to come. As we have seen, that process has required acts of taboo that, in the context of quasi-sacred ritual, prove not to be taboo at all.

We have also seen that the metaphysical "other world" continues to play a key role in this process, first by providing an appropriate setting in which to enact these rituals, calling down the presence of the gods and spirits to join with the human participants and lend their voices to the event. As is so common in Murakami fiction, however, the performance of ritual—of "killing" the father, for instance, to maintain connection with the gods—can also represent an act of rebellion *against* the gods. We have seen this in both *Kafka on the Shore* and in *1Q84,* wherein the destruction of the old collective narrative carries with it a rejection of the Will of the gods—fate—in favor of the will of the individual. This is the birth of Modernity itself, in which humankind discovers within itself the ability to think, to reason, and to act independently of God or the gods, determining our own fate. The real question that needs to be asked, as Tengo succeeds to the role of "hearer of the voices," is, will he still be listening to those voices? Or has he—have *we*—finally learned to listen to the "voice" within ourselves? It is a question to which Murakami returns in *Colorless Tsukuru Tazaki and His Years of Pilgrimage* and to which we will return in the fifth and final chapter of this book.

In the chapter that follows we will explore some of the ways in which the author has combined this logic of self-determination with the general truism, so succinctly summed up in the first chapter of *1Q84* by Aomame's taxi driver, that "'things aren't always what they appear'" (1:22). In the context of this novel he might well have been referring to Aomame's assumption that she knows the world in which she lives, but in the next chapter I will apply this logic to Murakami's response to real events, including the January 1995 Hanshin earthquake and the Aum Shinrikyō terrorist attack that occurred just two months later in Tokyo. What we will find is that, even within the context of nonfiction writing, Murakami has an urge to seek out the hidden stories and extenuating circumstances in order to provide the fullest possible explanation of events and those who cause them or experience them. His writing in this regard performs an interesting hybridization of fictional and nonfictional writing tropes, one that relies on the argument, stated repeatedly in this text, that all perceptions of reality are ultimately subjective.

FOUR

Murakami Haruki as Literary Journalist

> Why was it not enough that these unfortunates had had to suffer the injury of the sarin incident itself? Why should they have had to suffer twice, victim also of the violence of the ordinary society that surrounds us all?
>
> —Murakami Haruki, *Andāguraundo*

TO THIS POINT WE HAVE EXPLORED, through the metaphysical Murakami landscape, how language as narrative constitutes and shapes not only the realities external to the subject but those that lurk within the mind, in dreams and the imagination, even in the realm of the gods themselves. It is time, then, to bring the discussion back down to terra firma and, returning to our opening theme of constructed realities, test some of our hypotheses on those texts in the Murakami repertoire that touch upon current events. The purpose of this discussion is twofold: first, to examine Murakami's experiments with hybrid modes of writing that combine the literary tropes of fiction with current events reportage; and second, to explore how use of these hybrid modes leads to a confrontation between the individual inner narrative and the various collective external narratives that seek to supplant it. The hybrid modes to which I refer are literary journalism, for which there is a growing body of theoretical writing, and what I will term *journalistic fiction,* a genre of writing that I believe exists but has yet to be noticed until now. In the next few pages I will describe both modes of writing and some of the representational issues that will attend them, because while literary journalism is not so far "out in left field" as it was, say, twenty years ago, in the field of Japanese literature it remains virtually unknown, despite the fact that creative nonfiction—literary journalism, *reportage* (from the French; *ruporutāju* in Japanese, usually shortened to *rupo*), and fiction grounded in current events—makes up a remarkable percentage of what is published in Japan each year, as a visit to a Japanese bookstore or public library will clearly demonstrate.

What makes these genres both interesting and relevant to the current study is the tension that is created between the subjective and the objective when terms like *literary* and *journalism*—in practice understood to be mutually exclusive—are brought into proximity to one another. This, however, is a fallacy, for "objective fact" itself is a fallacy, and our ability to represent it remains illusory, not because we lack the will or integrity to seek out "the truth," but because working with the endlessly subjective, culturally bound tool of language to apprehend and express any given event or phenomenon, we are compelled to express individual truths rather than any single definitive one.

This should by no means discourage us, however, from seeking out truths, in plural, and the more the better. The mistake we make lies not in seeking facts but in imagining that we have got them definitively and are capable of sharing them, unabridged and in mirrorlike representation, with others. This is the part that proves more than we can manage owing to the clumsy nature of the linguistic tools we use.

Having posited the constitutive function of language in chapter 1 of this volume, let us now return to the scene of the crime and learn what good, if any, can be had from it. I propose that some of Murakami's nonfiction and certain works of his fiction contain discernible elements of recent or current events, and that these might be fruitfully reexamined now in terms of how they present the author's subjective apprehension of those events, with the result of recovering, to some extent, a sense of humanity—of actuality—for the participants thereof, while also providing a foil, as it were, to popular conceptions of these events that have been fed by a largely homogenous mass media system in Japan. Returning yet again to the Jerusalem speech, the "wall" is now the Japanese mass media, while the "egg" is the individual witness of events. Naturally, this includes Murakami himself.

Prior to entering this discussion in earnest, however, it is useful to rehearse—and where necessary, to adjust—current Western theories of literary journalism,[1] as well as to construct a clearer framework regarding what I am calling *journalistic fiction,* that is, fiction that has been grounded in current (or nearly current) events. Our first step is to establish a matrix that takes into account two principal issues: fidelity or infidelity to actual events (the "factuality" continuum), and subjective or objective narrative style (the "literary" continuum). The first of these places at one extreme a high level of fidelity to actual events, and at the other extreme, a high level of embellishment or liberty taken with those events. The former may be termed "nearly factual," the latter "nearly fictional." The second continuum places at one extreme a highly subjective, literary written style that places emphasis on not only what is said but how artistically or innovatively it is expressed; at the other extreme is the detached, unambiguous, and undecorated prose of the expository essay or conventional news story. The former is termed "literary," and the latter (for want of a better term) "expository."

I do not mean to imply that the study of writing and genre is something that can be accomplished with charts and a slide rule, of course, but matrices like these, when grounded not in evaluative but in descriptive terms, have been used effectively to identify more clearly other genre issues while breaking down traditional value judgments. A prime case in point is John Cawelti's use of such methods to reconsider the traditional dichotomy between "serious" and "popular" literature in favor of the less loaded (and less subjective) terms "inventive" and "formulaic." Cawelti pointed out, among other things, that by placing these two terms at extreme ends of a continuum, it could be readily seen that all texts lie somewhere in between them, but that none could be called completely inventive or completely formulaic.[2] One major advantage to this matrix is that it does not inherently privilege one type of writing over another.

What we will discover from the matrices I have proposed is that both creative nonfiction and journalistic fiction can be manipulated so as to highlight certain aspects of a case but not others, to draw attention to issues that mainstream reporting might deem irrelevant. Even a work that is nearly all fiction, containing only fragments of current events, can be highly effective in using those fragments as a deep underpinning in the text, enough to catch the reader's attention

"Literary"
subjective voice
elaborate style
emotional
entertaining

- creative fiction
- journalistic fiction
- historical fiction
- philosophical fiction

- literary journalism
- creative history
- editorial

manipulative of events/imaginative

fidelity to events/factual

- philosophy
- literary criticism
- theory
- essay

- orthodox journalism
- orthodox history

"Expository"
objective voice
undecorated style
detached
informative

"Literary" versus "expository"

but at the same time deflecting that attention toward a more important message about what those current events actually mean.

The matrix may also be used to draw some parallels between literary journalism and creative history and biography, on the one hand, and journalistic fiction and historical fiction, on the other. As the figure suggests, works that show a high degree of fidelity to events, yet are literary in tone and style, demonstrating their author's subjective stake in them, fall into the upper-right quadrant of the diagram, placing them closest to the various forms of creative nonfiction. Texts that show both a detached (objective) written style and a high degree of fidelity to the events (as far as they are known) conform variously to the orthodox "nonfiction" disciplines of history, journalism, and other forms of factual expository writing. On the left side of the diagram, creative, journalistic, and historical fiction have been placed in the upper quadrant but not the lower. This reflects my contention that while a writer might employ a detached style to almost anything, the idea of *creative* in and of itself suggests a high level of subjectivity, a close connection between the author and the tale she or he spins. In the lower-left quadrant, no doubt risking the wrath of many a colleague and friend, I have placed such ideas as philosophy, critical theory, essay, literary criticism, and so on. This reflects my conviction that most theoretical writing in areas of the humanities (as opposed to the hard sciences) is just one more "reading/interpretation" of a pattern of events; we may believe we are working with facts, but in the end much more comes out of our heads than from the pages of the text. (The present monograph is no exception, let us frankly admit.) Philosophy, similarly, is not so much a "search for truth" as it is a "construction of truths"; a certain way of looking at the world is constructed in the mind of the philosopher, who then tests it against the thought of other philosophers, codifies it by writing it down, and voilà! A new thought system is born. But the philosopher writes much as the expository essayist writes, much as *I* write, in fact: to inform, not to entertain. (Though happy are those who possess the knack for pulling off both.)

A few comparative examples—this time from historical discourse—will illustrate my point more clearly. Examining the works of historical novelists Gore Vidal and James Clavell, for instance, one discovers that both writers carried out considerable research in preparation for writing their various historical novels but with considerably different results. Vidal, on the one hand, scrupulously researches the events he depicts, from the Roman emperor Julian the Apostate to Abraham Lincoln to Aaron Burr, inventing as few characters and events as possible. And while he necessarily must take some liberties with individual thoughts and dialogue, and his approach to the characters and their events is far from objective (lionizing Burr, for instance, and lampooning George Washington), Vidal's command of the events he narrates and the detail with which he narrates them is considerable. And Vidal being one of those fortunate few, his writing style is exceptionally entertaining. His works would for the most part belong in the upper-right quadrant of my chart.

The works of James Clavell, on the other hand, while equally (or almost equally) entertaining, occupy a very different point on the chart. Clavell's 1966 novel *Tai-Pan,* concerning the Opium Wars and the founding of Hong Kong as a British colony, and his 1975 work *Shōgun,* about the seventeenth-century founding of the Tokugawa Shogunate, both create entirely fictional casts of characters. Some of these are clearly based on real persons (*Shōgun*'s "Toranaga" is obviously based on Tokugawa Ieyasu, and "Blackthorne" is meant to represent Will Adams, the first Englishman to reach Japan), but most are wholly out of the author's imagination. Clavell's approach, moreover, takes such liberties with actual events, characters, and certainly dialogue that his works are closer to epic romance novels than historical ones. Nonetheless, they are, in the most general sense, grounded in actual historical events. Clavell's novels would belong to the upper-left quadrant of the chart. (If one were to seek a parallel to Vidal-Clavell in, say, the area of creative philosophy, one might place Umberto Eco's *Foucault's Pendulum* in the upper right, alongside Vidal's *Burr* and *Lincoln;* Dan Brown's *Da Vinci Code* goes next to Clavell's *Shōgun.*)

And what do such texts accomplish? This, too, will depend to a greater or lesser extent on where they lie on the fidelity spectrum, but first and foremost, we must accept that they entertain while at the same time giving life and body to historical events that might otherwise remain localized or obscure. Clavell's *Shōgun,* though of little value as a historical text per se, nonetheless brings to life a moment in time—the unification of Japan under a single warlord in the year 1600—of which the average Western reader is likely unaware, as well as introducing certain facets of Japanese culture. At the time of its publication it undoubtedly helped, albeit in rather Orientalist fashion, to popularize Japanese culture just as the Japanese economy was poised to enter its "bubble" period (which has, however, long since "popped").

Vidal's texts, on the other hand, show such a high degree of fidelity to their events and major historical figures (all of whom are presented under their real names) that college history professors have been known to include them on their reading lists, if only to provide a more lively account for their students that does not stray massively from the facts as they are known.[3] Vidal's historical biographies, too, are hugely entertaining, bringing wit and humor to past events and even recovering a sense of humanity—of reality—for their participants; Lincoln becomes more than simply a sepia-toned photograph in the novel that bears his name, and readers are given a penetrating—if subjectively drawn—glimpse into his thoughts and actions, as well as those around him, during the American Civil War.

Similar arguments may be made concerning journalistic fiction, but we will find, I think, that this current-events parallel to historical fiction, particularly in Japanese writing, has a tendency to stray rather further from the events that ground it than does its historical counterpart. This has much to do with the liberating effects of the time that separates the present from the historical past, allowing authors a somewhat clearer view of the events they wish to narrate than is normally afforded writers of current events, whose subject matter is the immediate present, frequently misunderstood and often still developing.

Before turning to journalistic fiction, however, let us examine the more established genre of literary journalism, which differs from the former through virtue of its being, by definition, a nonfictional form. Here, too, nomenclature concerns us, for, as will be shown, even the relatively better understood literary journalism remains only imperfectly defined. Among our more important tasks initially will be to determine how, precisely, literary journalism is to be distinguished from other nonfictional forms, such as essay, editorial, or even the "I-novel."

Toward a Definition of Literary Journalism

The term *literary journalism* is a contentious one; few have wholly agreed on the true nature of this genre, whose "pedigree," as theorist Mark Kramer argues, is quite distinguished, dating at least from the eighteenth century, yet whose theorization is a relatively recent thing.[4] It is, in fact, only in the past few decades that the genre has been properly named, presumably in part as a response to the so-called New Journalism advanced in the 1960s by Tom Wolfe and other radical journalists.

The body of writing dedicated to defining and exploring literary journalism is nonetheless substantial, and our understanding of this deceptively complex genre grows apace. Superficially, literary journalism is made up of two terms that, while by no means simple or unproblematic, at least tend to conjure comprehensible images in the minds of those who hear them. It is when they are joined that friction develops, for they are—or have become in the minds of many of their practitioners—mutually exclusive endeavors. We understand "literary" prose to suggest subjective writing, expressed in an artistic, entertaining style that carries a strong aroma of the author's creativity, manipulation of language, setting, characters, plot, and so forth.[5] Style (including recent experiments with plainstyle) is nearly always a crucial factor; how something is said matters quite as much—and often more—than what is said.

Journalism, to the contrary, is reputed to be on the objective side of things, a claim made ever more stringently by practicing journalists as academic voices challenge whether language permits the existence of objectivity at all. In actual practice, journalism continues to focus on *what* is said, and to be interested primarily in four of the five famous *W*'s: who, what, when, and where; the *why*—motivation—is murky, messy, and speculative in too many cases to interest the fact-bent daily news reporter. Professional journalists, as a rule, avoid playing with style; are not (supposed to be) allowed to manipulate facts, quotes, or events; refrain from authorial commentary (except in editorial); and generally pursue a self-effacing approach that places events—never the author—at the forefront of the story.

So, how have these two apparently conflicting notions come together? How and why is literature also journalism, and vice versa?

In the first place, like most literary genres, the practice of literary journalism came long before anyone thought to ask what it really was. Some theorists trace the genre back to Daniel Defoe's (1660–1731) groundbreaking *Journal of the Plague Year* (1722), which purported to tell the story of the outbreak of bubonic plague in London in 1665. The work was presented as factual—and to some extent it was—yet also fictional.[6] Theorist and literary historian Lennard Davis, on the other hand, argues that news reportage began even earlier, with sixteenth-century "news ballads," single-sheet printings that covered events of their time, from floods and other natural disasters to the executions of criminals. These, Davis argues, were the first true "novels":

> [I]f we move backward . . . from the full-blown narratives of the eighteenth and nineteenth centuries to the earlier printed prose narratives, we arrive at a common point, what the sixteenth century called "novels"—that is, printed news ballads and tales. The first intersection of print and narrative that was

> a genuine product of the technology of moveable type (and not simply the printed version of earlier nonprinted forms) was the news ballad of the sixteenth century which was called, among others things, a "novel." The early prose narratives of the sixteenth century—tales of criminals, brief accounts of jokes and jests, Boccaccio-like love intrigues—were also called "novels."[7]

What Davis views as the origin of the modern novel, we may also see as an early form of literary journalism. It is, as Linda Hutcheon argues, only since the nineteenth century that literature and history have been considered mutually exclusive disciplines,[8] so why should journalism—history's close cousin—be different? In fact, in the early "news ballads" we see an urge to tell a story that is both new and news, a genre of writing that, even in its earliest days, surely relied for its very survival on an interested readership eager for fresh tales.

Modern literary journalism since that time has developed its own distinct parameters, despite its lack of a formal, universally accepted definition. Modern literary journalists in the English language—writers like Joan Didion, Tom Wolfe, Norman Mailer, Hunter S. Thompson, Truman Capote, and dozens more—trace their art back through Ernest Hemingway, George Orwell, Stephen Crane, Charles Dickens.

But why does literary journalism exist at all? Theorists have considerably differing views on the subject. Arguing that "literary" (here, imaginative) prose is unfairly privileged by an academic readership that disdains the ordinary and temporally bound text (as opposed to the "timelessness" of genuine Art), Phyllis Frus suggests that the genre serves as a means of narrowing the gap in respectability between the "imaginative freedom and creativity" of literary writing and the "discursive and mundane" nature of journalism.[9] Seeking to balance these two impulses while privileging neither, theorist Ben Yagoda argues that the genre assumes by its very nature a basis in fact and currency, and that its literary designs lie in the experimental, innovative efforts of its author. He writes, "Innovation is . . . important because, like portrait painting, rebounding, playing blues guitar, or doing quantum physics, high-level literary journalism is a tradition, with each practitioner standing on the shoulders of his or her predecessors."[10] While this is essentially correct, it lends a distinctly Modernist tone to the notion of literary journalism that is not necessarily shared by all. Kramer, for instance, while agreeing with Yagoda about the journalistic demands for factuality and currency, grounds the literary side of the equation in the writer's subjective "voice," which in the best cases expresses his or her position vis-à-vis the events narrated and, implicitly, the readers of the text as well: "the narrator of literary journalism has a personality, is a whole person, intimate, frank, ironic, wry, puzzled, judgmental, even self-mocking—qualities academics and daily news reporters dutifully avoid as unprofessional and unobjective."[11]

This sort of connectivity between reader and event, bridged by the literary journalist, also lies at the heart of Norman Sims's various discussions on the functionality of literary journalism, the ultimate purpose of which, in his estimation, is to bring a sense of depth and immediacy to a story that might otherwise be little more (to readers) than a series of nameless, faceless statistics. Its function, therefore, is to rehumanize those caught up in events larger than themselves and at the same time to show us "a very tiny part of the human condition," for "the facts of the case are woven into a story and consequently become secondary to the tale of the people involved."[12] In a similar vein, Shelley Fisher Fishken sees literary journalism as a social equalizer, for it frequently presents "the stories of people who were dismissed and devalued because they had the 'wrong' race, class, gender, ethnicity, or sexual preference. They were stories of the powerless, their pain invisible, their cries inaudible, their membership in the human community implicitly denied."[13] Paul Many, on the other hand, argues that it functions to preserve an appropriate intensity of emotional reaction to the events narrated, whereas the vaunted "objectivity" of conventional journalism actually leads to de-sensitization for reporters and readers alike. He writes, "What finally results from an over emphasis on such 'objectivity' is a gutless, institutional writing that causes readers to get cynical and jaded, and finally turns many off. Journalists also experience the same blunting of emotion in reporting such stripped-down stage sets of reality."[14]

What is gained from the literary journalist's subjective approach, in contrast, is frequently a story that gets a bit closer to the *truth* of what happened, if perhaps just a little further away from "the facts." Of what use are "the facts," after all, if we lose sight of the human presence embroiled in them? This is the implicit question behind any work of literary journalism, and given the challenges—indeed, we might say impossibility—of recovering "the facts" objectively at all, it may well be, to borrow Sims's lilting phrase, that "a very tiny part of the human condition" is all we are left with.

It is, I think, this "very tiny part of the human condition" that comes to interest us in our exploration of Murakami's brand of literary journalism, as it seems to connect solidly with his motivation both for returning to Japan following the Hanshin-Awaji earthquake of January 1995, and for interviewing survivors of the March 20, 1995, sarin gas attack in the Tokyo subway system, allegedly carried out by members of the Aum Shinrikyō cult. His first purpose, as we shall see, was to grasp more clearly the personal responses to the sarin incident of victims and cult members alike, but this was not all; rather, he was also driven by what might be kindly termed a perceived "lack of thoroughness" on the part of the mass media, but might be more accurately expressed as an incurable tendency on the part of the media to oversimplify their reporting in favor of a mentality that opposes "us" (society, normal decent people) to "them" (everyone who does not fit that description). A look at the current structure of the Japanese media, however, may suggest that this is not necessarily the fault of the average reporter in the street, who is bound, willingly or not, to professional organizations and systems that curtail his or her ability to report fully and accurately on the news of the day. Put another way, they, too, are trapped by "ready-made" narratives.

The Role of the Media

If literary journalism is written to shed additional light on stories reported in the so-called mainstream press, then there may be no place in which it is more abidingly important than in Japan, where the media has a reputation—frequently well deserved—for presenting one-sided and often hysterical reports that cast suspected (to say nothing of convicted) criminals into a maximally negative light, while reinforcing a view of society that is peaceful and tranquil and thus wholly apart from the sort of "antisocial" behavior exhibited by the suspect in question.

In fact, the integrity of the Japanese press has been called into question numerous times, for its perceived close relationship with the Japanese "System" of government and business and industry and also for its heavy reliance on so-called *kisha-dan* or *kisha kurabu,* "press clubs." This is worth discussing briefly here, if only to establish that when Murakami, and other novelists like him, engage in the production of creative journalism, whatever its form, they are in fact responding to what is widely perceived as a failure on the part of the mainstream Japanese press to get the full story or to tell it in a fair and objective manner. This makes Japanese literary journalism something of an anomaly, then, for whereas most literary journalism is intended to provide a more subjective perspective on a story that has been presented in too dry and detached a manner, Japanese literary journalists frequently find themselves restoring a sense of balance—even shades of the ever-elusive objectivity—to a story in which the media has whipped public opinion in one direction or another.

One of the most vocal critics of Japanese journalistic practice is Honda Katsuichi, himself a journalist, who describes his profession as "systematized" and blames the fact that journalism is always understood to be a business first, a watchdog for the public second. "The mass media's connection to the powers that be is a frightful thing indeed. Given the tendency of power to corrupt, it is necessary for journalism to continue to criticize the powerful almost as a matter of course. There cannot be a coincidence of interests."[15] And yet, big business and industry are essentially what keep much of the journalistic enterprise afloat, and thus, to critique such organs of Japanese power would be to bite the hand that feeds one. As just one example, Honda points out that weekly magazines are crippled by the lack of home delivery and are thus forced to depend for their survival on mass subscriptions purchased by the very businesses and companies on whom they ought to be reporting.[16] But the real problem, he admits, lies far beyond the mechanics of delivery; it is in the attitude of the reporters themselves, their complacency with a system that essentially tells them what to say. This points yet again to the press clubs and their general function as mouthpieces for the state. "If we are to have press clubs," argues Honda, "then we need to have a mechanism by which they can resist outside pressure."[17]

Murakami Gen'ichi is yet another critic of the press club system and of the manner in which Japanese journalism is practiced in general. While acknowledging that press clubs of various types exist round the world, including in the United States, Murakami Gen'ichi argues that Japanese press clubs throughout the modern period have always been a reminder that news and information, like most everything else in Japan, is "handed down" from those in power. This "handed-down" aspect—echoing "ready-made"—is, he argues, an archaic throwback to the early Meiji period, when imperial decrees were issued, a constitution "promulgated":

> In the fifth year of Meiji, the first imperial tour was conducted over the whole length of Japan. . . . Reporters had to be registered, and only those selected were permitted to attend. Reporters would wait in a special room, and an official from the imperial household would come out and give them the news. The reporters would receive this information reverently and write their reports from it.
>
> Call me cynical, but today's system of "press clubs" doesn't strike me as all that different.[18]

This, obviously, is one of the reasons that newspaper articles are virtually identical whether one reads the *Yomiuri,* the *Asahi,* or the *Mainichi Shinbun,* but the real difficulty, as both Murakami Gen'ichi and Honda would agree, is that members of press clubs—indeed, members of the journalistic profession in general—have little to no latitude to report independently. This is tied in part to access; those who criticize the "powers that be," as Honda has it, are barred from the press clubs and thus have no access to the information they need to write their stories. Both Yamamoto Taketoshi and Maggie Farley have argued convincingly that such pressures lead to severe limitations in what a reporter can say, and strongly discourage any sort of true investigative reporting for fear that it will implicate those whose patronage is essential for the press club to continue. "The *kisha* club . . . encourages dependence on sources and skews this balance in their favor. Unity is prized, entrepreneurial reporting is not," writes Farley. "The close relationships cultivated in and out of the club, therefore, may make the reporters more informed but leave the public less so."[19] The result is a media that cannot fulfill its primary function of disseminating information. William de Lange agrees: "The close and exclusive relationship between reporter and news source poses a direct threat to the integrity of reporting. . . . Needless to say that amongst the Japanese press clubs, where reporters are exposed to the intimations, intimidations, and insinuations of those in power on a daily and, almost as frequent, informal basis, the risk of an excessive and socially unacceptable level of self-censorship is—and has proven to be—very real."[20] Ironically, such uniformity in reporting accentuates the impression that the reporting is accurate; if all the major newspapers and television news outlets report a story at the same time and in the same manner, this is likely to increase the public's confidence in those news sources. When we factor into this the perception that the Japanese press tends to report stories in such a way that society itself is seen to be blameless, it is not difficult to imagine how something like the Aum Shinrikyō incident of 1995 would have been reported; in essence, the massively simplified reports that painted victims of the incident as (faceless) saints, and the perpetrators as demons were what brought Murakami into the game.

Underground and *Underground 2*

Murakami's first step was the 1997 nonfictional work *Andāguraundo*,[21] a collection of some sixty interviews with victims of the sarin attack. Murakami wanted to write about this incident for several reasons. First, he claims, was the fact that the event occurred underground, and the underground has always had a strong appeal for him. Second, having lived abroad in what he terms a "self-imposed exile," he notes that the distance at which he kept himself separated from his homeland established in him a desire "to gain a more profound knowledge about Japan."[22] This declaration was one of the first signs that the author was moving away from writing only about himself and his own personal dilemmas, beginning to focus more on the problems of the society that had created him.

Ultimately, however, *Underground* was born out of its author's sense that the victims of the sarin incident had been left out on their own after the media frenzy had died down. He describes how he happened to read in a magazine the letter of a woman whose husband, left partially disabled by his exposure to the toxic gas, had eventually left his job not because he could no longer work at all, but because his coworkers gradually grew cold toward him and his disability. "Like many people, I suppose," writes Murakami, "I closed the magazine with a sigh, and went back to my own life."[23]

But not for long. Claiming to have been nagged by the lingering sense that the victims of this incident had been peripheralized,

Murakami implicitly puts his finger on the very issue I seek to discuss here:

> Why wasn't it enough that these unfortunates had had to suffer the injury of the sarin incident itself? Why should they have had to suffer twice, victim also of the violence of the ordinary society that surrounds us all?[24]

What Murakami signifies by the expression "the violence of the ordinary society that surrounds us all" is the tendency of Japanese society to distance itself not only from criminals but also from their victims—indeed, from anyone perceived as different, as if they existed in a "separate world," as he expresses it. In other words, mainstream Japanese are uncomfortable with the notion of either criminal or victim existing in "ordinary" society, and thus seek to locate such things in some conveniently "other" space where they cannot threaten the illusion of tranquility and stability in Japan's so-called homogenous society.

One of the principal results of *Underground,* then, is that it narrows the gap between "ordinary society" and the "other," demonstrating that these events, though peripheralized, in fact spring from society, rather than existing in an external zone to threaten society from the outside. In this work, Murakami confronts his readers with the uncomfortable possibility that neither crime nor those involved with it are separate from ordinary Japanese, and thus ordinary Japanese can no longer afford to imagine that they transcend such matters. Put another way, he confronts them with their own implicit culpability as members of a flawed society.

This point becomes clearer in Murakami's follow-up work on the subject, *Yakusoku sareta basho de: Underground 2* (1998; At the place that was promised: Underground 2), in which the author presents interviews with members of the Aum Shinrikyō in an effort to learn more about what motivated them to join an organization that would be responsible for such an act. His purpose here is twofold: first, to portray the cult members not as psychologically flawed beings but as ordinary members of society seeking an alternative to the confining rules of the Japanese social structure; and second, to expose the fundamental lack in mainstream society of an alternative to what I have been terming the "group narrative" of the Japanese system, for those who reject this "group narrative" as unfulfilling or even as false have few socially acceptable means by which to develop their own individual narratives free from mainstream ideology. This, in part, is what leads people to turn to the likes of Asahara Shōkō and the Aum Shinrikyō; Japan's social system does not provide them with anything better on which to rely. As Murakami writes in *Underground 2*,

> Our reality is that beneath the main "system" of Japanese society there exists no subsystem, no safety net, to catch those who slip through the cracks. This reality has not changed as a result of the [sarin] incident. There is a basic gap in our society, a black hole of sorts, and no matter how thoroughly we stamp out the Aum Shinrikyō, similar groups are certain to form in the future to bring about the same kinds of disasters.[25]

The author is not defending the Aum Shinrikyō or its actions; indeed, he is careful to express his own outrage at their behavior. "I still feel deep anger toward . . . those members of Aum Shinrikyō who carried out the sarin incident in the subways,"[26] he writes in his prologue, but he is also inclined to view the question of guilt and innocence here as a complex one, encompassing not only the cult and its members but the social systems—particularly the education system—that have in a sense forced them either to conform to the collective system/narrative or to seek a system/narrative that lies outside social boundaries, on the periphery. Murakami attacks the simplistic portrayal in the mass media of the cult as "evil," and the victims—indeed, the rest of Japanese society—as "pure." This is clear throughout the epilogue to *Underground*, in which he writes:

> The perspective of the mass media in disseminating information about this incident has taken the form of a simplistic opposition, consisting of "our side," meaning "victims=purity=justice," and "their side," meaning "criminals=befoulment=evil."[27]

Obviously the question is not so simple for Murakami, who seeks to restore a sense of identity to the victims of the incident and at the same time recognizes, none too comfortably, certain likenesses between himself and the cult members, particularly in his sense of being somehow different from others in Japanese society in his rejection of social conformity. Writing of his interviews with cult members in *Underground 2*, the author admits that "sitting side by side talking with them, I could not escape the sense that there were points of similarity between what I seek in writing novels and what they sought through their religion."[28] What Murakami has always sought in his writing, as I have argued repeatedly in this monograph, is a means to make sense of the world around him and his own role in it. In a word, he seeks to connect with a more intensely profound, even spiritual, aspect of his identity, to connect with his individual inner narrative, and he hopes to show others, if not exactly how to do this, then at least that it can be done and that such inquiries can help his readers to understand their role in the world, too.

This, he argues, is also what the cult members sought in their religious beliefs, but in the end they failed to find their own inner narrative and instead gave themselves up to the twisted, "cure-all" ideology of Asahara Shōkō. A number of present and former members of Aum interviewed by Murakami echoed the statement of Kano Hiroyuki, who told him that "'no questions remain. Every question is answered fully. Everything has been solved. If you do this, then this will be the result. Whatever question you might pose, the answer comes instantly.'"[29] This sense of being able to ask any question and have a clear, definitive response must have been extremely attractive, particularly to people who had sought out involvement in religion due to overwhelming doubts about the purpose of life; it would also have made it easier, however, for those same troubled people to abandon the quest for their own internal narratives—the answers that lay within themselves—in favor of yet another type of "ready-made" narrative.

Murakami does not suggest absolution for the Aum cult, but he does present a new and more understanding view of its members, many—perhaps most—of whom in the end simply fell under the same sort of spell that captures most members of society, that of the "group narrative" presented as absolute fact, Barthes's "myth" yet again. His comparison with the Japanese militarist state of the 1930s and 1940s is telling here; he notes to the same interviewee that "'a segment of the Japanese population regarded the emperor as a god and were willing to die for him,'"[30] but in raising that "certain segment of the Japanese population," does he not also evoke the memory that the entire nation followed that "certain segment" into the most destructive war (for Japan and the victims of its aggression) in Japanese history? This was yet one more "group narrative," infinitely more devastating than that of the Aum cult. While appearing to expose the absurdity of the Aum members' acceptance of Asahara's "ready-made" narrative, then, Murakami reminds his readers indirectly that in the not-so-distant past, the entire nation did something very similar. And thus, without stating anything outright, this text has the potential to stir empathy, if not actual sympathy, toward those in Japanese society who, in seeking an alternative to "acceptable" group narratives offered by society, stray into the web of other, less acceptable ones. Such people, he seems to say, are not so different from everyone else. They were simply driven into the waiting arms of Asahara Shōkō because mainstream society offered no real answers to their particular questions.

Accordingly, Murakami urges his readers to look at the unusual, the unfamiliar, as a potentially valuable part of their world, rather than as something threatening that lurks outside it. He challenges them to look for the flaws, the gaps, in their own system that force some members of Japanese society to reject its structure and seek something more unique, individual, and meaningful. He indicts the rigidity of the dominant social system and, more importantly, questions the validity of its motivation in preserving the so-called *kanri shakai,* or "managed society." At the same time, he implicitly indicts the mass media's symbiotic relationship with the powerfully homogeneous and homogenizing social system it serves.

Works like *Underground* and *Underground 2* thus represent an essential part of that implicit challenge, for they offer an alternative view of a major event in which public sentiment is powerfully biased and emotional. We might liken this to public sentiment in the United States in the months following the 9/11 attacks; would any professional journalist in his right mind have dared present a side of the story that attempted to understand (let alone empathize with) the motives of the terrorists? Yet it is precisely in such cases, when questions of "right" and "wrong" seem established beyond the capacity for doubt, that expressions like these are needed most, for literary journalism is very likely the only form of an "opposition press" Japan will ever have.[31]

From Creative Nonfiction to Journalistic Fiction

Perhaps even more interesting than Murakami's literary journalism is what I am calling journalistic fiction, that is, purely fictional texts that are to a greater or lesser extent grounded in current or recent news events. This type of writing, I suspect, will prove somewhat more contentious as a genre than literary journalism, if only because it lacks any body of theoretical writing to support it, a "proper pedigree," as Kramer expresses it. Even the name is little more than an expedient constructed for purposes of this text.

Nomenclature aside, one could probably make the argument that *all* works of fiction contain traces of the events that were current during its writing; does this mean that those works are also journalistic fiction? In my view this would be a weak argument, but it is not difficult to see how such a genre could run the same theoretical gauntlet as something like autobiographical fiction, given that virtually *any* text will contain traces of its author's life and experiences. Yet few would be foolish enough to suggest that every text is autobiographical. It does seem quite clear, nonetheless, that some texts, wittingly or not, do have greater potential than others to awaken in their readers' minds a connection with current, newsworthy events. I would further argue that in numerous cases this is intentional, the purpose being to raise public awareness about an event (perhaps without seeming to do so) and at the same time to retell that event from a new perspective, perhaps even with different results. For true though the current events may be upon which the work of journalistic fiction is founded, in the final analysis such texts are still fiction and are thus liberated from the constraints of fidelity to fact that (normally) govern literary journalism and other types of creative nonfiction.[32]

If, then, we apply the same logic and motivation for literary journalism to this close cousin we are calling journalistic fiction, we may note two things: first, that the motivation is virtually identical, that is, to tell the story in a more in-depth and revealing manner than is possible using orthodox journalistic methods; and second, that the parameters—the "rules," so to speak—of journalistic fiction prove to be considerably more liberating even than those of literary journalism. This is because the author is now freed from literary journalism's first principle, namely, that the story must adhere to the basic facts of the case. Abandoning this principle means that a story may be constructed using some or all of the actual conditions that apply in a current event—in fact, it must by definition contain some of these elements, and they must be sufficiently current in the public mind for the genre to achieve its purpose—yet may be couched in a new narrative altogether. What such works do, in essence, is re-create the conditions present in a story told in the media but explore it from a much more imaginative perspective. For example, at a time when truancy *(futōkō)* was becoming a serious social problem in Japan, Murakami Ryū (one of Japan's most prolific writers of journalistic fiction) took up the topic in his novel *Kibō no kuni no ekusodasu* (2000; Exodus to the promised land), in which he posited the question, "what might happen if several hundred thousand junior high school students suddenly refused to attend school?"[33] A number of his other works from the late 1990s and into this century work in similar areas. His response to a series of horrific murders targeting homeless people and teenage prostitutes in the Kabuki-chō district of Tokyo resulted in the novel *In za miso sūpu* (1997; In the miso soup), while "compensated dating" (*enjo kōsai,* a euphemism for teenage prostitution) and its causes are discussed in *Rabu & Poppu* (1996; Love & pop). The *hikikomori* (shut-in) phenomenon is explored in *Kyōseichū* (2000; Symbiotic worm), the end of which is chilling, as it mimics the execution of the sarin gas attack against the Tokyo subway system, complete with vinyl bags full of liquid nerve gas being punctured with pointed sticks (the Aum perpetrators used the sharpened ends of umbrellas).

My point is that writers *are* incorporating current events into their fiction, and that these intrusions of the actual world are not incidental but actually drive the narrative forward and, more importantly, raise readers' expectations about how the narrative will develop based on their knowledge of those current events.

In the case of Murakami Haruki, *Kafka on the Shore* could be read in these terms. Murakami's decision to narrate the story through the eyes of a fifteen-year-old boy rather than his customary thirtyish, lackadaisical underachiever probably surprised many readers and certainly caught the attention of critics, some of whom suggested that Murakami was trying to "look back upon his own youth,"[34] while others claimed he meant to "return to his own beginnings as a novelist."[35] This may also be true, but why would he choose this particular time to go back to his roots? If we historicize *Kafka on the Shore* in the context of the infamous Sakakibara incident of 1997, on the other hand, we gain a different perspective on Murakami's young hero.

It was the Sakakibara incident that brought the expression "Shōnen A" (Youth A) into the consciousness of the public at large.

"Shōnen A" is a generic term used by police and the media to refer to underage criminal suspects, whom the law does not permit to be identified by name, and this is how the teenage suspect in the murder of Hase Jun, a primary school student, was known after he allegedly abducted the boy, then killed and dismembered him, leaving his head in a plastic bag in front of a nearby elementary school. Accompanying this gruesome artifact was a note, emblazoned with a swastika, that read, "The game begins . . . Stupid police stop me if you can . . . I enjoy killing so much I can hardly stand it."[36] Eventually the boy *was* caught, and his case began a public debate that lasted for several years concerning the perception that Japanese young people were more violent and out of control than at any other period in history. This public discussion would have coincided with the time Murakami was writing *Kafka on the Shore.*

The Sakakibara incident—named for the Osaka suburb in which it took place—was so horrifying, in fact, that this particular Shōnen A became, for all intents and purposes, *the* Shōnen A in the public mind, and those who used the term in casual conversation for years after the incident could be understood to mean the fourteen-year-old boy who had killed Hase Jun. A variety of books emerged in the immediate aftermath of this case, most attempting to explain how a mere teenager could commit so vicious an act, and a variety of details about the home life of Shōnen A became public knowledge. Among those who had the chance to interview this boy was Takayama Fumihiko, much of whose reportage in recent years has focused on young people and the challenges they face in contemporary Japanese society. Among other things, Takayama learned that the boy's home, while not particularly unusual, did show a certain proclivity for isolating its members; each room in the house had at least one television/video combination, so that family members could and did pass considerable periods of time without interacting at all. The one thing they *did* share was a powerful hostility toward cats, shooting with a BB gun at any unfortunate stray who wandered into their garden, ostensibly because the cats ate the food put out for the family dog and left feces all over the garden.

Shōnen A, however, appears to have taken the matter further and from an early age made a habit of killing and dissecting slugs and frogs, later expanding his mutilations to cats unfortunate enough to wander too close, until "by the time he graduated from elementary school there was not a stray cat to be found in his neighborhood."[37] Takayama also notes the boy's obsession with Hitler—that he had read *Mein Kampf* multiple times and was fascinated by documentary videos about the Holocaust—and his habit of inscribing swastikas all over his bedroom.

Into the context of such public disclosures, then, Murakami introduces Tamura Kafka, a recently fourteen-year-old boy (the novel begins on his fifteenth birthday) who, albeit by proxy, becomes responsible for the bloody murder of his own father. And while the practice of mutilating cats has now been transferred to the father rather than the son, its prominent role in the novel is nonetheless noteworthy, and one cannot help reflecting that we are unlikely to find any stray cats in *his* neighborhood, either. Later, as Kafka hides out from the police in the cabin belonging to Ōshima's older brother on the edge of the very metaphysical woods we have already explored at some length, he discovers and reads with considerable interest not Adolf Hitler's *Mein Kampf* but rather a history of the trial of Adolf Eichmann, the logistical brains behind Hitler's "final solution." This leads him to consider the nature of the relationship between responsibility and imagination, and he reasons by association that the murder of his father, which appears to have occurred in the realm of the imagination, is in fact his own responsibility, marked by the blood he has quite literally on his hands.

This is, admittedly, what a court of law would call "circumstantial evidence" of a causal connection between the Sakakibara incident and *Kafka on the Shore,* and it is only fair to disclose that Murakami himself, asked directly by me whether he had been thinking of Shōnen A as he wrote *Kafka on the Shore,* responded casually that it had not crossed his mind.[38] However, even if we set aside the fact that, as a novelist, Murakami is a professional teller of lies (and an extraordinarily good one), we cannot ignore the fact that authors do not exert total control over what goes into their works. We therefore ought not to exclude the possibility that, on a subliminal level, the author's humanist concerns for the youth-related problems, forefront in Japan's collective imagination at the time, found their way into this scenario in which a young man, though evidently responsible for his father's death, is still redeemable.

Subliminally or not, Murakami fiction does not serve to excuse criminal behavior nor does it deny guilt. What it *does* do is to imagine a similar set of conditions or characteristics, while offering readers an in-depth look inside the mind of the principal character (and it would be difficult to deny that we have a *very* detailed look at the inside of Kafka's mind), thus allowing them to understand better what has motivated his behavior. It may well be true that Murakami never had the original Shōnen A consciously in mind (and let us again emphasize the word *consciously*) while writing Kafka, but this does not finally matter; some of his readers undoubtedly *were* thinking and wondering about that boy as they engaged the character of Tamura Kafka, and this matters very much.

We see a similar impulse, though with rather less specific clues, in *After Dark,* which like a lot of Murakami's writing in recent years deals with trauma, but which also touches on some of the more common social issues capturing the attention of the mass media and public at large. Unlike Murakami Ryū, who is fairly explicit about the current events that fuel his novels, Murakami Haruki tends to weave such matters more subtly into the overall narrative, so that they are apt to go unnoticed by some readers, while catching the attention of others.

One social issue that was in the news around the time Murakami was writing *After Dark* was a dramatic rise in the number of Chinese nationals illegally residing in Japan, many living in dangerously cramped conditions (six or eight people in an apartment designed for one). Even more disturbing, however, were the stories of Chinese smuggled into Japan to work in prostitution rings and "sweat shops" operated by Chinese gangsters. Public opinion, following the media, tended at this time to lump such illegal immigrants together, focusing more on the fact that they were in Japan against the law than the fact that they were victims of human trafficking, inhumanely treated and living in substandard conditions. Even in cases where the media acknowledged the desperate conditions at home that had led these people to risk illegal entry into Japan, they tended to overlook the fact that a booming trade existed—and probably still exists—that exploited such people, either as cheap labor or as workers in the sex trade. In telling the story of Guo Dong-li, then, and in giving us even a tiny glimpse of her situation, Murakami puts before his readers not only the fact that she is a human being in an inhuman situation, but that she is caught between two extremely dangerous entities: the Chinese mafia and a brutal Japanese customer, who is apparently immune from punishment.

If Guo Dong-li represents a "non-person," outside the protection of Japanese law, Mari herself occupies a position in Japanese society that lies somewhere on the periphery. We learn midway through the novel that Mari's fluency in Chinese comes from the fact that she could not cope with the Japanese school system and that she became a *futōkō,* one who refuses to attend school. This, too, was a major issue, not only for the Japanese media but for local PTA chapters as well. In the summer of 2002, for instance, it was reported that the Japanese truancy level had doubled during the previous decade and had risen 3 percent in just the previous two years.[39] Rampant bullying, severe competition among students, and overpowering pressure to conform are frequently cited as the principal causes of this phenomenon, and Mari's comments to the manager of the love hotel might have been made by any of the more than one hundred thousand children refusing to attend school at the time *After Dark* was being conceived:

> "I never much liked competing with others for grades. I wasn't good at sports, had trouble making friends, and I was bullied, so by my third year in elementary school I just couldn't go anymore."
>
> "You refused to go to school?"
>
> "I couldn't stand the idea of it, so I would vomit up whatever I had eaten, upset my stomach horribly."[40]

In the same conversation, Mari explains that she finally elected to attend a school for Chinese children in Yokohama, and expresses what might well be Murakami's own idea of progress in the Japanese education system: "'Half of the classes were taught in Chinese, but unlike in Japanese schools, you didn't have to scrabble around for grades. . . . You didn't have to have special qualifications or anything.'"[41]

Mari explains that her parents never liked the idea of her attending this Chinese school, nor were they particularly excited by her prospects afterwards. "'They were hoping I'd go on to some famous prep school, eventually be a lawyer or a doctor or something.'"[42] There is nothing particularly troubling in and of itself about parents indulging such dreams for their children, but Murakami touches on a more basic and insidious reality in the Japanese education system: that there is but one path to true success, and it leads through one of the various socially identified and accepted "good" schools. Where Mari was peripheralized at her Japanese school for not being good at what the other children were good at (and what the adults wanted them to be good at), she found acceptance and friendship among the children of an "alien" race, like all foreigners kept carefully outside of mainstream Japanese society. Like those who, seeking alternatives, joined the Aum cult, Mari has been forced to live out her life "underground," first in Yokohama and later in the dark and mysterious scenery of Tokyo's after-hours, reading novels at all-night Denny's restaurants, taking the occasional break to rescue a Chinese sex slave beaten up by a customer like Shirakawa, who represents the successful types who went to the "right" national universities.

Fictional Realities and Real Fictions

From time to time one finds a novelist offering dual works—one in the literary journalistic mode, the other written as journalistic fiction—on exactly the same story. These cases, while admittedly rare, permit us an opportunity to examine some of the merits and limitations of each mode of writing and to consider what the point might be of using both. In all the cases of which I am aware, the work of literary journalism comes first, followed, after some interval, by the journalistic fiction version thereof. This is not surprising, given that journalism is more concerned with immediacy than fiction needs to be.

One highly interesting and useful example of Japanese journalistic fiction from the twentieth century comes from novelist and journalist Kaikō Takeshi (1930–89), who debuted at almost exactly the same time as 1994 Nobel laureate Ōe Kenzaburō (b. 1935). Kaikō never enjoyed the exalted literary reputation that Ōe attained, in part because he never altogether matched Ōe's imaginative or intellectual genius, but probably also in part because he diverted his talents toward commercial writing—Kaikō spent several years writing public relations copy for Kotobukiya, the company that later became Suntory—as well as journalism. In the latter field, Kaikō made a name for himself when he traveled to Jerusalem to cover the trial of Adolf Eichmann in 1960.

In 1964, however, Kaikō achieved real acclaim as a creative journalist. In November of that year, Kaikō accepted an assignment to travel to Saigon to report on the increased U.S. military presence in South Vietnam following the Gulf of Tonkin incident the previous

August. He remained in Saigon until late March of the following year, publishing regular reports—chiefly on the lives of Vietnamese living in and around Saigon—in the *Asahi Shinbun*. Many of his reports were humorous and frequently featured himself, fishing in the Mekong River, trying local foods, using the open-air toilets ("philosophy huts") that Vietnamese farmers made above the irrigation ditches that surrounded their fields.

Aside from the almost daily rumors of coup d'état plots in Saigon, most of Kaikō's reports read more like travelogues than accounts of a shooting war. Just two events occurred that reminded readers unmistakably that this *was* a war: one was the execution by firing squad of Le Van Khuyen on January 28, 1965, which Kaikō witnessed and reported with considerable shock and horror; the second, which involved him more directly, was the poetically named Operation Fallen Leaves, a rather unpoetic search-and-destroy mission carried out by two hundred South Vietnamese army regulars in the jungle areas north of Ben Cat, roughly thirty kilometers north of Saigon, on February 14, 1965. Shortly after noon the unit was ambushed by Vietcong guerillas, caught in a murderous cross fire, and cut to pieces. Running for their lives back to the base camp at Ben Cat, Kaikō and his photographer managed to survive, along with just seventeen of the original two hundred ARVN troops. A week later the two Japanese flew home, and within a month Kaikō had published a book of literary journalism titled *Betonamu senki* (1965; Vietnam war journal). The work was an instant best seller.

Three years later he published the novel *Kagayakeru yami* (1968; translated as *Into a Black Sun*), a work that covers precisely the same period of time and in fact many of the same events, including the execution of Le Van Khuyen and Operation Fallen Leaves. However, the fictional work adds certain new elements. First, Khuyen's execution is now written as two executions, on consecutive days; witnessing the first, Kaikō's protagonist responds with revulsion, much as he did in the *Betonamu senki*, but in the second he shows almost no emotion at all, as though he has now been desensitized to the violence that only yesterday caused him such angst.

A second major development in *Into a Black Sun* is the inclusion of fully developed characters, most or all of whom are composites of the many people Kaikō met while he was there. These characters include the protagonist's errand boy, named Tran, whose conscription into the South Vietnamese Army becomes a point of anguish; and Tran's older sister, To-nga, who provides romantic interest for the protagonist. Kaikō may have been imitating Graham Greene's Fowler and his Phuong in *The Quiet American,* or perhaps he had in mind his colleague Okamura Akihiko (1929–85), whose own work of creative nonfiction *Minami Vetonamu sensō jūgunki* (1965; Record of an embedded reporter in the South Vietnam War) begins—and is punctuated from time to time—with Okamura's letters to his lover in Thailand, a woman named Soo-nee.

Kaikō's two works are useful here because they allow us to examine comparatively two texts—one of literary journalism, the other of journalistic fiction—by a lone author on a single set of events, and in doing so to consider key questions about the relative strengths and limitations of each genre. Why was it necessary to write a second work, this time a fictional one? What, specifically, was Kaikō able to share with his readers in *Into a Black Sun* that could not be adequately told in the *Betonamu senki?*

The simplest response to this is that he is able to redirect the energy of the story and its events in a direction that is simply not possible in a work of journalism, even if it *is* couched in the tropes of creative writing. Despite the fact that Kaikō is a constant presence in the *Betonamu senki,* as authors frequently are in literary journalism, in the end the story is about the war itself and the myriad people who are caught up in it. Kaikō may record his reactions to it, but he cannot, finally, make it about himself, and as a novelist this is among his favorite and most compelling topics. However, what happened to him as he watched the execution of Le Van Khuyen and as he ran for his life out of the jungle back to Ben Cat was profound and life-changing for him, and in the fictional framework of *Into a Black Sun* he is able to explore those events more freely. This helps us to understand why the "young terrorist" in his story must be shot twice in *Into a Black Sun:* the first time is to record the actual event and his response, while the second allows us a look at a second Kaikō, the one who is (now) unaffected by such events, a cool and detached reporter who remains aloof, an observer, a voyeur.

Kaikō experienced considerable angst with regard to his observer's role, and *Into a Black Sun* allows him to bring this issue to the forefront of the narrative on an existential level, to interrogate his commitment to the world outside himself and how this affects the meaning of his own existence. As the narrator of *Into a Black Sun* observes the people of Saigon, coping with poverty, corruption, and the war itself, he wonders why he is incapable of taking a side. It occurs to him that if he could kill with his own hands, then this might give him an understanding of the conflict and the men fighting it, and at the same time, he would gain the sense of *being* that comes with making a choice. This becomes the motivation for his narrator's participation in Operation Fallen Leaves, now no longer just a news story for the *Asahi Shinbun* but an existentialist exercise in choice, action, and consequence. Unfortunately for Kaikō's narrator, when the bullets fly and the moment for action is upon him, he proves incapable of firing a shot even in defense of his life, and leaves Vietnam a broken man.

Cases of this type of "double exposure" reporting are admittedly rare, but fiction that takes up a semijournalistic role is not as unusual as we might imagine. In the wake of the 1923 Tokyo earthquake a number of interesting works of fiction and nonfiction emerged, from the "reports" of major writers such as Akutagawa Ryūnosuke and Kikuchi Kan (the latter of whom, in true Modernist form, displays an erotic fixation on accounts of nude women rushing into the streets to escape the flames and destruction),[43] to poet Nagata Mikihiko's (1887–1964) novelistic memoir *Daichi wa furuu* (1923; The great earth shakes).[44] This writerly response to disaster occurred after the 1995 Hanshin-Awaji earthquake (better known outside of Japan as the Kobe earthquake) as well, with the production of texts like Tanaka Yasuo's *Kōbe shinsai nikki* (1996; Kobe earthquake diary), an account of Tanaka's volunteer efforts following the disaster; Oda Makoto's *Fukai oto* (2002; Deep sound), a fictional work detailing how and why relief efforts proved ineffectual in the first hours and days after the earthquake; and of course Murakami Haruki's *Kami no kodomotachi wa mina odoru* (2000; translated as *After the Quake*), a fanciful collection of short stories that seldom touch upon the Kobe earthquake directly but deal more with the posttraumatic stress, and in some cases the *pre*traumatic stress, of a nation that lives in constant threat of natural disasters.

Japan's most recent disaster, the Tōhoku earthquake and tsunami of March 2011, has also occasioned a number of reports, including one interesting example of this sort of "double exposure" fiction. It comes in the form of novelist Kawakami Hiromi's (b. 1956) short story "Kamisama" (1993; Gods), a simple fairy tale of a woman who is invited out for a picnic by a friendly bear somewhere in rural northern Japan. While out, they take a pleasant stroll along a riverbank crowded with people fishing, and enjoy a picnic. Later the woman naps, and upon awakening discovers that the bear has brought her a gift of fresh fish. At the end of their day together the bear wraps her in his massive arms and pronounces a kind of benediction: "'May the blessings of the Bear God be showered upon you!'"[45]

Three months after the tsunami and not long after the meltdown at the Fukushima Daiichi nuclear reactor, *Gunzō* republished this story, along with the updated "Kamisama 2011," in which virtually the same story is presented but with certain significant alterations. In the new version, an ominous occurrence known as "that event" *(ano koto)* is constantly foregrounded: "in early spring I *had* gone out, dressed in protective clothing, to observe the snipe, but this was the first time since 'that event' that I had come out in normal clothing, exposing my skin, with a picnic lunch."[46] As the woman and bear approach the river, there are still people out fishing but only adults, all wearing radiation suits, protective masks, and rubber boots up to their hips. The narrator admits she is envious of the bear, since "'you are hardly affected at all by strontium or plutonium,'"[47] and when she returns home, the bear's benediction strikes the reader as rather pointless as the woman uses her personal Geiger counter to check her skin radiation levels.

This retelling of the original pleasant fairy tale as a kind of nightmarish sci-fi horror story never mentions by name the nuclear disaster that was even then unfolding at the Fukushima Daiichi power plant, yet it powerfully foregrounds this "event," whose real implications for Japan's natural environment and for the people living in that area are still not fully clear. It is a study in contrasts, paradise and paradise lost, and while it differs from the Kaikō Takeshi example in that both stories are fiction, it does illustrate how a work of journalistic fiction, particularly when used in this "double exposure" manner, can signify a great deal while saying nothing explicitly. For her own part, Kawakami noted the following in her brief epilogue to the two stories:

> I did not write this story in order to warn people about the dangers accompanying the use of nuclear power. Rather, I

wanted to say that our everyday life would continue, and yet, there was a chance we would see great alterations in certain aspects of that everyday life, and I wanted to express the shock that would accompany that realization.[48]

Despite the obviously fictional nature of the work, the pointed intrusion of "that event" at key points in the narrative ironically lends this fantasy tale a greater sense of immediacy and reality than a news story might be able to do. In reminding us that we can no longer take for granted the pleasure of walking along a riverbank, having a picnic, catching fish, Kawakami tells us nothing particularly new about the Fukushima meltdown, yet she has somehow concretized a story that had been reduced, in the mainstream news, to a series of statistical reports that taught the general public words like *becquerel* but could not tell them how the disaster might affect them in their daily lives.

Double Exposure: *1Q84*

Murakami, too, succeeds in creating a kind of "double exposure" in *1Q84,* and while I do not suggest that we read this novel merely as a fictionalized retelling of the stories in *Underground* and *Underground 2,* it *is* possible to discern some of the issues Murakami unearthed in those two nonfictional works in *1Q84* as well, and thus I propose to read the work from the perspective of journalistic fiction to see whether any fresh insights become apparent. The working assumption of this section is that the cult portrayed in *1Q84* as "Sakigake" is a fictional depiction of the Aum Shinrikyō, or a cult very like it, in its earliest phases.

Unlike Kaikō Takeshi, Murakami is not particularly interested in redirecting any of this story back onto himself in *1Q84,* chiefly because none of his protagonists actually represents him, but also because, unlike Kaikō, he was never directly involved in the events that become prominent in these narratives, that is, the formation of the cult itself and the rise to quasi-sacred status of the cult's leader. For this reason, Murakami is able to remain focused on the process by which these two phenomena develop, and offer an imaginative, highly revealing scenario for them.

In so doing, there can be little question that the voices of the various Aum Shinrikyō members Murakami interviewed for *Underground*

2 made their way, with or without the author's awareness, into the narrative flow, along with some of the media and public attitudes that attended the Aum case. There were intellectuals and manual laborers, artists, schoolteachers, and engineers in Aum; some sought meaning in life; others, merely change from their everyday existence. Quite a number sought actual salvation and genuinely believed in the sacred powers of Asahara Shōkō. Some of these people are shown in the novel through generalized descriptions—chiefly provided by Professor Ebisuno, Fukaeri's guardian after she fled Sakigake—of the types of people who joined that organization in its early days. "'People with farming skills, healthy people who could handle harsh physical labor were sought. . . . There were also professionals with higher education. Doctors, engineers, educators, accountants—people like that were also welcomed into the collective since their skills were useful.'"[49] Characters like "Ponytail" and "the Monk," the Leader's bodyguards, are probably typical: highly devout and spiritually committed but basically stupid, unimaginative, and amateurish. Finally, of course, there is the Leader himself, who bears little resemblance to Asahara Shōkō, it is true, but whose charisma and power—including actual spiritual power—seem to represent the beliefs of Asahara's followers. (Asahara's widely touted ability to levitate is transformed in *1Q84* to the Leader making a stone clock float in midair before Aomame's eyes.)

As noted, Murakami has expressed no interest in recuperating the image of the Aum Shinrikyō specifically, and least of all Asahara Shōkō; what he does succeed in doing through *1Q84* is to suggest how the story might have turned out with an *actual* spiritualist as a leader, someone who truly *could* hear and interpret the voices from "over there." A second, but no less critical, motivation for Murakami is to offer an alternative image to that provided in the Japanese mass media, if only to demonstrate that their simplistic "good versus evil" construct is not the only way to conceptualize the cult and its members. Public opinion toward the Aum Shinrikyō was so uniformly negative in Japan following the media blitz (which, to be fair, was fed by public cries for vengeance) that former members could not find work or even apartments to rent, for they were, in most people's eyes, guilty by association. Murakami suggests through his narrative that merely belonging to a cult (a highly loaded term to begin with) does not make one a criminal, and (somewhat more riskily) that not all the members of Aum were bad. Most, like his characters "Ponytail" and "the Monk," were simply unimaginative.

A reading such as this does carry with it certain risks, foremost of which is the suggestion that eavesdropping on the author's thinking during the act of creation is advisable or even possible. This is particularly true when dealing with Murakami Haruki, who has always maintained that he does not plan out his narratives but allows them to flow organically from his imagination. But planning the narrative and selecting its subject matter are two different things. Murakami notes, for instance, that when he was preparing to write *A Wild Sheep Chase*, "'I used "sheep" as a key word, but the only thing I was sure of was that, at the end of the story, "Boku" on this side and "Rat" from the other side would be brought together.'"[50] We can just as easily imagine him saying, "I used 'cult' as a key word, but the only thing I was sure of was that at the end of the story 'Tengo' and 'Aomame' would be brought together. . . ." Whereas the "Sheep" in *A Wild Sheep Chase* has every appearance of a random image, the notion of the cult is anything but random, and the similarities between the formation of "Sakigake" and that of Aum Shinrikyō are difficult to ignore.

More importantly, if we choose to read a work like *1Q84* for its quasi-journalistic qualities, then the very nature of journalistic fiction, as with historical fiction, fairly demands that we acknowledge the role of the writer as selector and organizer of the events to be presented, and it is necessary to assume that such writers—including Murakami—must make choices with regard to characters and descriptions, even in an "organically evolving" narrative, if it is to accomplish its purpose. Why, for instance, does Murakami elect to depict the Leader as a man of such physical and spiritual size and power yet, ultimately, as a mere tool to be used by the cult? Why are "Ponytail" and "the Monk" shown to be bungling amateurs? And why, in fact, are *all* the characters, from Tengo and Aomame to Ayumi and Tamaru, presented as somehow "slightly off," standing just outside mainstream society? Is it not because so many of the people Murakami met from the Aum Shinrikyō actually fit that description in some manner or other? All were looking for something, just as everyone in *1Q84,* whether actually or figuratively, is looking for something, including its two heroes; Tengo seeks his inner wellspring, his "narrative," and Aomame seeks him. Both Tengo and Aomame are somehow "outside" the mainstream, and it is not difficult to imagine that even these two, given the right circumstances, might have been drawn to the Leader—a "true prophet"—for their spiritual guidance. Where else, after all, are they to seek it?

Among those Murakami interviewed from the Aum cult for *Underground 2,* young Kanda Miyuki seems to have made a particularly strong impression on him. Reflecting that she was only sixteen when she joined the Aum cult, and apparently an actual mystic, Murakami not only understands why she joined a group like Aum but argues that Japanese society should make a place for her, and soon. "I can think of no reason why there should not be a few people in our world who think seriously about matters that are not directly useful to society. The problem is, besides the Aum Shinrikyō, there are few effective 'nets' in which to catch such people."[51]

It is only natural that Murakami would be drawn to someone like Kanda, who describes her dreams and her reality as being indistinguishable. Is this an expression of schizophrenia, or is she actually channeling the "other world" directly into her conscious mind? Murakami himself does not presume to know, but he is clearly impressed with her apparently natural ability to attain what many seek through ascetic practice and he, as a novelist, must seek through daily toil, that is, direct connection with his inner mind—his dreamscape—while writing in a conscious state. If we attempt to connect her to *1Q84,* Kanda reminds us of Fukaeri, whose direct link to the Little People—the gods themselves—makes her, as we saw earlier, an ideal oracular mouthpiece but also (like dreams themselves) an enigma in the ordinary, secular world. Put another way, Fukaeri, like Kanda, is problematic in a society that has no particular objection to fantasy fiction or virtual reality but is intolerant of anyone with the temerity to claim that her "visions" might actually be real.

This returns us to an important thematic point from the previous chapter, wherein individual spiritual experience was contrasted with shared, inherited doctrine. Mirroring the inherent inability of industrialized societies to accept direct divine experience as valid, one of the central ironies present in *1Q84* is that many—maybe most—of the same people who pursue religious traditions that began with direct mystical experiences are nonetheless intensely mistrustful of—even hostile toward—living people who claim to have had similar experiences. There is no place in modern, "normal" society for those who have left their bodies, visited other worlds, found enlightenment, conversed with God. Such events belong to ancient times, or to fiction; suggest otherwise and one is dismissed as a mental case. One of the deeper messages of *1Q84* is thus identical to one of the deeper messages of *Underground 2*, namely, that in a world where our choices are limited to the homogenizing consumerist System of Japan, Inc., or the likes of Asahara Shōkō, in order to find meaning in life, we do ourselves a disservice indulging in oversimplified oppositions of "us versus them"; rather, there are benefits to be found in the recognition that there *may be* those in our world who really do "hear the voices," who are not mental cases, and sometimes they should be listened to. And where, finally, are these "voices" to be found in the actual world in which we live? Here, too, I think we could substitute "inner narrative" for "voices" and have a clearer idea of what Murakami has been trying to accomplish as a writer all these years. From his most bizarrely magical realist fiction to his most realistically grounded nonfiction, he has tried again and again to demonstrate to his readers the importance of looking within themselves, engaging their own inner "voices," and using these to perceive and remake the world that surrounds them.

This chapter—indeed, this book—began with the assertion that concepts like "truth," "fact," and even "reality," grounded as they are in the snares of individual perception, filtered through the imperfect tool of language and culture, are to be viewed with skepticism. I have not sought to suggest that the world around us does not exist, so much as to suggest that it cannot exist *meaningfully* without first passing through the various filters of our perception apparatuses. If this is true, then it becomes ever more important for each individual to examine and explore the unique apparatus with which he or she perceives *and reconstructs* the world and its various events. This is why genres like literary journalism and journalistic fiction are so useful, for they acknowledge the constitutive role of language, of our internal narrative, in the production of the *external* narratives we project into and share with the rest of the world. It is Kanda Miyuki's acute awareness of and connection to a strong internal narrative that Murakami responds to so powerfully; it is the lack of such narratives that seems to link so many other Aum Shinrikyō members with whom he spoke as he compiled *Underground 2*. A great many of these people admired Asahara Shōkō and his upper echelon—particularly Jōyū Fumihiro—for their ability to respond with great precision and certainty to their questions; yet, one can hear Murakami asking implicitly—and at times, almost explicitly—how can anyone answer questions about the "other world," about *our* purpose and place in the world, about existence itself, with precision or certainty? Are these not the very things every individual must discover for himself? The greatest flaw Murakami identifies in the Aum Shinrikyō, then, is that it gives its members answers to intensely personal questions that can only truly be approached *from the inside,* through our own individual narrative. Ultimately, cults like the Aum Shinrikyō behave much as the homogenizing state or "System": they supply an overarching narrative of the world, how it works, what its values are, what it means to be successful, happy, enlightened, and they present that narrative to their members, fait accompli, as an inalienable truth. Rat expresses this central theme at the outset of *Hear the Wind Sing* when he complains that "thinking your way through fifty years, truth be told, is a lot more tiring than spacing out for five thousand years."[52] Today, more than three decades after writing that line, Murakami continues to pit the empty bliss of blind conformity against the greater challenges—but also greater rewards—of maintaining an individual stance toward the world, accepting our imperfections, thinking for ourselves, connecting with our inner narrative, and finally deciding on our own what the world is, what it means for us, and what our role in it should be.

Connecting *1Q84* to the actual development of the Aum Shinrikyō cult, then, exposes more clearly how this novel brings Murakami's most important original theme up to date, a theme whose mode of expression has changed a great deal in three decades but whose essential message has not. What have we seen in *1Q84* but a plea from the author to make up our own minds? To think for ourselves? Tengo and Aomame both emerge as heroes in this novel, but only after they determine of their own free will to break away from the tasks that have been set them, tasks that, they are told, are morally right and correct; it is only when both strike out on their own and choose for themselves that they are able to shake off the delusion of predetermined fate and begin to fulfill a destiny that, both actually and figuratively, they are in the process of writing themselves. At the same time, Murakami presents the Sakigake cult to us not as a monolith of "evil" but as individuals seeking answers to life's questions. Some of them have the gifts required to "hear the voices," to gain the wisdom of the gods, but most can only await that wisdom, perhaps never realizing that the means to discovering it already exists within themselves, in their own narrative. In the context of our discussion of journalistic fiction, Murakami's voice seems to urge us as readers to take each character as he or she appears, to judge for ourselves their guilt or innocence, their good or evil, based not on loaded terms like *cult* but on what we see occurring in the story. And finally, if we listen carefully, we may even hear Murakami's own "voice," whispering to us, reminding us that the realities we find in the novel are not, finally, so different from the realities we find in the real world. The most important thing is to judge for ourselves, against the inner narrative *we* carry, for only in this manner can we truly grasp what radio journalist Paul Harvey (1918–2009) used to call "the rest of the story."

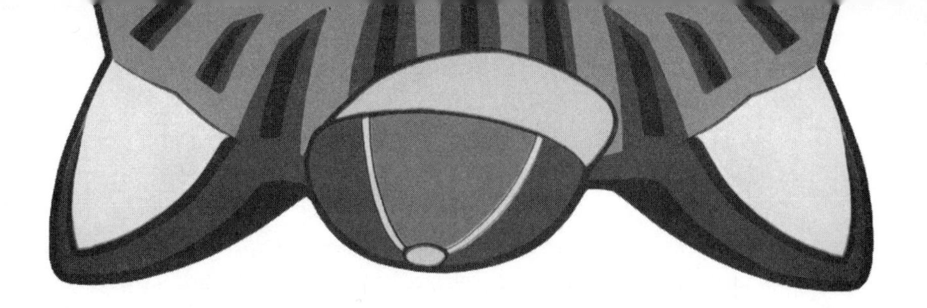

FIVE

Forbidden Dreams from "Over There"

> Some kinds of dreams . . . are more real than reality itself.
> —Murakami Haruki, *Shikisai o motanai Tazaki Tsukuru to, kare no junrei no toshi*

HAVING SPENT THE PAST FOUR CHAPTERS examining how language constitutes realities and what sorts of realities are created, not only in the fictional framework but through actual world examples of literary journalism and journalistic fiction, I will end this volume with a close reading of Murakami's most recent work, *Shikisai o motanai Tazaki Tsukuru to, kare no junrei no toshi* (2013), for which Murakami conveniently appends the English title, "Colorless Tsukuru Tazaki and his years of pilgrimage."[1] As we will see, this work is structurally most similar to *Norwegian Wood,* in that the "other world" never makes a full-blown appearance in the way it does in works like *The Wind-Up Bird Chronicle* and *1Q84,* and yet it is particularly appropriate as a closing text for two important reasons: first, it places front and center the role of dreams; and second, it seems—almost consciously at times—to revisit almost every major motif in Murakami fiction, from embedded narratives to the "nostalgic image." It also shows us, as Andō Reiji notes, "where Murakami is headed from here,"[2] and while he does not fully elaborate, we might note that new motifs include a depiction of the human core identity (the soul) in the form of light and colors, and a more explicit awareness of what I termed "divine" characters in the previous chapters, but here might simply be called "the gifted." Murakami also writes his first homosexual sex scene.

Given that *Tazaki Tsukuru* is a brand-new work, this chapter will break formation with previous chapters to some extent and focus almost exclusively on it, with a considerably more in-depth summary than I have provided for earlier works. And while we will spend some time exploring how the work continues to express some of the important features and characteristics of the "other world" we have seen in previous works, the broader mission of this final chapter is to explore how dreams are used in this text not merely as "psychic energy" or, less subtly, messages from the inner mind, but as products of language that, in their turn, construct new realities of their own.

Structurally speaking, *Tazaki Tsukuru* is similar to much previous Murakami fiction in that it tells two stories: one current, the other in retrospect. The author makes liberal use of embedded narratives, much as he does in *Pinball, 1973; A Wild Sheep Chase;* and *The Wind-Up Bird Chronicle,* and in one case he has a second long narrative embedded within the first. He also continues his contrastive opposition of Tokyo as an urban emblem of the contemporary, and Nagoya, Ōita, and finally Finland as not-altogether-metaphysical expressions of "over there." In its most superficial terms, the work may be read as the story of a man traumatized by an incident at the age of twenty who, having suppressed his memories of that time for some sixteen years, must now embark on a journey to confront those who traumatized him. His goal is to discover the truth about what happened to him and why, and in so doing heal the inner part of himself that remains injured.

The Early Narrative

Tazaki Tsukuru grew up in Nagoya, and during his high school years belonged to a tightly knit group of five friends. The other four—two males and two females—all have colorful names: the women are Kurono (black field) and Shirane (white root), while the men are Akamatsu (red pine) and Ōmi (blue sea). In typical Japanese fashion, they are addressed by their respective colors: Kuro, Shiro, Aka, and Ao. Only Tazaki lacks any color imagery in his name and is thus jokingly referred to as "colorless Tazaki Tsukuru." Jokes aside, however, his lack of color actually troubles him, causes him to feel out of place in this colorful group, and irrational though it may be, he often wonders why the others accepted him as a member.

The group itself is significant, according to Tazaki's own description, in that it operates under certain unspoken rules, first and foremost of which is that they must always do everything together. Explaining it to his girlfriend, Kimoto Sara, in the present narrative, Tazaki calls their group "'an orderly, harmonious team,'"[3] but it would be more accurate to describe it as a kind of hermetically sealed, utopian closed circle, and there is an implicit curse set against any who might disrupt its perfection.

Tazaki is the first to break this commandment when he elects, unlike the others, to leave Nagoya and attend college in Tokyo, the only place he can obtain the specialized training he will need to design and construct railway stations. The other four show him support in his endeavor, but the unspoken curse has been invoked, and less than two years after leaving Tokyo, returning home during vacation, Tazaki discovers he has been unilaterally expelled from the group. Asking Aka—who is tasked with informing Tazaki of his expulsion by telephone—why this has happened, he is told that he should "ask himself" that question. Feeling that further inquiry is pointless, Tazaki returns to Tokyo.

For the next five months following this incident, Tazaki thinks chiefly of death. It is not unnatural that he should consider suicide, but in his case he goes beyond just thinking and seems to place himself precisely on the border between the worlds of the living and the dead. He does not, so far as we know, take the one final step that would cast him into the world of death, but this is a little ambiguous in the narrative, even to Tazaki himself. He has barely eaten in the five months of his confinement, and looking at his emaciated appearance in the mirror, he finds himself resembling a corpse more than a man. "In some sense, I might *truly have been* on the brink of death. Like the shell of an insect, still stuck to a tree branch, I could have been blown into oblivion by a good strong wind, just barely clinging to life in this world. . . . Or maybe—the thought struck Tsukuru—maybe I really did die" (44–45).

What brings Tazaki out of his long reverie on death is a dream, in which a woman he does not know—yet desperately desires—offers him her body *or* her soul, but not both, for the other will be given to someone else. Assailed for the first time in his life by powerful jealousy—a fact that in itself should arouse our interest—Tazaki tries to tell the woman that he must have all of her or none of her, but she is unrelenting. As his frustration grows to rage, a pair of powerful hands grip him and squeeze, as though the marrow will be crushed out of his bones, until the anger is driven out. Tazaki then awakens, bathed in sweat. From this point on he steps away from the brink of death, puts the Nagoya incident behind him, and begins to strengthen his weakened body through healthy meals and regular exercise taken at the university pool. He is, however, conscious that this "new" Tazaki is not the same as the old. His five-month brush with death has transformed him into a new and more formidable man.

While swimming at the pool one day, Tazaki meets Haida, a fellow student two years his junior, who studies physics but whose true passion lies in philosophy. Haida, a handsome youth with what appears to be the scar of a deep knife wound at the nape of his neck, takes a liking to Tazaki, which once again surprises the latter, partly because they are very different but also out of his habitual assumption that he has nothing to offer the relationship, no "color" (Haida's name, which means "gray field," is also colorful, and more than once Tazaki mentally transposes his name as "Mister Gray"). In contrast with Tazaki, whose first name means "to make/create," and who is indeed adept at creating "things that have form" (53), Haida's true interest lies in the abstract, in the freedom that comes with leaving the world of the flesh behind. During one of his regular visits to Tazaki's apartment, where the two young men talk, cook, and listen to classical music, he explains his philosophy on the separation of flesh and spirit (a theme given considerable development in *The Wind-Up Bird Chronicle* and *Kafka on the Shore,* as noted previously), reminding us of the woman in Tazaki's fateful dream:

> "To think freely about things is also to separate ourselves from the flesh we are crammed into. To escape from that limiting cage that is our flesh, to break free of our chains and take flight into pure reason. In reason lies the natural life. That's what is at the core of freedom of thought." (66)

Haida's implied ability to divide flesh and spirit is given graphic demonstration that very night. Awakened by what he thinks is a noise in his room, Tazaki finds himself immobilized (echoing the Leader and Tengo in *1Q84*). And while the room is pitch dark, he somehow *knows* that Haida is in the room with him. The scene is quite similar to that in which Naoko visits Watanabe Tōru in *Norwegian Wood;* unable even to turn his head to see the clock at his bedside, time is eliminated from this space between the worlds of "this side" and "over there." Meanwhile, Tazaki concentrates on Haida, but he senses that this is not Haida's physical form. Rather, "he could not tell whether the Haida who stood there was the real Haida. Maybe the real, physical Haida was still out there in the other room, sound asleep on the sofa, and this was only Haida's alter ego, separated from his body" (113). Tazaki is not afraid of Haida, only puzzled about his purpose and concerned about his sudden paralysis. But he senses that Haida is frustrated with him. "It seemed as though Haida had something he wanted to tell him. He had some message that he needed to convey at all costs. But for some reason that message could not be converted into real words. This was irritating his wise younger friend" (115). At length Tazaki falls asleep and has a vivid erotic dream in which Kuro and Shiro, both still in their teens, make love to him, in turns and together. As he approaches climax, however, the two girls suddenly disappear, replaced by Haida, who takes Tazaki's penis into his mouth, whereupon Tazaki ejaculates violently. He awakens somewhat abashed the following morning and is surprised to discover no residue of the dream in his underwear or bedclothes, leading him to wonder whether this truly had been a dream at all. Either way, he has the uncomfortable sense that Haida is somehow aware of what has happened, "that perhaps Haida had, that night, with those sharp eyes of his, seen straight through him to something lurking at the bottom of his consciousness. Maybe he had felt the remnants of doubt within him. . . . Haida had examined and dissected, one by one, all the delusions and desires that Tsukuru had kept hidden away" (125).

Not long after this dream Haida disappears. Tazaki is left, not unnaturally, with questions about his own sexuality and is somewhat relieved to have his first sexual experience shortly thereafter in the waking world, with a real, flesh-and-blood woman. He brings the thing off successfully.

Haida's role in the narrative, then, is to awaken in Tazaki an awareness of the nature of his inner sexual desire, but it is also to connect him more concretely to his memories and desire of Shiro. This is clear in his introduction to Tazaki of classical music, and one piece in particular: Franz Liszt's *Le Mar du Pays,* roughly translated into English as "Homesickness," but more fully explained by Haida as "'a kind of reasonless melancholy that a pastoral scene calls forth into the soul'" (62).

This also happens to be the piece, Tazaki realizes upon hearing it again, that Shiro always played when she wanted to get away from the world. It is an unusually obscure and challenging piece for a high school girl to play, but those melancholy strains come to represent Shiro, indeed, to contain her very soul, even after death.

The Present Narrative

We now flash to the novel's present. Much of the story above, minus the parts about Haida, is related to Kimoto Sara, Tazaki's new girlfriend and, significantly, the first woman Tazaki has seriously considered marrying. Sara listens to Tazaki's narrative with great interest, then declares that he must confront this past, for clearly it has caused wounds that have not yet healed. Although Tazaki has, in the intervening years, largely suppressed his memories of the Nagoya incident, the matter becomes more urgent when Sara issues an ultimatum of sorts. She can sense that Tazaki is not wholly with her when they are in bed, that there remains something twisted inside him. Sounding very much like Tengo, explaining to Fukaeri the deeper meanings of George Orwell's *Nineteen Eighty-Four,* she tells Tazaki that "'however well you've hidden your memories, however deeply you've buried them, you can't erase that history.' Sara looked straight into his eyes. 'You should remember that. You can't erase history, and you can't change it. It would be the same thing as killing your own existence'" (39–40). This statement becomes a recurring mantra throughout the text.

As a result, Sara sends Tazaki out on a mission to confront his former friends, to determine what happened and why, and thus heal that "twisted" part of himself. She does the preliminary research, learning that of the four friends, Ao and Aka are still in Nagoya. Ao is an award-winning Lexus salesman, while Aka runs a company that trains company workers to think more independently. Kuro, meanwhile, has married a Finnish man and moved to Helsinki; Shiro, however, has been dead for six years.

Tazaki initially travels to Nagoya, confronting Ao first at his Lexus dealership. Ao does not recognize him at first—a pattern that repeats itself with each of his friends—but after an initial period of awkwardness, the two men are able to discuss the past. The first thing

Tazaki learns is that his expulsion from the group was the result of a serious allegation made against him by Shiro all those years ago:

> "Shiro said she had been raped by you," Ao said uncomfortably. "She said you had deliberately forced her to have sex with you."
>
> Tsukuru tried to say something, but no words would come out. He had just taken a sip of water, but his throat was painfully dry.
>
> Ao spoke. "I couldn't believe you would do something like that. The other two were the same, Kuro and Aka. No matter how we thought about it, you weren't the type to force yourself on anyone, and even less the type who would use violence to do it. We knew that. But Shiro was dead serious, and she was taking it really hard. She said you had two faces, one on the surface and another underneath. Shiro said you had an inner face that no one could ever imagine from the outer one. We couldn't think of any way to respond to that. (163)

Ao claims—and later Aka will confirm this—that the question of his guilt and expulsion was largely determined by Kuro, who stood determinedly on Shiro's side. Asked why they went along with his betrayal (Tazaki uses the verb *kiru,* "to cut"), both men answer that of the five friends Tazaki seemed like the one best equipped to handle the consequences of being cut from the group. As Ao puts it, "'you lived with both your feet firmly on the ground, and that gave the group a sense of quiet stability. Like the anchor of a ship'" (169), while Aka describes him as "'emotionally tougher than the rest of us. Remarkably so, more than you looked'" (196). Both of these comments, needless to say, come as a surprise to Tazaki.

Finally, Tazaki embarks on his greatest and most unnerving journey, a trek to Finland to confront Kuro, who was, according to Aka and Ao, the real driving force behind his expulsion from the group sixteen years earlier. When he arrives in Helsinki, however, he finds she has gone with her family to spend the summer at their country cottage in the woods surrounding the tiny town of Haemeenlinn, famous as the birthplace of composer Jean Sibelius. To reach this town, he must drive some distance, and in this journey, too, we find a kind of *michiyuki,* not quite as dramatic as those of *Pinball, 1973* or *A Wild Sheep Chase,* to be sure, but nonetheless discernible. He drives through wooded areas of birch trees, great birds circling above them in search of prey on the ground. Finding the town of Haemeenlinn poses no particular difficulty, but on his arrival he realizes that locating this one cottage in the middle of a great forest will be no mean feat. Fortunately he meets an old man on a bicycle, who, asked for directions, without preamble or invitation climbs into Tazaki's car and shows him the way. The old man's fearsome appearance and demeanor are worth notice: "an old man of small stature . . . wearing an old hunting cap and long rubber boots. Great tufts of white hair emerged from his ears, and his eyes were red and bloodshot. Like he was filled with rage at something" (268). The man's language is confusing as well; he speaks a variety of languages all at once—English, German, Finnish, and at one point, "a language Tsukuru could not place. From its sound it did not seem to be Finnish" (269). Upon reaching the cottage, the old man turns around and storms off without a word and without looking back, "like the death god who guided the departed onto the path to the underworld" (269). The old man bears certain similarities to the "Gatekeeper" who removes Boku's shadow at the outset of *Hard-Boiled Wonderland and the End of the World,* but his function is more like the two soldiers who guide Kafka into the forest to meet Saeki in *Kafka on the Shore.* In both appearance and manner he is clearly marked as a guardian spirit of the forest and gives us our best indication that Tazaki has at last reached his destination "over there." This is not, however, the same "over there"—the same metaphysical forest—as we have seen in previous Murakami fiction, for when Tazaki finally meets Kuro, he discovers her to be living, with her Finnish husband and her two daughters. This is not the underworld per se. And yet, as Tazaki and Kuro face one another, preparing to confront their shared past, Murakami offers a subtle clue to indicate that this is not entirely the world of the living either: Kuro, as a wife and mother, wears her hair pinned up, but just before they begin to talk in earnest, she removes the pins and lets her hair down so that "her bangs now covered her forehead. Now she looked more like the old Kuro" (284–85). It is an updated version of the flickering back and forth between the teenage and the middle-aged Saeki confronted by Kafka at the end of *his* quest.

To Tazaki's surprise, Kuro (who prefers now to be called by her adult name, "Eri," and suggests that they refer to Shiro by the grown-up name of "Yuzu" as well) confesses that, like Aka and Ao, she never truly believed that Tazaki had raped Shiro; she pursued his expulsion, rather, for the sake of Shiro, who was tottering on the brink of madness. But this was only one of the reasons. She confesses at length that she had always loved Tazaki, knowing all the while of his desire for Shiro. Partly out of awareness of Shiro's beauty—"'she was Snow White and I was the Seven Dwarfs'" (295), she quips—Kuro was simply afraid to confess her love. "'I lacked confidence in myself as a woman. No matter how much I loved you, I figured you would never take someone like me as your partner. Your heart was set on Yuzu. That's why I was able to cut you out so mercilessly. It was in order to cut out my feelings for you'" (313).

In between catching up and Kuro's confession to Tazaki, the two also discuss what had really happened to Shiro. Like Aka and Ao, Kuro notes that Shiro's injuries were real; she truly had been sexually violated, but she hints that the incident may have occurred in the metaphysical world: "'there is a certain kind of dream that is more real than reality itself,'" Kuro explains. "'She had a dream like that'" (295). Somewhat later Kuro suggests that Shiro "'had an evil spirit in her . . . it was always hovering at a slight distance behind her, breathing its icy breath on her neck, steadily pursuing her'" (304).

Tazaki learns that Shiro had gone off to the mountains to hide out while awaiting the arrival of her child—she could not consider an abortion, because she was firmly against the practice—but had miscarried. After this, she drifted further and further from human contact, gradually cutting herself off from society. Like Tazaki, she starved herself to dangerous levels, until even her menstrual periods stopped coming.

What Kuro describes is Shiro's gradual but inexorable shift from flesh to pure spirit, a drive toward death that made it impossible for anyone to anchor her to this world. In the end Shiro moved to Hamamatsu to live by herself, but given her helpless state, Kuro interprets this as an act of suicide. When Shiro is murdered, found strangled to death on the floor of her kitchen, the circumstances are inexplicable; her room is locked from the inside, there is no sign of struggle or break-in, and nothing has been stolen. Tazaki is again assailed by the possibility that it was his own inner self that killed Shiro, perhaps in the "other world":

> Just as Shiro said, maybe I have another face, one no one can imagine, lurking just beneath the surface. Like the far side of the moon, forever cloaked in darkness. In some other place, without my ever knowing about it, in a totally different kind of time, maybe I really did rape Shiro, slicing deeply into her soul. Despicably, with all my strength. And maybe that dark inner side will eventually rise up, completely overwhelm the surface me, swallowing it whole. (228)

Tazaki cannot dismiss such fears, if only because his past experiences—particularly with Haida—have convinced him that flesh-spirit separation is possible, and that he probably does carry within him a darker self, capable of doing things his outer self would never consider. And yet, he also has a vague notion that this was what was supposed to happen all along:

> Tsukuru had never in his life felt the urge to kill anyone. But maybe he had meant to kill Yuzu in the abstract. Tsukuru himself had no way of knowing what sort of dense darkness lurked within his soul. All he was sure of was that Yuzu had the same sort of dense darkness within herself. Perhaps their two darknesses had connected somewhere deep beneath the surface. And maybe being strangled by Tsukuru was exactly what Yuzu had wanted. Maybe he had heard her pleas through their connected darkness. (318)

He does not, however, tell all this to Kuro, opting instead for the more ambiguous statement that "'I might actually have killed Shiro'" (318). The meeting between Tazaki and Kuro ends shortly after this scene, marked by Kuro pinning her hair back up, signaling the return of the present and the recession of the "other world." At this moment Tazaki reflects that "the flow of time became just a little lighter" (319).

One important question that lingers here is why Shiro sought death. This is never resolved properly in the narrative, but Tazaki himself has a plausible answer: she simply could not face the idea of growing up. "In their high school days the five of them had lived in perfect, tightly knit harmony. They accepted each other as they were, and understood one another. Each of them felt a sense of profound happiness in that. But such happiness could not go on forever. . . . Shiro's spirit probably could not handle the pressure of what must come"

(363). This also helps us to understand Shiro's determination not to become pregnant again—indeed, her general horror of sexuality—for these belong to the realm of the adult world in which, as Tazaki puts it, "each person must grow up at their own pace, and in their own direction" (363). He concludes that Shiro's urge toward death—using himself as a stepping stool—represented a flight from that inevitable destiny. From our vantage point, it may be added that Shiro's drive toward the "other world" is an attempt to escape the effects of time, of growth and change, and remain the young and innocent girl she has always been. This relates directly back to the "perfect, utopian circle" that we have seen again and again in Murakami's writing, most prominently in *Norwegian Wood* and *Kafka on the Shore,* a perfect space in which nothing can disrupt the ideal happiness of Kizuki and Naoko, or Saeki and her boyfriend; yet we have also seen—in the village where the fifteen-year-old Saeki continues her unchanging existence—that this is a realm in which individual growth and development come to a halt. This realm represents perfect peace, but such peace is meaningless without the existence of conflict to define it.

Once More into the "Other World"

The account above suggests that the ontological stance of this novel is closer to *Norwegian Wood* or *South of the Border, West of the Sun* than it is to some of the more metaphysically imbued texts discussed in this volume; in short, it is what might be termed a near-realistic text. Its narrative structure supports this, lacking the regular rhythm of alternating narratives that marks the works up through *The Wind-Up Bird Chronicle* but also lacking clear-cut forays into the forbidding darkness of the "other world." Instead, much as we see in *Norwegian Wood,* Tazaki Tsukuru's ventures into the "other world" are symbolically portrayed in his visits to Nagoya, his imagining of Shiro's final home in Hamamatsu, his internalization of Haida's story about a hot spring resort in Ōita, and, most obviously, his journey to the village of Haemeenlinn, not far from Helsinki, to meet Kuro at her summer home in Finland. None of these locations is truly representative of "over there"; rather, like Hokkaido (as opposed to Rat's villa) in *A Wild Sheep Chase,* it is their status as being "other than Tokyo" that marks them as likely settings for close encounters with "over there." And if we are denied the familiar explorations of the "other world" that made works like *A Wild Sheep Chase* and *Kafka on the Shore* so intriguing, we are perhaps compensated by the unnerving, yet thrilling sensation that the "other world" is constantly, unblinkingly, observing *us*.

Incursions of "over there" are most prominently depicted in the early sequences of this novel, particularly those that detail Tazaki Tsukuru's peculiar transformation, from a youthful, naive idealist suddenly faced with expulsion from a group that, in many ways, defined who he was, into a detached loner, or what he finally describes, at novel's end, as a "defector from his own life" (357). This transformation is brought about, physiologically speaking, through five months of near starvation, as the traumatized Tazaki flirts with the idea of suicide and does not take the trouble of feeding himself. During this time, his perception of the world around him is about as close as we get to a description of "over there" in this work:

> As far as he could see, the ground was strewn with shattered boulders. There was not a drop of water, not a blade of grass growing. No color, no light. No sun, nor any moon or stars. Probably no direction either. The bizarre twilight and fathomless darkness traded places at regular intervals. It was the ultimate frontier of consciousness. (41)

As we have seen in previous chapters, the lack of sun and moon, indeed, of light itself, suggests the timelessness of that realm, its dark and forbidding nature. His description, within the context of the novel's structure, could be read as a metaphorical representation of the darkest despair, but I am more inclined to read this passage as a hint that Tazaki Tsukuru, facing the abyss of death and the unknown, actually exists more inside his mind than outside it during these five critical months. It is in this gloomy no-man's land, on the border between the world of the living and that of the dead, that he loses his youthful idealism and becomes a new man. And when at last he does emerge, his appearance is altered significantly and appropriately for a man who has faced the brink of death and returned. It is not, to be sure, quite the same level of transformation one finds in the earliest texts—he has not become a talking pinball machine, for instance—but enough that people who know him are shocked by the change. Not only has his body wasted away, but "his face had also changed. Looking at himself in the mirror, no traces remained of the soft face of that mediocre, unfocused youth. The face looking back at him was that of a young man, whose protruding cheek bones were sharp, like they'd been carved with a garden trowel" (50). His body and face have at last transformed to match the change in his core self, so that Tazaki Tsukuru is an entirely new man, inside and out. And this new "him" is wholly without regrets for the passing of the old; indeed, we even catch a hint of the dark determination that lurks beneath the surface of this sharply featured new man. Significantly, it is precisely at this moment that we catch another glimpse of that hidden forest that so many previous Murakami heroes have found, for better or worse:

> Look at it how you may, the youth who had been Tazaki Tsukuru was dead. He had gasped out his last breath in desolate darkness, and was buried in some tiny forest clearing. Secretly, quietly, while everyone else slept. With no headstone. He who stood here breathing was a "new Tazaki Tsukuru," whose contents had been completely replaced. But no one besides himself knew this, nor did he have any intention of telling anyone the truth. (51)

Words such as "contents" *(naiyō)* remind us yet again that the physical body in Murakami fiction is frequently little more than a container *(yōki),* housing a core identity—a soul, a *kokoro*—that is by no means permanently fixed to that container. This was a prominent motif in *Kafka on the Shore,* as we have seen, and casts into sharper perspective the reasons for Kafka's loathing of his own body; while the "contents" of that body may well be the "soul" of Nakata, the vessel itself is the product of Johnny Walker, and as such it bears the *physical* curse of that origin. Clearly a similar operation goes on in *1Q84* with the construction of the *dōta* ("daughter") characters, mere empty vessels destined to receive the seed of the Leader in the hopes that that material will be conveyed to yet another type of container: the womb. This last image strikes a resonant chord with *Tazaki Tsukuru,* for in his transformation, Tazaki himself is in a sense "reborn"—a term Andō uses as well—from the dark and mysterious "womb" of "over there."[4] It is a function of the metaphysical world we have already seen employed with considerable effect in *Kafka on the Shore, After Dark,* and *1Q84,* namely, as a symbolic location for growth, gestation, and eventual reemergence into the light as something new. Beginning with Tamura Kafka and continuing through Tazaki Tsukuru, the hero who ventures into that dark and unsettling place has the potential to emerge stronger and better able to cope with the world than before.

But this is not always the case. Shiro, for her part, is the one other character in this novel who almost certainly encounters the world "over there," and she is destroyed by it. Of the five friends in this novel, clearly Shiro is the most fragile; a delicate, sensitive musician, Shiro struggles with a general tendency to withdraw from interaction with others. Perhaps due in part to her father's profession as an obstetrician gynecologist, she has developed a basic fear of sexuality, which fits in well with Tazaki's perception that their high school group avoids any romantic entanglements among the various parties. In any case, as Kuro tells Tazaki near the end of the novel, Shiro (now called "Yuzu") never felt sexual attraction for anyone. "'Yuzu had a powerful loathing for anything sexual that bordered on terror'" (296). This is why, following her rape and miscarriage, Shiro virtually starved herself. "'It was because she wanted to stop her menstrual periods,'" Kuro explains. "'When you drop below a certain weight, your periods stop. That's what she wanted. Not only did she want to ensure she would never get pregnant again, but she probably wanted to stop being female altogether. If it had been possible, she would have liked to remove her uterus'" (297).

These feelings are worth pursuing for just a moment, because if we observe Shiro's situation dispassionately, we see certain similarities with Tamura Kafka. Recall that Kafka's primary source of discomfort is the irrefutable fact of his genetic connection to his father, whom he considers to be evil; Shiro, too, is to some extent uncomfortable about her father's chosen profession. Why, we might wonder, did Shiro never consult her father regarding her condition? Presumably it is because, as Kuro explains to Tazaki, she could never have considered terminating the pregnancy. "'Whatever the circumstances, there was no way she could have killed anything. . . . From way back she was highly critical of the fact that her father also performed abortions. We used to argue about that a lot'" (292). This fits the overall profile of Shiro's character, particularly her abhorrence of sexual contact, and lends a certain pathos to the fact that the assault upon her was of a sexual nature.

There is, however, another important aspect to consider regarding Shiro, namely, that if Tazaki Tsukuru possesses a "darker inner self hidden by his outer mask," who is to say that Shiro herself does not have the same sort of "dark inner self," one that—like that of the "nine-fingered girl," of Naoko, of Kumiko, of Aomame, indeed, of Tazaki himself—is grounded in bestial emotion and raw sexuality? If Tazaki's inner self is grounded in this uncontrollable sexual desire—is, in fact, the very "evil spirit" of whom Kuro spoke—then we have no reason to assume that Shiro did not also possess an inner sexuality that drove her into the hands of that evil spirit, to the horror of her conscious self. In other words, we cannot rule out the possibility that Shiro's dreams were quite as erotic—as "forbidden"—as Tazaki's own.

If this is so, then Shiro's absolutist stance against sexuality and its natural result speaks of a basic resistance to something within herself; thus, her gradual movement toward the world of death is finally an effort to resolve the dilemma within herself, which must end either in the restoration of her "innocence" within the other world or in the triumph of her inner demon. Furthermore, it is not difficult to see that same struggle occupying Tazaki as well. We recall that Tazaki, prior to his expulsion from the group, fought to suppress his growing sexual desire for Shiro (which he did not feel for Kuro). "'I always did my best not to be conscious of her as a member of the opposite sex. I was careful not to be alone with her'" (217), he tells Sara, an admission that may shed light on the fact that following his expulsion, Tazaki regularly dreamed about having sexual relations with both women, yet—puzzling even to himself—when the climactic moment came, he inevitably ejaculated into Shiro's body rather than into Kuro. On the unconscious—the metaphysical—level, Tazaki Tsukuru was equally a prisoner of his own "evil spirit," whose sexual desire for Shiro could no more be stopped than Shiro's secret desires (for Tazaki? It is unclear) could be suppressed. Within the model of the "other world" we have constructed throughout this text, then, it is quite plausible that Tazaki Tsukuru's concerns about a dark inner self are correct, that he has acted out his inner fantasy, within the inner dreamscape, and caused irreparable harm to the woman he wanted more than any other. But was it all perhaps just a dream?

By novel's end Shiro's pregnancy is left as one of the several unanswered riddles to which we are now accustomed in Murakami fiction. Did Shiro's dark inner spirit really connect with that of Tazaki Tsukuru, leading to their sexual liaison? Did Tazaki really rape, and later murder, the woman he loved most? Or was Shiro's condition, as

Andō suggests, just another "immaculate conception,"[5] the result of her own powerfully repressed sexual urges? All we can say with any certainty is that the fact of that conception forced Shiro to confront the "evil spirit" that lurked within her, a confrontation she could not hope to win. And yet, not all has been lost, even for Shiro. In one of the more moving scenes in the novel, as Kuro and Tazaki reminisce about Shiro at Kuro's summerhouse in Haemeenlinn, they hold a sort of impromptu funeral for her—neither was able to attend her actual memorial service—by playing a recording of Liszt's *Le Mar du Pays.* We can almost feel, as Tazaki and Kuro seem to do, Shiro's presence joining them once more through this melody, and Kuro tells him that "'in a lot of ways, she still goes on living'" (307). One of those ways, in spirit, at least, is through Kuro's daughter, whom she has named "Yuzu" in honor of their friend. Once again the "other world" functions symbolically as the womb, in conjunction with Kuro's actual womb, to facilitate the "rebirth" of Shiro.

Through the Doors of Perception

One of the more diverting aspects of Murakami criticism has been the flurry of speculation about direct literary "influences" and "antecedents" that seems to attend each new work. This actually goes back to *Pinball, 1973,* whose title looked like a parody of Ōe Kenzaburō's *Man'en gannen no futtobōru* (Football, 1860; translated as The Silent Cry), and to works like *Dance Dance Dance, Norwegian Wood,* and *South of the Border, West of the Sun,* all of which are named after popular songs. The diversion lies in trying to decipher how these antecedents have exerted their "influence" on the author and text, an exercise that is likely to yield about as much insight as trying to prove that *The Sputnik Sweetheart* is really about the Russian space program. Still, *Kafka on the Shore* no doubt had plenty of critics scurrying to dig out dusty editions of *The Metamorphosis* and "In the Penal Colony," and *1Q84* probably led more than one curious reader to delve back into Orwell's *Nineteen Eighty-Four,* just in case. . . .

Tazaki Tsukuru has been no exception to this kind of interest, not for its title but because of the prominent color imagery that seems to demand a bit more than the usual attention. Works of fiction offered by Japanese critics as having possible connections with *Tazaki Tsukuru* include "The Pursuit of Mr. Blue" in G. K. Chesterton's Father

Brown mysteries, Paul Auster's *Ghosts,*[6] and certain works on color by Johann Wolfgang von Goethe and Rudolf Steiner.[7] These last two, suggested by Numano Mitsuyoshi, are not far off the mark, as we shall see. And while I customarily avoid these games, not wishing to become embroiled in yet another wild sheep chase, I would be ready to wager a small sum on the relevance, if not the definitive influence, of Aldous Huxley's nonfiction work *The Doors of Perception,* for reasons that will be made clear below.

On the evening prior to Tazaki's second dream, the topic of his discussion with Haida turns to the nature of death, a subject to which Tazaki has given quite a bit of thought, and this occasions Haida to share a peculiar story he claims to have heard from his father, but which he tells so expertly that Tazaki suspects it may actually be his own. During the 1960s, as the story goes, while still a university student, Haida's father grows tired of the constant strife among the various radical student factions and leaves school to go on a one-year walking tour of Japan (resembling Rat's journey in *Pinball, 1973* and *A Wild Sheep Chase*), eventually landing at a secluded hot spring resort in the mountains of Ōita Prefecture. There he meets a jazz pianist named Midorikawa (green river), a middle-aged man who has determinedly avoided unnecessary human contact while staying at the inn. He takes a liking to Haida's father, however, particularly after the latter guides him to a nearby public school to use the piano in their music room. While performing a spellbinding rendition of Thelonius Monk's "'Round Midnight," Midorikawa keeps a small pouch on the piano. Asked what it is, he responds first that it is "a kind of talisman," then clarifies that "'you might call it my other self'" (79).

But Midorikawa has far more interesting secrets to tell. He confides that he is a carrier of something known as the "death token," and while we are never told clearly what this means, to be chosen as its carrier, one must first accept the responsibility of facing death willingly. In exchange for this, one is granted special powers of perception not given to ordinary people. In Midorikawa's case, it is the ability to see the "lights and colors" that surround all people like an aura. What this glow represents is open to interpretation, but I am inclined to agree with Numano's contention, leaning on Goethe and Steiner, that these represent the actual "souls" of the individuals he sees. For Midorikawa this "gift" is very much a mixed blessing, however; it was because he was sick of seeing into men's souls that he came to this isolated mountain retreat, where he now awaits his own death, due to arrive within the next two months. The carrier of the "death token" is given but one chance to avoid his impending death: he must find someone—a person with the just right sort of color and glow, "'maybe one in a thousand, or two thousand'" (88), as Midorikawa puts it—who will, in full knowledge of the consequences, take up the burden of the "death token" for him.[8] Asked what sort of person willingly accepts such a fate, Midorikawa says it might be "'the sort of person who is unafraid of making a great leap'" (89).

Presumably, Midorikawa has shared this tale with Haida's father because he sees that special "light and color" in him as well. He does not, however, invite the young man to take up the death token in his place; he merely offers him a few avuncular words of advice, simple, yet moving: Midorikawa tells him that he is different from most people, that he is not meant simply to live and then die "like a cat, alone, in some dark place" (94). Rather, he must strive always to live fully. "'Soon you will return to your life in Tokyo, I suppose,' Midorikawa told him in a quiet voice. 'Then you will go back to your real life. Live that life fully. Even if you meet with frivolity and monotony, there is value simply in living this life'" (94). The following day Midorikawa disappears for good, and Haida's father never learns what became of him.

Why does Haida tell Tazaki this story? On the surface it is a chance to introduce his friend to the idea of a heightened, indeed transcendent, sense of perception and to give graphic narrative expression to his theory of free thought. In terms of driving the novel forward, it serves to highlight the existence of certain "gifted" persons in the world, much as we saw in *1Q84*, who possess extraordinary powers of perception. Midorikawa describes his own heightened perception as follows:

> "At the moment you have agreed to take up the burden of death, you possess an unusual quality. You could call it a special ability. The ability to read the various colors given off by people is only one of those functions. At the root of it, you are able to expand your perception. You push open that 'door to perception' that Aldous Huxley talked about. And then your perceptions are pure and genuine." (89)

Midorikawa's reference is to a series of experiments Huxley carried out in the early 1950s with the drug mescaline, a derivative of peyote, and while Huxley's experiences were temporary and artificially induced, his descriptions of them resonate with much that is expressed in *Tazaki Tsukuru* by those characters who possess the gift of a wider perception. As Huxley observes the various objects in his study—his books, a desk, a chair, a flower arrangement—he becomes aware that he is no longer a distinct entity among these other entities, but rather that they have all become one. Interestingly, the familiar themes of temporal and spatial suspension also surface, part of his overall pseudomystical experience:

> I saw the books, but was not at all concerned with their positions in space. What I noticed, what impressed itself upon my mind was the fact that all of them glowed with living light and that in some the glory was more manifest than in others. . . . I spent several minutes—or was it several centuries?—not merely gazing at those bamboo legs, but actually *being* them—or rather being myself in them; or, to be still more accurate (the "I" was not involved in the case, nor in a certain sense were "they") being my Not-self in the Not-self which was the chair.[9]

Colors, too, are so intensely alive that he is surprised to find how much he has been missing. "Mescaline raises all colors to a higher power and makes the percipient aware of the innumerable fine shades of difference, to which, at ordinary times, he is completely blind" (27). But not all people are blind to these visions, even at "ordinary times"; rather, Huxley suggests that there are those who possess the ability to see the world thus all the time; artists such as Van Gogh and Botticelli "had looked at draperies with the same transfigured and transfiguring eyes as had been mine that morning. They had seen the *Instigkeit,* the Allness and Infinity of folded cloth and had done their best to render it in paint or stone. Necessarily, of course, without success. For the glory and the wonder of pure existence belong to another order, beyond the power of even the highest art to express" (34). But this experience, this exquisite perception, in itself is only part of the game; in the process of becoming "one" with everything around him, Huxley recognizes a profound disinterest in human interaction, and this troubles him. "How could one reconcile this timeless bliss of seeing as one ought to see with the temporal duties of doing what one ought to do and feeling as one ought to feel?" (35). The answer, he reasons, is that only the rarest of mystics—he compares them with *arhats,* enlightened beings who have reached Buddhahood but, out of compassion, choose to come back to earth to help others—will seek ways to communicate some of what is in that infinite realm back to the masses of the unenlightened: "The *arhat* and the quietist may not practice contemplation in its fullest; but if they practice it at all, they may bring back enlightening reports of another, a transcendent country of the mind; and if they practice it in the height, they will become conduits through which some beneficent influence can flow out of that other country into a world of darkened selves, chronically dying for the lack of it" (44).

This admittedly lengthy detour into the mescaline-induced visions of Aldous Huxley does have a point, for in Huxley's description of the compassionate enlightened ones, we may also discern an apt description for Midorikawa, and indeed Haida as well. Kōnosu wants to see Midorikawa as a kind of Mephistopheles,[10] and insofar as he does offer Haida a glimpse of the world that lies beyond normal perception, without deceit, this is a defensible reading. And yet, Midorikawa shows Haida these things not to offer him a choice—he has no intention of asking Haida to take up the death token for him—but merely to make him aware that this greater reality exists and that those with the ability to perceive it ought not to ignore it. This is why he urges Haida, despite the banality of the world around him, to live fully and find meaning in that process where he can. Midorikawa is not Mephistopheles tempting Haida with a choice, but an *arhat* acting out of an abundance of compassion; his purpose—to judge from the results—is to awaken Haida to his own special ability. If Tazaki's suspicion is correct and Haida's "father" in the story is really Haida himself, perhaps in astral form, then Midorikawa's act of kindness has been successful; the time Haida spends with Tazaki Tsukuru represents his own compassion, his return to the "world of darkened selves," to help Tazaki Tsukuru, quite literally, "see the light."

If Midorikawa and Haida represent "the elect," so to speak, those who possess a special light and color that permits them heightened powers of perception, then it is Aka and Ao who represent and minister to the "ordinary people" who do not have these powers. This is most explicitly expressed through Aka, whose business is educating new company employees and reeducating those in midcareer. Aka sees himself as a visionary—"'I wasn't made to be used by others'" (186), he rather smugly informs Tazaki—and believes that his company performs a noble service, training workers to think for themselves. This liberation of the mind, however, has its limitations. "'We are trying to create a workforce that can say, "I can use my own head to think about things" *while continuing to work within the expectations of the company*'" (188; my emphasis), he tells Tazaki. Whether Aka's goal is people who actually *can* use their own heads or simply people who can *say* that they do is a matter of some ambiguity; that their thinking must remain "within the expectations of the company" is a not very subtle way of reminding us that whatever illusions of free thought they may have, such people are still pawns of the System.

This, of course, places some limits on what sorts of people are suitable for the kind of System-approved training Aka has to offer. As a matter of expediency he divides his potential clientele into three categories:

> "There are quite a lot of people who can't accept our program. I divide them into two types: first is the antisocial person. The English term is 'outcaste.' These people reject established attitudes, they won't accept them. Or else they won't be bound up by collective rules. Working with them is a waste of time. We can only ask them to leave. The other type is the person who truly can use his head and think. We can leave them alone. Better not to fiddle with them and screw them up. Every system needs a representative like that. If they stay on the path, they eventually end up in charge. But in between these two groups, there is a layer of people who simply take orders and carry them through, and they occupy a large chunk of the population—I would estimate about 85% of it. Our business is built on the foundation of that 85%." (188)

Aka's clientele, then, are the mediocre, the ordinary, and they are implicitly opposed to those like Midorikawa and Haida, both of whom are capable of looking and thinking beyond accepted boundaries. In contrast to the "expectations of the company," Haida's philosophy requires a willingness to break out of those expectations, to reach escape velocity and shoot for unknown galaxies. "'All things have a framework,'" he tells Tazaki. "'Thought also has its limits. There is nothing to be feared in boundaries, but we also must not be afraid to smash those boundaries. In order for humankind to be free, this is more important than anything. Reverence and abhorrence for limits. Everything important in human life is grounded in this duality'" (68). Clearly Haida represents the "incorrigible" group, for his refusal to "stay inside the lines." Aka, on the other hand, represents the cream of society's mediocrity, creating not freethinkers but the illusion of freethinking, for he is still bound up by the rules. Ao, too, for all his expressed distaste for the kind of company Aka runs, is part of this great mediocrity. Ao sells the Lexus brand—Toyota's luxury model, meant to tap into the middle class's desire to enjoy the illusion of being upper-class. It is fitting that Ao's mobile phone ringtone is "Viva Las Vegas," for if ever there was a city that embodied the facade, the false front, it surely must be Las Vegas. Ao harbors no illusions about this, admitting that the brand name of Lexus "'has no meaning at all. It's just a made-up word. Something a New York advertising firm came up with in response to Toyota's request for a name that sounded high class and meaningful, with a nice ring to it'" (176).

And what of Tazaki Tsukuru? It would be safe to say that Tazaki begins the work, more or less by accident, in the same group as Aka and Ao, but that the traumatic experiences of his youth prove transformative for him, nudging him closer to his true destiny, which is to join the "elect." This, one suspects, is the message that Haida wished so fervently to convey to Tazaki on the night of his second dream—the very reason, in fact, that he told Tazaki the story of Midorikawa in the first place. Tazaki, however, is not yet prepared to receive and decipher that message, so Haida finds another way of getting his attention, of demonstrating the separation of spirit and flesh. . . .

Having come this far, let us now pause to reexamine some of the earlier Murakami characters who possess remarkable abilities and use those talents to assist others: the clairvoyant ear model Kiki from *A Wild Sheep Chase* and *Dance Dance Dance;* Naoko and her attunement to the world of the dead in *Norwegian Wood;* the clairvoyant girl Yuki in *Dance Dance Dance;* Okada Tōru's ability to divide flesh and spirit; Nakata and Saeki in *Kafka on the Shore;* Tengo, Aomame, Fukaeri, Ushikawa, and the Leader in *1Q84*. It is not until *1Q84,* however, that we begin to see an acute consciousness of these gifts on the part of the characters they adorn, as well as some inkling of the consequences that must attend those gifts—including the willingness to be sacrificed for the sake of the greater good, as occurs with the Leader and Ushikawa, and very nearly with Aomame and Tengo as well.

In many of these instances, the "gifted" person possesses some physical sign of his or her ability. The clairvoyant from *A Wild Sheep Chase* has ears so exquisite that those who see them are likely to experience spontaneous orgasms. Okada Tōru bears a mark on his cheek. Tengo and the Leader have their extraordinary size; Aomame, the imbalance in the size of her breasts (and her frightening grimaces); and Ushikawa, his ugliness. Haida has the scar on his neck, while Midorikawa carries something in a pouch with him wherever he goes.

In *Tazaki Tsukuru,* the physical manifestation of this special quality is symbolized through a discussion of the "sixth finger." As Tazaki and Sakamoto, his assistant at the construction company, chat with a stationmaster one day, the conversation drifts to the sorts of things that have been discovered left behind on trains. Among the more ordinary forgotten items one might expect are some rather unusual ones—wigs, a false leg, a box of cremated bones, a live pit viper, and even a dead human fetus in a Boston Bag. One of the more mysterious discoveries in recent memory, the stationmaster tells Tazaki, was two severed fingers floating in a jar of formaldehyde. Thinking this might be part of some crime, the station employees informed the police and were later told that these two fingers had likely been surgically removed from someone who was born with one additional finger on each hand. As it turns out, having an additional finger on each hand is not particularly unusual; perhaps one person in five hundred is born this way. In most instances, however, worrying about what others will say, parents of such children arrange for early amputation. This leads to a discussion of the relative pros and cons of having additional fingers; in evolutionary terms, is it an advantage or a disadvantage? Tazaki speculates that for a pianist, an extra finger might be quite helpful, and suddenly he has the wild idea that the pouch carried by Midorikawa might have contained the preserved remains of his own sixth fingers, symbols of his own "gift."

So, what *are* the advantages to having a sixth finger on each hand? What are the advantages to *any* of the "gifts" with which Murakami's extraordinary characters have been endowed? Did clairvoyance prove an advantage to "Kiki" or "Yuki"? Did Boku/Watashi's gift of mental calculation bring him satisfaction in *Hard-Boiled Wonderland and the End of the World*? What were the ultimate fates of Nakata and Saeki? As one runs the gamut of these "gifted" characters, it is difficult not to conclude that, with very few exceptions, their "gift" is more of a curse.

This motif remains largely intact in *Tazaki Tsukuru* as well. Among the characters, it is not difficult to identify the four who possess something special, beyond the abilities of ordinary people, as Shiro, Haida, Midorikawa, and, of course, Tazaki himself. All four of these characters have in common a connection with the world of death. Midorikawa, as carrier of the "death token," stares that world in the face daily, awaiting its advent; Haida, as suggested previously, is probably dead already; Shiro, for an unspecified period of time—perhaps her whole life—has been communicating with the world of the dead, gradually moving herself closer to it; and Tazaki, following his expulsion from the group, carries a mental imprint of the abyss into which he stared for five long months. And while their "gifts" are not as dramatic as those of Aomame, Tengo, or the Leader, they are nonetheless remarkable. For Shiro, the gift is musical; what she lacks in mechanical technique she makes up for in feeling and emotion as she plays the deceptively difficult *Le Mar du Pays*. Midorikawa possesses the ability to see the "light" and "color" that surrounds all people—in short, he can see their souls. Haida, like Okada Tōru, is able to divide his flesh and spirit and thus to move beyond the boundaries of ordinary human thought. And what is Tazaki's "gift"? It takes him the better part of the novel to realize it, but his gift is to be an empty container, a refuge for those who need a safe place to rest as they struggle through the world, the metaphysical sign for which is his sexual climax. This is why Tazaki has attracted, and been attracted to, women who were "on their way somewhere else," but also why Sara—and perhaps Tazaki's previous sexual partners—can sense his emptiness when she holds him, for it is in this moment of intense physical and emotional release that his emptiness is most clearly revealed:

> Maybe I am an empty human, with no content, Tsukuru thought. But it's just because I don't have anything inside me that I've had people come to stay with me, even just for a little while. Like a solitary, nocturnal bird needs the attic of some uninhabited house to rest in during the day. The birds probably

> appreciate that empty, gloomy, quiet space. If that were true, Tsukuru thought, he ought to rejoice in his emptiness. (245)

This is not easy, for Sara, a woman he truly loves, is not looking for a temporary refuge; she wants a permanent structure, a "station" of her own, and she wants Tazaki to build it for her with his own hands.

But Tazaki's gift cannot be cast aside so lightly, for its true beneficiaries are not the living but the dead; his true function is to provide a refuge for the souls of Haida, Shiro, and even Midorikawa, whose physical vessels are gone. Giving himself to Sara will mean stepping away from these shadows of his past and moving boldly into the future. Returning to Haida's duality, Tazaki must choose to respect the boundaries of thought or, alternately, choose to break free of them. Either will require an act of courage and sacrifice.

Forbidden Dreams from "Over There"

It has become clear that *Colorless Tsukuru Tazaki and His Years of Pilgrimage* contains many of the same structures, themes, and motifs found in previous Murakami fiction, and while the "other world" remains, as it does in *Norwegian Wood,* largely unexplored in this work, always lurking just "over there," that it nonetheless plays a key role in this narrative is beyond dispute. In its close juxtapositioning of "this side" and "over there," its revival of the "nostalgic image" (Haida—"Mr. Gray"—could be read as a rather unsubtle projection of Tazaki's memories of "Miss White" and "Miss Black"), its exploration of the tension between inner and outer "selves," this work does indeed, as Andō says, "show us where Murakami has been."

But *Tazaki Tsukuru* also places a new emphasis on dreams and their function, not merely as flashes of our inner minds nor even messages from the gods, but as a powerful means to constitute new realities. In the pages that follow, then, we will explore some of the more prominent dreams, including the dream that Shiro is suspected to have had, that drive this narrative forward.

Dreams are not new to Murakami fiction, but they have developed, much like the metaphysical world itself, from a curiosity, somewhat peripheral to the primary structure of the work, into an essential part of the narrative as Murakami's fiction has progressed.

We see this clearly when contrasting Murakami's early dream portrayals with his more recent work. *A Wild Sheep Chase,* for instance, includes a scene in which the protagonist falls asleep in the back of a limousine. He dreams of a cow carrying an electric fan, which the cow offers to trade to him for a pair of pliers. And while the protagonist philosophizes on the "symbolic" content of dreams, readers are apt to conclude—rightly, I think—that this absurdist dream has no particular meaning or necessity in the story, unless it is symbolic of the protagonist's equally absurd quest for the Sheep.

Dreams can also serve as harbingers of the approach of the metaphysical world. In the short story "Nemuri" (1989; translated as "Sleep"), a woman dreams that an old man stands at the end of her bed, pouring water over her feet from a jug that seems never to run dry. As the woman begins to fear that her feet will eventually rot away, she awakens and soon realizes that she no longer needs to sleep. In all likelihood, however, she is asleep still, and the life she leads now is merely part of the same dream, so indistinguishable from her waking, everyday life that she cannot tell the difference. In this story, then, a dream is used to signal the onset of permanent entrapment in the "other world," echoing the fate of the protagonist of *Hard-Boiled Wonderland and the End of the World.* In "Sleep," however, the endless dream leads the woman to the realization that her life as a wife and mother has itself been little more than a very dull dream; it "awakens" the inner self she has kept suppressed out of consideration for the demands of that role, and in many ways strikes her as preferable to her waking life.

Dreams begin to play a much more significant role in *The Wind-Up Bird Chronicle,* as we have already seen, and to some extent they do reveal certain key points in the novel. Okada Tōru's erotic dreams about Kanō Creta—in one dream she fellates him, while in another they have intercourse—demonstrate his own repressed desires, much as Tazaki Tsukuru's dreams do for him, but they also foreground his prudish refusal to engage in suggestive talk with the "telephone woman," who is actually Kumiko, trying desperately to reveal to him the raging sexual desire that lurks in her inner self. Tōru's mulish refusal to read these signs—to acknowledge her sexuality as well as his own—keeps Kumiko in the limbo of the unconscious hotel.

We also find dreams playing an important role in *The Sputnik Sweetheart,* in which a young novelist named Sumire travels to the

Greek islands and disappears. Her best friend, K., a young man, goes hunting for her, his only clue a set of notes she has left behind. In them she describes a vivid dream about her long-lost mother, beckoning to her from atop a high tower. Sumire climbs the many stairs to reach the top of the tower, only to find her mother trapped in a tube in the floor, looking up at her. Her mother wishes to convey something vital to her, but as she begins to speak, she is sucked into the hole and disappears. K. finally concludes that Sumire must have gone into that hole herself, into the "other world," presumably to find her mother.

While dreams in Murakami fiction are not always sexual, as this discussion demonstrates, the release of sexual energy does nonetheless prove a dominant theme in many cases. We have already seen this theme used to advantage in *Kafka on the Shore,* wherein Kafka's dream of raping "Sakura," the girl he fantasizes to be his long-lost sister, leads on a metaphysical level to her taking on that role for him, much as his seduction of Saeki forces her to take on the role of his mother. Kafka's dream is particularly significant in that it enacts the deliberate transgression of a sexual taboo—incest—thus revealing Kafka's darker "inner self," fulfilling its depraved, hitherto suppressed libido.

It is not my intention here to attempt a definition of dreams; such matters lie well beyond the scope of this discussion and are best left to professional scholars of the mind. We might note in passing that Jung suggested a "compensatory" function to dreams, that is, that they assist the dreamer in managing psychic overloads that result from events that occur in waking life. For Jung, dreams are the result of psychic energy that rises to the surface when the compensatory content is too intense for the inner mind to handle.[11] This content is frequently grounded in desires (often sexual in nature) that may not be confronted in the waking world. Citing Freud, Jung notes that "the wishes which form the dream-thought are never desires which one openly admits to oneself, but desires that are repressed because of their painful character; and it is because they are excluded from conscious reflection in the waking state that they float up, indirectly, in dreams."[12]

This assessment agrees with my own contention that dreams, briefly stated, express the dreamer's deepest desires as well as his or her worst fears, and in this sense they mirror, on the individual level, the nature and function of mythology. This, no doubt, is one reason that dreams, like mythology, frequently contain taboo content, the difference being that whereas in mythology taboos are expressed in a prohibitive manner, in dreams taboos are enacted freely, without retribution, for they express the desire of the inner self—the baser side of our psyche—which in the dreamscape is permitted to have its way.

And yet, if dreams express (and in effect, reveal to us, the dreamers) our deepest fears and most powerful desires, taboo and otherwise, it must also be said that these are precisely what attract us within the dream world. Dreaming of a "forbidden" sexual act we are apt, in our dreams, to feel the tug of our waking conscience, to fear waking social mechanisms (the concern about being seen, of "getting caught"), yet we are also inexorably drawn to that very act, precisely because it *is* forbidden. In a similar way, when pursued by terrifying demons, threatened by monsters, frightened of a dark and forbidding place, we feel the conflicting urges of flight and fascination; should we run, or should we stop and gaze upon what frightens us? In fact, we often bring what frightens us into being simply by imagining it, initiating a willing confrontation, an expression of our inner self's fascination with those things that lurk in the pitch-black depths of our own mind. We peer into the dark mouth of the cave, down the stairs of the basement, around the next corner, knowing that something awful lurks there. Yet we cannot *not* look. . . .

We see this fixation on desire and fear played out in the various dreams that drive the narrative of *Colorless Tsukuru Tazaki and His Years of Pilgrimage,* as well. There are three dreams in particular that relate to Tazaki himself, as well as the implied dream in which Shiro is raped, that not only carry the narrative forward but in fact *create* the new realities in which each character must now live. For Tazaki these are the dream of the flesh-spirit woman, his erotic dream involving Shiro-Kuro-Haida, and his dream of playing the piano at the end of the novel. We will close this final chapter by looking in detail at these "forbidden" dreams from "over there" in order to determine what they reveal to Tazaki about himself, and how they function to create him and the world around him.

The first dream, in which Tazaki meets a woman he does not know but for whom he feels uncontrollable desire, is important for two reasons: first, because it establishes the idea in his mind of separating flesh and spirit, a key concept throughout this novel; and second, because it introduces him to the sensation of jealousy, an emotion stemming from (unfulfilled) desire. These two issues are, of course, linked for him, since the very fact of separating flesh and spirit means that it is possible for him to possess one without the other, and he senses the meaninglessness of such possession. The woman herself *probably* represents Shiro herself (rendered unrecognizable through Tazaki's suppression of his desire for her), who is of course unavailable to Tazaki either in flesh *or* spirit owing to the unspoken rules of the group against pairing off, but also due to her powerful aversion to sexual contact. She can therefore only appear before him in the dreamscape. An alternative reading would be that the dream woman is both Shiro and Kuro, one an object of (suppressed) physical desire, the other a friend; one could even read the woman as Kuro alone, offering Tazaki either sex or friendship but not both. In the end, however, the identity of the woman is not the point of the dream; rather, its purpose is to show Tazaki the connection between desire and jealousy, both of which exist forcefully within his inner self.

This is why Tazaki's claims of unfamiliarity with jealousy should catch our attention, for it would imply first that he has never consciously felt desire, and second, that he has never experienced the frustration of not being able to act upon or even express that desire. Given the utopian nature of that perfect, hermetically sealed circle in which the five friends exist, one may easily imagine the disruptions that would have resulted had jealousy been introduced into it.[13] And yet, by forcing his true feelings deep underground, Tazaki in effect gives greater strength to the "compensatory contents" of his inner world, which now reach an intensity so great that they are forced out not only into his dreams but into the waking world as well. Indeed, it is this intensity of emotion that finally brings about Tazaki's transformation into an other—his own other—in the conscious world. His transformative experience of jealousy is his first act of rebellion against the rigid structures of the System—the circle of friends—that continues to govern him. Nevertheless, this dream is constructive rather than destructive, for although it destroys the old Tazaki, with his slavish adherence to social convention, at the same time it occasions his rebirth as a new and stronger individual. As noted earlier, this new and stronger individual is reflected physically as well as emotionally, as Tazaki himself can see when he looks into the mirror at a man rather than a boy. This is the new reality that has been brought into existence by his first dream.

The second dream is actually part of a series of recurring erotic dreams for Tazaki that, until the sudden intrusion of Haida, have featured Shiro and Kuro alone. Within this recurring dream we find certain constants that reveal much to Tazaki. We note first that both girls appear in every dream; it is never just one or the other. This reflects the perfection of the utopian circle in which all are equally members. And yet, while both girls caress him, when the time comes for his climax, he *always* ejaculates into Shiro, never Kuro. This causes him some concern. "Why did it always have to be Shiro?" he wonders. "The two of them ought to have been equal. The two of them *should have been* one existence" (117; emphasis in the original). We read in this the rather unsubtle message from his inner mind that the two women are *not* equal, but Tazaki's conscious mind in these instances is no wiser than Okada Tōru's, for he cannot see the most obvious things in front of him. It is not until he meets Kuro in Finland, in fact, that Tazaki is able to admit openly to her—and to himself—that he had loved Shiro. By then it is, of course, too late, and Tazaki comes to believe that the net result of suppressing his true feelings was to unleash a far less dainty version of himself on the hapless Shiro in the dream world. It is a simple revelation but one that reminds Tazaki of the risks of sacrificing his true desires in order to conform to the rest of society. This is also the quintessential Murakami message.

If this is the case, what is the purpose of Haida's sudden appearance at the end of the second dream? Here, too, we see Haida as an object of both fascination and discomfiture for Tazaki, a part of his inner self and an expression of his most deeply suppressed desire. Whether we choose to read that desire as a homoerotic one or merely as a nostalgic displacement of Kuro and Shiro, it proves useful to Tazaki, whose determined suppression of desire has led in his waking life very nearly to a *literal* mortification of the flesh, and in his dreamscape to homosexual fantasy. This is what prompts Tazaki to seek out his first sexual encounter with a woman, "not out of passion, nor because he especially liked her, nor even to relieve the daily loneliness he felt," but rather "in order to prove to himself that he was not homosexual, that he was capable of ejaculating into an actual, flesh-and-blood woman, not just in dreams" (133). Tazaki's anxiety over his sexual orientation is not particularly unusual considering his youth and the nature of the dream he has had, but in the end it will not matter where his sexual orientation lies; what does matter is that this second dream has driven him out of the world "over there," back to this side, where he begins to engage in actual relationships with real women instead of merely with his memories of the lost women in his dreamscape. We see in this instance, too, an expression of the decision Tazaki must make as "empty vessel," whether to provide haven for living souls of the present or lost souls from the past. It is significant that once Tazaki begins a physical relationship in the waking world, his erotic dreams featuring Kuro and Shiro vanish.

Thus far, then, we have seen Tazaki's first dream act as a means of rebirth for his character, as well as reveal to him emotions—desire, jealousy—that lurk deep within his inner self. It also demonstrates for him the possibility of separating spirit and flesh. The second dream, on the other hand, spurs Tazaki into sexual action, showing him once again the various objects of his desire but at the same time driving him out of the metaphysical realm to enact his desires on actual people. These two "forbidden dreams" have largely positive effects on Tazaki, guiding him in the construction of both a new outer self and a new sexuality to go with that self. While he does nail down his elusive sexual orientation, however, he fails to find lasting fulfillment with the various women he encounters, for none of them fully displace the memories of the past that still lurk deep within his heart—until Sara comes along, that is.

Tazaki's third dream once again connects him to Shiro, and in turn connects her to Midorikawa, and through him, to Haida. In this dream, Tazaki sits at a piano (an instrument he does not actually play in waking life), performing an impossibly complex piano sonata for an unappreciative audience. Seated beside him, turning the pages of the score for him, is a woman in a black dress, but though he is curious about who she might be, he cannot take his eyes from the score to look at her face. Just prior to awakening from the dream he notices that she has six fingers on her hand, connecting her to his mental image of Midorikawa—and thus to Haida, who has "created" Midorikawa for him through his narrative. The presence of Shiro is implied, first through the piano itself, and second through the evocation of Midorikawa/Haida, the latter of whom is linked to Shiro through the second dream. Whether Shiro actually had six fingers on each hand is of little consequence; the superfluous fingers are merely a symbol—not a literary one but a symbol within Tazaki's own mind—of the ambiguous nature of being "gifted." One important message from this dream, then, is that Shiro, too, was "gifted."

There is, however, a more important revelation here, one that carries the first and second dreams to their logical conclusion. If those dreams showed Tazaki the absurdity of suppressing his natural sexual and emotional desires in the name of protecting an essentially fallacious utopian dream, then the third dream, at its most basic level, demonstrates the impossibility of perfect communication, of perfect human understanding, even under the most ideal conditions. Tazaki plays his part flawlessly, and yet his audience cannot understand the music, causing him later to reflect that "life was like a complicated musical score. . . . even if you could get all the notes right and produce the correct sounds, there was no guarantee that listeners would get the right meanings and assign the correct values to them" (343). And yet, in spite of the impossibility of conveying exactly what the music is supposed to communicate, of his audience's rejection of his efforts, and of the countless distractions, in his dream Tazaki is determined to play this piece through to the end. Herein he expresses a new variation on Midorikawa's final admonition to press on with the act of living, the search for meaning, even in the face of the mundane and the frivolous. This final dream suggests that Tazaki has finally "got it."

But *what,* exactly, has he understood? Through his various dreams and the self-reflection they engender, Tazaki discovers by novel's end that meaning in life lies not in the perpetuation of perfection, the endless preservation of harmony and stasis (which is impossible in any case), but in the acceptance of imperfection and the celebration of hardship and discord as catalysts for growth and change:

> At that moment he was at last able to accept it. In the deepest part of his soul, Tazaki Tsukuru understood. People's hearts were not connected only by harmony. They were, rather, deeply bound together by injury. They were joined by pain, by their fragility. There was no tranquility that did not contain cries of grief, no forgiveness without spilled blood, no acceptance that did not pass through acute loss. This was what truly lay at the root of harmony. (307)

This passage is, in my opinion, one of the most important in the entire work and, indeed, in the overall body of Murakami fiction, for it clearly expresses an exceedingly simple idea that is found in almost every major Murakami work in one form or another: that imperfection is not only permissible but *desirable.* It is this imperfection that Rat seeks to protect when he destroys himself and the Sheep at the end of *A Wild Sheep Chase,* the same complication and turmoil from which Kizuki and Naoko flee directly into the arms of death in *Norwegian Wood,* the same conflicts that Okada Tōru tries to restore in Kumiko at the end of *The Wind-Up Bird Chronicle.* And why is it desirable? Simply because it is our imperfections, our quirks and flaws, even our weakness and mediocrity, that make us unique and uniquely human. It is through our attempts to solve the puzzles of our lives and the mysteries of our world that we grow and develop. Carried but a step further, it might be read as Murakami's understanding of the purpose of reading/writing literature, recalling the first words of *Hear the Wind Sing:* "There is no such thing as a perfect text." Extended beyond the scope of this narrative, we might even find in it an allegorical comment on contemporary Japanese society and its continued efforts to project an image of tranquility and order, when in fact these, too, are utopian.

Shiro's Forbidden Dreams

One of the major ironies in *Tazaki Tsukuru* is that while we are never entirely certain that Shiro's dreams actually took place, we can nonetheless see their effects rippling through the narrative, driving it forward. I would argue, in fact, that Shiro's implicit dreams create more "realities" than any others in the novel. This, of course, is accomplished with a little help from her friends.

Chronologically speaking, Shiro's first dream begins everything. As noted earlier, Shiro claims that she dropped by Tazaki's apartment while visiting Tokyo, that he slipped something into her drink, and then forced himself on her while she was helpless. Each of the three remaining friends gives Tazaki essentially the same story, and each one asserts that Shiro meant her story, that she believed it. "'Yuzu truly believed to the end that this had happened to her,'" Kuro tells Tazaki, "'that you had forcibly taken away her virginity at your place in Tokyo. For her *that became the last version of reality*'" (295; my emphasis).

But it very nearly becomes the "last version of reality" for everyone else as well. Returning to my original theme in this volume, we must confront the fact that Shiro's dream is constructed of language, as is the narrative through which she passes it along to her other friends. And despite the fact that none of the three remaining friends entirely believes the story, it nevertheless has very real consequences, not merely of a temporary kind, but consequences that lead, as Tazaki himself sees it, to the "death" of the old him and the "birth" of the new. We could hardly ask for a more dramatic example of the constitutive function of language. What makes Shiro's dream exceptional, however, is the fact that Tazaki himself eventually joins himself to it, constructing his own role from the imagination, quite as if he truly *were* channeling Shiro's spirit through himself:

> Even if it were no more than a dream, he could not help feeling that he was in some way responsible. And not just her rape. Her murder, too. On that rainy night in May, *something* in himself, without his ever knowing about it, had gone off to Hamamatsu and strangled her lovely, swan-like neck.
>
> "Open up, will you? I need to talk to you." The scene in which he knocks on her apartment door floated up in his mind. His raincoat is black and wet, heavy with the scent of the night rain.
>
> "Tsukuru?" Yuzu says.
>
> "There's something I've got to talk over with you. It's important. That's why I've come to Hamamatsu. It won't take long. I want you to open the door," he says. He continues speaking to the closed door. "Sorry to come without warning. But I figured you'd never see me if I got in touch first."
>
> After a moment's hesitation, Yuzu silently releases the chain. In his pocket, his right hand tightly grips the length of cord. (317)

Is this vivid scene the result of an overactive imagination, or is Tazaki "remembering" the constructed memory of Shiro herself? The answer is, of course, both. Shiro's imagination, seeking to find some solution to the dilemma of growing up, facing sexuality, constructs the narrative of Tazaki as monster, but that narrative is grounded in her own suppressed sexuality, held back by the same "mortification of the flesh" that traps Tazaki himself; once that narrative is released into the wider world, however, it develops a life of its own, co-opting

Tazaki's own inner self in the process. If, meanwhile, we are willing to bear in mind that time, particularly that connected with the metaphysical world, does not always move in a straight line nor in just one direction, there is no particular difficulty in seeing how Tazaki's inner self is written into the role of Shiro's rapist—and her murderer—in retrospect. Through the suspension of physical time in the metaphysical realm, Shiro's narrative succeeds in placing the trial before the crime, and for Tazaki, the conviction invents the convict.

Tazaki Tsukuru does indeed show us where Murakami has been and where he is headed. We see in this work yet another instance of the "other world" exerting its influence on "this side," and at the same time we see how that influence has grown less destructive as Murakami's heroes press forward with the process of redefining themselves independently of established convention. The same "dark inner self" seen in works like *The Wind-Up Bird Chronicle* and *Kafka on the Shore* remains a powerful force in that process, and while its purpose still seems to be domination of the outer self, that domination takes on a liberating aspect that began with Kafka's exit from the forest, continued to develop with Aomame's rescue of Tengo at the conclusion of *1Q84,* and reaches its most explicit expression in *Tazaki Tsukuru.* The target, as we have demonstrated, is the "same" utopian illusion we saw in *A Wild Sheep Chase,* and yet not quite "the same," for it is a much more realistic portrayal of that illusion, one that is played out among countless groups of friends in countless schools throughout the world. As with Kafka, Aomame, and Tengo, the final goal for Tazaki Tsukuru is simply to grow up and, in so doing, to outgrow the childish notion that *any* dreams from "over there" should ever truly be forbidden.

EPILOGUE

The Roads ~~Not~~ Taken

> I'm just a novelist. If I write something acceptable to myself, whether it has a reason or not, that is enough.
>
> —Murakami Haruki, *Wakai dokusha no tame no tanpen shōsetsu annai*

IN ADDITION TO HIS WORK AS A NOVELIST, Murakami is a widely acclaimed writer of nonfiction as well as a highly prolific translator. Aside from the works of literary journalism discussed in chapter 4 (which clearly have social and political agendas attached), his nonfiction output includes travelogues, collections of essays, miscellanies, and even a literary guide for young readers; his work as a translator focuses on English-language texts by recent or contemporary authors, from F. Scott Fitzgerald to John Irving. Since in this epilogue I intend to make a few remarks about these and other genres that did not make it into this volume, I should also note that Murakami has written a number of fictional works that are clearly tongue-in-cheek, collaborative works that combine the talents of *manga* artists and the author's own creative genius, such as *Hitsuji otoko no kurisumasu* (1985; The Sheepman's Christmas), with illustrations by Sasaki Maki; and *Fushigi na toshokan* (2008; The weird library), also by Murakami and Sasaki, in which the Sheepman returns as a character. Both works might be read as modern fairy tales, and while the stories (like most fairy tales) have a slightly dark and sinister underpinning, readers can hardly help but be charmed and amused by the "cute" Sheepman, so different from the filthy, unshaven one whose illustration appears in *A Wild Sheep Chase*. Works like the two mentioned here are, one suspects, meant to siphon off some of the creative energies for which Murakami finds no outlet in his more serious fiction, but they also reveal, somewhere in the dark interior of his inner mind, the heart of a writer of children's fiction.

Murakami's travelogues, on the other hand, are charming, often lighthearted, and always fun to read. *Moshi bokura no kotoba ga uisukii de atta nara* (1999; If our words were whiskey) is a photographic journey through Ireland and Scotland, with photographs by Murakami's wife, Yōko. In his opening remarks, titled "Maegaki no yō na mono to shite" ("Something like a foreword"), Murakami writes that

> in any journey, to a greater or lesser extent, there is an underlying theme. While in Shikoku, I decided to destroy myself with daily infusions of *udon;* in Niigata I determinedly tried to taste every kind of the profoundly pure *saké* produced in the area. Seeing as many sheep as possible was my goal in Hokkaido, whereas my crossing of the United States included an attempt to eat as many pancakes as possible (once was enough, so I wanted to eat pancakes until I was sick of them).[1]

In *Henkyō/kinkyō* (1998; Frontiers near and far), the author details his journeys around Japan, other parts of Asia, and North America. Choosing just one of these journeys at random—his "camping trip" to an uninhabited island in the Inland Sea of Japan, just eight hundred meters from the coast—we find both humor and pathos. Traveling to this island by boat with the photographer Matsumura Eizō, Murakami expects this to be a pleasure trip but soon learns that deserted islands are not resorts. After setting up their tent, the two men turn to the beautiful waters; Murakami is immediately stung by jellyfish (stirred up by a recent typhoon), while Matsumura, walking in the shallow surf, manages to cut his foot on a razor-sharp oyster shell, and in the process of steadying himself, does the same to the palm of his hand on a rock. He also ruins his prized vintage Leica camera. After using up their stores of first-aid supplies disinfecting and binding Matsumura's wounds ("It's not like you can just swim over to a nearby drugstore,"[2] Murakami quips), the two settle in to eat and watch the sunset. But with the sunset come millions of hungry insects. . . .

Even in works like this, we find echoes of the author's fictional world. As the two men take refuge inside a zip-up tent from the myriad types of insects that invade every part of their campsite, Murakami reflects that a deserted island has its very own ecosystem: "we didn't notice it so much in daylight, but when the sun went down and the place turned pitch-black, we were fully enveloped by *it*."[3] In these works, we gain a vivid sense of the sights, sounds, and smells that accompany the author's journeys into unknown places.

As an essayist, Murakami has been active almost from the start of his career. *The Scrap: Natsukashi no 1980-nendai* (1987; The scrap: the nostalgic 1980s) contains a series of interesting vignettes, each of two pages or so, followed by the author's impressions of Tokyo Disneyland (which opened in 1983), and a strange segment titled "Orinpikku ni amari kankei nai orinpikku nikki" (Olympic diary with very little to do with the Olympics). This work, which seems to move more or less at random across some of the events, themes, and figures of the 1980s (Reagan's politics, Linda Ronstadt, paparazzi, and so on), might qualify as a modern-day "pillow book" of sorts, similar to the miscellanies of Heian Japan (of which the best known is surely Sei Shōnagon's *Makura no sōshi,* or "pillow book"). Others are less easily classified; Murakami himself does not know exactly what to call his series of vignettes with Itoi Shigesato titled *Yume de aimashō* (Let's meet in a dream), stating at the outset (a little helplessly) that "it is not a short story collection, nor a collection of essays, nor even a gathering of random manuscripts . . . it is, from the start, a book that houses weirdness."[4] The book's organization is equally puzzling: beginning with "A," the entries continue in alphabetical order to the end of the Japanese syllabary at "Wan." It is little wonder Murakami had no idea what to call it; reaching the end of the book, the reader is likely to be just as puzzled as to what he or she has just finished reading. Works like these are primarily pleasure works, some lying more than others in the realm of "pop" culture, while others would likely make good punishments to be inflicted on disobedient graduate students. . . .

Other nonfictional works by Murakami *are* intended to be instructional, albeit in a somewhat less than formal manner. The author's 1997 work *Wakai dokusha no tame no tanpen shōsetsu annai* (Guide to short fiction for young readers) contains brief introductions to and impressions of specific works by six modern Japanese writers: Yoshiki Junnosuke (1924–94), Kojima Nobuo (1915–2006), Yasuoka Shōtarō (1920–2013), Shōno Junzō (1921–2009), Maruya

Saiichi (1925–2012), and Hasegawa Shirō (1909–87). But Murakami is clear—and characteristically humble—about the scope and nature of his "introduction" to Japanese literature:

> I'm not a literary scholar nor a critic. I'm just a novelist. If I write something acceptable to myself, whether it has a reason or not, that is enough. That's how I am. I don't know any of the difficult terminology used to explain literature, and while it's nothing to brag about, my understanding of literary theory is pretty much zero. . . . this is not literary criticism, nor is it a message or a statement. It's just me, as a novelist, saying "here are some works I read and found to be interesting," an ego-centric "personal guide for reading."[5]

As the author further notes in his introductory remarks, this "guide" grew out of the classes he taught at Princeton and Tufts universities in the early 1990s, but one strongly suspects that it was also part of his overall push after 1995 to be more committed to the Japanese society that had made him famous (particularly its younger members), and his concerns about it in the post-Aum era. As I noted in the introduction to this book, Murakami has never shown much interest in playing the "typical" role of the novelist in Japan—appearing on talk shows to offer his intellectual insights to society's problems, engaging in literary debates, serving on literary prize committees—but he seems to have been comfortable with this less formal, more personalized function of helping young readers become engaged.

One aspect of Murakami's writing that does merit further study—and has been receiving quite a lot of attention in Japan in recent years—is his voluminous body of translation work. One might imagine that the author's efforts in this regard are secondary to his work as a novelist—I freely confess to such an inclination myself—but in terms of actual quantity, as Miyawaki Toshifumi points out, this is not wholly true: "Whether he realizes it or not," writes Miyawaki, "in terms of volume Murakami is an established translator. He has done that many translations. As a writer he is a rarity. Of course there is nothing unusual in itself about a writer engaging in translation, but I cannot think of another writer in the world who has sent more translations out into the world than Murakami."[6] The list of authors whose works Murakami has translated includes some illustrious names, to be sure: in addition to Fitzgerald and Irving, noted above, we may add Truman Capote, Raymond Chandler, Raymond Carver, Tim O'Brien, J. D. Salinger, Paul Theroux, and many more. Not surprisingly, his translations gain considerably more attention than those of other translators, even those who make this their sole profession. Niimoto Ryōichi points out the unusual fact that new translations by Murakami usually bear his own name on the cover (as translator) in print quite as large as that of the original author.[7] This means, in essence, that Murakami's name (as novelist as well as translator) is used to market works by writers who may be otherwise unknown to Japanese readers. In one sense this is a good thing; Murakami's strong following in Japan will thus serve to expose Japanese readers to a variety of Western authors who might otherwise never have seen the light of day there. In another sense, however, it is disquieting, for if readers flock to Murakami's translations over those of others, does this not mean that he has the potential to exert undue influence over what is read in translation by the Japanese public? Insofar as Murakami (like most translators) chooses works and authors that interest him personally, we see the possibility that a whole generation of Japanese readers—particularly young readers—will simply end up mirroring Murakami's own taste in Western fiction, to the exclusion of other, equally deserving writers and their works. Still, faced with the equally likely possibility that such readers will never read any Western literature at all, this may well be the lesser of the two evils.

As to the quality of Murakami's translations, this is generally thought to be rather good but also heavily colored by the author's own writing style and worldview—again, probably like most translators. One of the more virulent debates about Murakami's own fiction centers on its *mukokuseki* (nationality-less) style, as I noted in my introduction; in other words, the fact that there seems to be nothing particularly "Japanese" about it stylistically, save that it happens to be written in that language. This is not unique to Murakami, according to Miyawaki, who argues that it merely reflects "the lifestyle of the vast majority of contemporary Japanese,"[8] and this is no doubt true, but it does raise an important issue that every translator must confront at some point, namely, whether to preserve a text's "foreignness" through something closer to literal translation (wholly literal translation being virtually impossible and certainly unadvisable most of the time), or to "naturalize" the text to the point that readers have no sense of its origins as they read.[9] Murakami tends somewhat toward the former in his preservation of sentence length and structure, as well as his use of pronouns (in which he often challenges the Japanese idiom),[10] but toward the latter in his utilization of certain linguistic mannerisms that are clearly part of his own personal repertoire. Numano Mitsuyoshi notes, for instance, that in translating Capote's "Children on Their Birthdays" (1949), Murakami renders Capote's phrase "From their faces you would have thought that they'd never seen a girl before" as *sono kao o mitara, kono kodomotachi wa umarete kono kata onna no ko to iu mono o ichido mo me ni shita koto ga nai n ja nai ka, to anata wa omotta koto darō;*[11] it is the use of *anata wa omotta* for "you would have thought" in particular that catches our attention, for it is in Japanese an extraordinarily awkward and unnatural expression. In one sense this strategy preserves something peculiarly "American" about the language of the original, giving Japanese readers a distinct sense of reading something foreign, exotic, and fulfilling what Walter Benjamin argued was the only truly legitimate function of translation, namely, to expose the gaps and differences between various languages.[12] Murakami also leans toward literalism in his handling of Holden Caulfield's asides in Salinger's *Catcher in the Rye,* using the second-person pronoun *kimi* ("you," familiar/intimate), but who is being addressed here? "Murakami himself told [translator] Shibata Motoyuki in one of their discussions that he is acutely conscious of the 'you' that exists opposite the narrating 'I,'"[13] says Numano, but whether this "you" represents the reader, another character, or merely a voice in Holden's own head (something like "the Boy Called Crow," perhaps?) is unclear. On reflection, even native speakers of English who use the pronoun "you" in this manner probably do not really know whom they are addressing.

On the other hand, some of Murakami's favorite phrases *do* manage to infiltrate these translations. Numano cites Murakami's continued use of an old favorite, *yareyare,* an expression of mild exasperation, as well as *iyahaya,* in both Salinger (for Holden's frequent curses) and in Raymond Carver (for roughly the same sorts of words), to some extent naturalizing the texts for Japanese readers with such commonplace expressions. Their use also lends these texts, however, a particularly "Murakami-esque" flavor, and for regular readers of Murakami fiction, Koshikawa suggests, serves to lessen for readers the sense of *iwakan,* or "incongruity,"[14] or what Russian Formalists might have termed "differentiation," in the translated texts.

Further discussion on this topic is best left for another time, and another text. Here it will suffice to conclude that Murakami Haruki the translator is quite as creative and innovative as Murakami Haruki the novelist, and in that spirit I suggest that the "dark, inner world" that informs so much of his fictional work comes significantly into play in his production of translations, travelogues, illustrated stories, and even his reader's guide. This could hardly be otherwise; insofar as his visions of the places he has seen, both in and out of his mind, remain as ever firmly grounded in his experiences, culture, and above all his language, that dark place "over there" will always be the final arbiter for any discourse he attempts.

This book has focused chiefly on Murakami's fictional works, and I believe this is appropriate. For it is in Murakami's fiction—particularly his long fiction—most of all that we catch a glimpse of his "other world," not merely as a grounding for other visions but as a fictional setting in its own right. By examining the most recurrent themes and motifs of that mysterious, metaphysical realm, we have begun in some manner to map that world, much as the protagonist of *Hard-Boiled Wonderland and the End of the World* maps "the Town" in which he is trapped. Such a diagram will serve, one hopes, as a template for deliberations on the nature of our own "dark, inner worlds." What truly lurks in the gloom of these metaphysical realms? To quote Bogart's final line from the film *The Maltese Falcon,* it is "the stuff that dreams are made of."

NOTES

Introduction

1. Murakami Haruki, "Yume no naka kara sekinin wa hajimaru," interview with *The Georgia Review,* Autumn 2005. Cited here from Murakami, *Yume o miru tame ni maiasa Boku wa mezameru no desu,* 333.

2. Murakami gave this speech, in English, on 15 February 2009, at the International Book Fair in Jerusalem. Available at http://www.salon.com/2009/02/20/haruki_murakami/.

3. I have been directly involved in these preparations as well, and this comment has been made more than once during our various discussions.

4. This is the final line of Murakami Haruki, *Kaze no uta o kike.*

5. Uchida, "Kyōkaisen to shishatachi to kitsune no koto," 174.

6. Rubin, *Haruki Murakami and the Music of Words,* 14–15. Readers interested in the personal life of Murakami are strongly encouraged to read this excellent work, for Rubin enjoys a close personal friendship with Murakami and probably knows him better, as a person, than any non-Japanese in the world. My own relationship with Murakami is strictly professional, and while I have had the good fortune to interview him several times, our discussions have focused chiefly on his writing, rather than his life.

7. Murakami Haruki, interview by author, 22 October 1994, Cambridge, Mass.

8. Rubin, *Haruki Murakami and the Music of Words,* 13.

9. Murakami, interview.

10. Ibid.

11. Murakami, *Yagate kanashiki gaikokugo,* 215.

12. These first responses came from the Gunzō Prize committee, which

named Murakami best new writer in 1979, launching his career. Cited in Tōyama, "Doitsu ni okeru gendai Nihon bungaku no juyō," 267.

13. Cf. ibid.; Kim, "Kankoku ni okeru Murakami Haruki no juyō to sono kontekusuto."

14. Ōe Kenzaburō, in Ishiguro and Ōe, "The Novelist in Today's World," 173.

15. Chang, "Taiwanjin no Murakami Haruki," 37–38.

16. Kim, "Kankoku ni okeru Murakami Haruki," 27–28.

17. Noted in Rubin, *Haruki Murakami and the Music of Words*, 36.

18. Koshikawa, Numano, and Niimoto, "Murakami Haruki-yaku o yomu," 286.

19. Kazamaru highlights this rhythmic quality in part through a side-by-side analysis of Murakami's translation of a work by Paul Auster and Shibata Motoyuki's rendering of the same piece. See Kazamaru, *Ekkyō suru "Boku,"* 244–45.

20. Murakami, interview.

21. Ibid.

22. Tanaka Masashi, "Naibu to gaibu o kasaneru sentaku," 22–23.

23. Kawai Toshio, *Murakami Haruki no "monogatari,"* 16.

24. Kawai Hayao, "Gūzen no shinjitsu," 311.

25. The Aum cult, originally grounded in acetic practices of yoga but taking its "philosophical" inspiration from the doomsday account in Revelations, as well as various occultist writings on the end of the world, became a major organization in Japan, boasting thousands of members. It has been designated a terrorist organization by Canada, the European Union, and the United States but continues to exist in Japan even following the sarin incident in 1995. For more on the organization's history, see Robert Jay Lifton, *Destroying the World in Order to Save It: Aum Shinrikyo, Apocalypse Violence, and the New Global Terrorism* (New York: Holt, 1999); and David E. Kapland and Andrew Marshall, *The Cult at the End of the World: The Terrifying Story of the Aum Doomsday Cult, from the Subways of Tokyo to the Nuclear Arsenals of Russia* (New York: Random House, 1996). For more on the revival of the cult, see Andrew Marshall, "It Gassed the Tokyo Subway, Microwaved Its Enemies and Tortured Its Members. So Why Is the Aum Cult Thriving?" *The Guardian*, July 14, 1999.

26. Murakami, *Andāguraundo*, 26.

27. Murakami, interview.

28. Murakami, *Andāguraundo*, 701.

29. Murakami, "Rongu intabyū," 16.

30. Kamata, *Shintai no uchūshi*, 12.

31. Iwamiya, *Shishunki o meguru bōken*, 97.

1. New Words, New Worlds

1. Toews, "Intellectual History after the Linguistic Turn," 881–82.
2. Ibid., 901–2.
3. Barnstone, *The Poetics of Translation,* 19.
4. Eco, *Foucault's Pendulum,* 189–90.
5. Ibid., 89–90.
6. Ibid., 168–69.
7. Ibid., 533.
8. Eco, *Baudolino,* 35; emphasis mine.
9. Ibid., 111.
10. Eco, *The Mysterious Flame of Queen Loanna,* 73.
11. Ibid., 419.
12. Interestingly, Saleem Sinai in *Midnight's Children,* following a head injury caused by artillery, loses track of his own name and attempts to bring it back by reciting his story: "it becomes apparent that he is struggling to recall something particular, something which refuses to return, which obstinately eludes him, so that he gets to the end without finding it . . . Padma, the buddha had forgotten his name" (Rushdie, *Midnight's Children,* 437).
13. Eco, *The Prague Cemetery,* 86.
14. Ibid., 77.
15. Ibid., 219. It is well known that the slogan *"arbeit macht frei"* was placed at the entrances to numerous Nazi concentration camps, including those at Auschwitz and Dachau. The expression "final solution" *(die Endlösung)* became synonymous with the Nazi plan to exterminate the Jews, a shortened version of Adolf Hitler's own phrase, "final solution to the Jewish question" *(Endlösung der Judenfrage).*
16. Ibid., 423.
17. Murakami, *1973-nen no pinbōru,* in *Murakami Haruki zensakuhin,* 1:126; hereafter *Murakami Haruki zensakuhin* is cited as *MHZ.*
18. Ibid., 1:135.
19. As will be noted in greater detail in the next chapter, this "half-asleep" place Naoko describes is part of the "other world."
20. Baudrillard, *The Illusion of the End,* 121–22.
21. Shimamura, "'Kuronosu' to no kōsō," 88.
22. Huxley, *Time Must Have a Stop,* 222.
23. Ibid., 253.
24. Ibid., 250–51.
25. Murakami, *Hitsuji o meguru bōken,* in *MHZ,* 2:23.
26. Murakami, *Dansu dansu dansu,* in *MHZ,* 7:282.
27. Ibid., 7:541.
28. Murakami, *Nejimakidori kuronikuru,* 2:235.

29. One might suggest, with justification, that Okada Tōru's healing activities, in which he sits passively in a dark room and permits psychologically traumatized women to lick a magical mark on his cheek, are a symbolic form of this; by receiving the ministrations of these women, who become active subjects to his passive object, Tōru in effect "reads" them, while also allowing them to "read" him, acknowledging their existence and restoring their sense of self. For more on this method of healing, see my reader's guide to this book, esp. 54–56; Strecher, *Murakami Haruki's* The Wind-Up Bird Chronicle. See also Rubin, *Haruki Murakami and the Music of Words,* esp. chapter 11.

30. In his *Meditations on First Philosophy,* René Descartes posits the "evil genius," a deceptive intelligence who tricks Descartes into believing that the world external to his mind is real, when in fact it—including Descartes himself—is all a figment of the evil genius's imagination. Interestingly, Carl Jung, after dreaming of a UFO, had a similar thought about interterrestrials: "Still half in the dream, the thought passed through my head: We always think that the UFOs are projections of ours. Now it turns out that we are their projections. I am projected by the magic lantern as C. G. Jung. But who manipulates the apparatus?" In Jung, *Memories, Dreams, Reflections,* 323.

31. Murakami has himself expressed dissatisfaction with the English term *shadow* for this complex idea, which may explain his more recent preference for terms like *kokoro* (heart/mind) and *tamashii* (soul).

32. Murakami, Yukawa Yutaka, and Koyama Tetsurō, "*Umibe no Kafka* o chūshin ni" in Murakami, *Yume o miru tame ni maiasa Boku wa mezameru no desu,*" 129.

33. Murakami, *Umibe no Kafka,* 1:290–91; hereafter page numbers are given parenthetically in the text.

34. Murakami, "Hibi idō suru jinzō no katachi o shita ishi," in Murakami, *Tōkyō kitanshū,* 141.

35. Ibid., 145.

36. Ibid., 147.

37. Murakami, "Shinagawa saru," in Murakami, *Tokyo kitanshū,* 202.

38. Murakami, *Shikisai o motanai Tazaki Tsukuru to, kare no junrei no toshi,* 60.

39. Murakami, *1Q84,* 1:274; hereafter page numbers are given parenthetically in the text. This type of ostracism, as I shall note at the end of this volume, is known as *nakama-hazure* (exclusion from the group) and is, in fact, a not uncommon form of bullying.

40. Murakami, "Murakami Haruki rōngu intabyū," 44.

41. Just which of the two—the original Fukaeri or her replica—has escaped the compound is a question that will be taken up in chapter 3.

42. Barthes, "Myth Today," in *A Barthes Reader,* 130–31; originally published in 1956.

43. Derrida makes a case of this sort in *Des Tours de Babel* in his interpretation of Genesis 11 (the Tower of Babel myth) as an attempt by man to wrest the grounding and control of language from God and unto himself, leading to God's confounding of human understanding. See Derrida, "From *Des Tours de Babel*," 218–27.

2. Into the Mad, Metaphysical Realm

1. Hawking, *A Brief History of Time*, 149.

2. Iwamiya, *Shishunki o meguru bōken*, 130.

3. Freud, "The Anatomy of the Mental Personality," in *New Introductory Lectures on Psycho-Analysis*, 104.

4. This is noted in Tsuge, "Media to shite no 'ido,'" and by Komori in Rubin and Komori, "*1Q84* to Sōseki o tsunagu mono."

5. Campbell, *The Masks of God*, 88. See also Campbell's *The Hero with a Thousand Faces*, esp. chapter 2 ("Initiation").

6. Jung, *Modern Man in Search of a Soul*, 122.

7. Jung, *Memories, Dreams, Reflections*, 191.

8. In *Dance Dance Dance*, Boku is told that the "other world" is a place created solely for him. See *Dansu dansu dansu* in *MHZ*, 7:128.

9. Murakami, *Kaze no uta o kike*, in *MHZ*, 1:106; hereafter page numbers are given parenthetically in the text.

10. I have translated *kokoro* as "inner self," though the more common meaning for the term is "heart," or occasionally even "soul."

11. Tsuge, "Media to shite no 'ido,'" 51.

12. Murakami Haruki, interview by author, 22 October 1994, Cambridge, Mass.

13. See Katō, *Murakami Haruki*, esp. 10–11.

14. Murakami, *1973-nen no pinbōru*, in *MHZ*, 1:151.

15. Ibid., 1:181–82; my emphasis.

16. Ibid., 1:173.

17. When the Ainu guide asks some fellow Ainu he comes across the name of the place, they respond, *konna ketsu no ana mitai na tochi ni namae nante aru wake nai ja nai ka*, which the English translation renders humorously and accurately as "'do you really think this asshole of a terrain even deserves a name?'" See Murakami, *Hitsuji o meguru bōken*, in *MHZ*, 2:255; cf. *A Wild Sheep Chase*, 201.

18. Murakami, *Hitsuji o meguru bōken*, in *MHZ*, 2:292; hereafter page numbers are given parenthetically in the text.

19. A footnote to the story of the Ainu youth is that he married one of the settlers of Jūnitakichō and had a son, who was later killed in the Russo-Japanese War of 1904–5.

20. Most recently, in the course of explaining to an interviewer why he named his characters in *Norwegian Wood,* Murakami noted that "I intended very deliberately to write a realistic novel, so not to use names would have been out of the question." See Murakami, "Murakami Haruki rongu intabyū," 22.

21. Odaka, *Kindai bungaku igo,* 53.

22. Murakami may have felt he had not exhausted this theme, as two years later he wrote the short story "Warera no jidai no fōkuroa: Kōdo shihonshugi zenshi" (1989; translated as "A Folklore for My Generation: A Prehistory of Late-Stage Capitalism"), in which a man recounts a very similar relationship with a high school sweetheart who feels compelled (a) to remain a virgin for marriage, and (b) to marry a man several years older than herself. Thus, she makes the rather bizarre promise to her boyfriend that she will have sex with him but only *after* she has married someone else. When that moment arrives, however, both back away. See "Warera no jidai no fōkuroa: Kōdo shihonshugi zenshi," in Murakami, *TV piipuru* (1990); an English translation may be found in Murakami, *Blind Willow, Sleeping Woman.*

23. Murakami, *Noruwei no mori,* in *MHZ,* 6:135.

24. By far the most dramatic of these "guards" is the Gatekeeper of "the Town" in *Hard-Boiled Wonderland and the End of the World,* who slices away Boku's shadow before admitting him; other figures of this type we have seen or will see include the Sheepman in *A Wild Sheep Chase,* two soldiers who guide Kafka to the forest village in *Kafka on the Shore,* the "faceless man" in *The Wind-Up Bird Chronicle,* the nurse who tends Tengo's father in *1Q84,* and an old man who guides the protagonist to the secluded summer home of a friend in Finland in *Colorless Tsukuru Tazaki and His Years of Pilgrimage.* More will be said on this subject later in this chapter and the one that follows.

25. Murakami, *Noruwei no mori,* in *MHZ,* 6:191; my emphasis.

26. This is a motif we will see repeated in *1Q84* with "Fukaeri," the replica of a girl held captive in her father's cult, whose ears and sexual organs appear unnaturally perfect to the protagonist.

27. Murakami, *Noruwei no mori,* in *MHZ,* 6:206.

28. Murakami, *Nejimakidori kuronikuru,* 1:187; hereafter page numbers are given parenthetically in the text.

29. Or rather, it *has* borne fruit; for readers seeking an in-depth and sophisticated analysis of the specifically Jungian and Lacanian aspects of Murakami's work, including the anima/animus question, I recommend the excellent doctoral thesis of Dil, "Murakami Haruki and the Search for Self-Therapy."

30. Iwamiya, *Shishunki o meguru bōken,* 107.

31. Murakami, *1973-nen no pinbōru,* in *MHZ,* 1:182; my emphasis.

32. Murakami, *Hitsuji o meguru bōken,* in *MHZ,* 2:297.

33. Crows, viewed in Greek mythology as divine messengers, are frequently present in Murakami's metaphysical sequences as well, though they seldom do anything beyond observing the action.

34. Murakami, *Sekai no owari to hādo-boirudo wandārando,* in *MHZ,* 4:197; hereafter page numbers are given parenthetically in the text.

35. Murakami, *Umibe no Kafka,* 1:235; hereafter page numbers are given parenthetically in the text.

36. Kawai Hayao, "Kyōkai taiken o monogataru," 239.

37. The connection between these two novels is by no means tenuous. In an interview given shortly after the release of *Kafka on the Shore,* Murakami stated that he had originally meant to write a continuation *(zokuhen)* to *Hard-Boiled Wonderland and the End of the World,* not because he regretted the ending he had devised in that work, but because, as a writer, he was now in a position to try out different solutions. See Murakami, "Rongu intabyū: *Umibe no Kafka* o kataru," esp. 34–35.

38. See C. G. Jung, "Phenomenology of the Self," in *The Portable Jung,* 145–46.

39. Iwamiya, *Shishunki o meguru bōken,* 132–33.

40. Murakami, *Afutādāku,* 3; hereafter page numbers are given parenthetically in the text.

41. Murakami, *1Q84,* 2:271–72; hereafter page numbers are given parenthetically in the text.

42. Ibid., 3:462. This is related in the narrative sequence of "Ushikawa," an unsavory detective type who will be discussed further in the next chapter.

3. Gods and Oracles, Fate and Mythology

1. Bulfinch, *The Age of Fable or, Beauties of Mythology,* 1.

2. Most Japanese taboos were prophylactic in nature, intended to maintain good health, but in a tradition that valued and required high rates of birth, it is not surprising that contact with women during pregnancy, nursing, or menstruation—those times when they are unlikely to become pregnant—was avoided. In this, too, traditional Japanese animist belief shared many of the taboos of the ancient Hebrews. Chapter 18 in the book of Leviticus specifies many similar taboos, adding homosexuality, sodomy, and bestiality, all of which share the characteristic of being nonprocreational sex acts.

3. Campbell, *The Hero with a Thousand Faces,* 38; his description of the archetypal structure noted above occurs in the same text, 36–38, and 245–47. For a discussion of these archetypes in the context of literary criticism, see Frye, *Anatomy of Criticism,* esp. 131–242.

4. As we have seen in the Introduction, this tension between culturally

specific and globally diffuse runs parallel to the stylistic features of Murakami's writing that are called *mukokuseki,* or "without nationality." Murakami is a "global" writer in the sense that he writes in Japanese, but he is "natural" for readers in almost any language, from almost any cultural background.

5. Here and elsewhere it will be important to distinguish religion from spirituality. Religion, as I use the term, assumes organization, a belief system held to be true by many (or at least more than one), usually some type of doctrine or codification of truths. Spirituality may exist having none of these, representing merely the desire and efforts of humankind to come into direct contact with the metaphysical realm. An acetic mountain hermit is undoubtedly spiritual; she or he may or may not be religious.

6. Murakami, *Umibe no Kafka,* 2:96.

7. Rubin and Komori, "*1Q84* to Sōseki o tsunagu mono," 185.

8. Uchida, *Mō ichido Murakami Haruki ni go-yōjin,* 61.

9. Rubin, *Haruki Murakami and the Music of Words*, 210. Cf. Napier, "Meet Me on the Other Side," 51. Connections between Murakami fiction and both the Orphean legend and the *Kojiki* have also been made by Suzumura Kazunari and Susan Fisher. See Suzumura, *Murakami Haruki kuronikuru 1983–1995,* 119; and Fisher, "An Allegory of Return," esp. 161.

10. Kawai Hayao, *Mukashibanashi to Nihonjin no kokoro,* 170–72.

11. Murakami, *Umibe no Kafka,* 1:242.

12. Hesiod, *The Homeric Hymns and Homerica,* 365–67.

13. Kawai Hayao, "Kyōkai taiken o monogataru," 239.

14. Kamata, *Shintai to uchūshi.*

15. The proscription against eating the food of the dead is echoed in Greek myth as well, wherein Persephone, abducted by Hades, cannot return permanently to the world of the living because she has eaten a handful of seeds from a pomegranate given her by a resident there.

16. Other mythical journeys into the underworld are to be found in the lore of ancient Sumeria (Gilgamesh), the Norsemen (Baldr), the Mayans (Hunahpu and Xbalanque), as well as in the Buddhist, Hindu, and indeed Christian traditions. Most, though not all, are unsuccessful, reminding those who hear them that death is irreversible and that contact with the dead is inadvisable (presumably both for reasons of ritual pollution and for actual hygiene).

17. Murakami, *1973-nen no pinbōru,* in *MHZ,* 1:212; hereafter page numbers are given parenthetically in the text.

18. This is strongly reminiscent of Ōe Kenzaburō's 1968 novel *Man'en gannen no futtobōru* (Football in the year 1860), whose title is parodied by this Murakami novel. In Ōe's novel one of the principal characters makes a thick-walled storehouse the site of his death and his final testament to the

world. English readers should see John Bester's excellent translation, titled *The Silent Cry*.

19. Here, as elsewhere, we might recall Odysseus visiting the realm of the dead, meeting many well-known characters whose deaths are told in *The Iliad* (including Agamemnon and Achilles), to say nothing of his own mother. Though he offers them words of comfort, however, there is never any question of his bringing any of them back. See Homer, *The Odyssey*, Book XI.

20. Kamata notes the legend of "Miminashi Yōichi" (Earless Yōichi), the hapless lute player of lore who has his ears torn off by the spirits of vengeful Heike warriors, eager to hear his beautiful ballads about their deaths. This was the only part of him visible to the spirits, because the priests who attempted to protect him by writing sutras all over his body neglected to write anything on his ears. See Kamata, *Shintai no uchūshi*, 269–73.

21. Ibid., 273–74.

22. Ibid., 274.

23. Rubin, *Haruki Murakami and the Music of Words*, 4.

24. Readers of the short story collection *Blind Willow, Sleeping Woman* may recall that in the title story, one of Murakami's early works, the narrator escorts his nephew to the hospital to have his ears checked; the nephew's hearing alternates between being almost normal and almost totally absent. In this instance, however, it is less the cousin than the narrator himself who is drawn powerfully into his own memories. The original story was published as "Mekura yanagi to nemuru onna" in the December 1983 issue of *Bungakukai*.

25. Murakami, *Hitsuji o meguru bōken*, in *MHZ*, 2:293.

26. Murakami, *Sekai no owari to hādo-boirudo wandārando*, in *MHZ*, 4:43–44.

27. Murakami, *Noruwei no mori*, in *MHZ*, 6:138.

28. Murakami, "Kami no kodomotachi wa mina odoru," in *Kami no kodomotachi wa mina odoru*, 73; hereafter page numbers are given parenthetically in the text.

29. *Jingū* is another word for a Shintō shrine, literally, "hall of the gods."

30. Campbell, *An Open Life*, 37.

31. Murakami, *1Q84*, 1:83; hereafter page numbers are given parenthetically in the text.

32. Murakami, *Hitsuji o meguru bōken*, in *MHZ*, 2:356.

33. Murakami, *Umibe no Kafka*, 2:66. The word I am translating as "vessel" is *iremono*, "container."

34. Kawai Hayao, "Kyōkai taiken o monogataru," 236.

35. Murakami, *Umibe no Kafka*, 2:374.

36. Ibid., 2:382–83.

37. Numano, Uchida, and Tokō, "Murakami Haruki no 'ketsudan,'" 162.

38. It will be useful here to note Mircea Eliade's assertion that among premodern cultures, "myth" is understood to be a true story, rather than the fictional (often allegorical) legend it has come to be in industrialized societies. See Eliade, *Myth and Reality.*

39. Frazer, *The Golden Bough,* 628.

40. Ibid., 634–35.

4. Murakami Hakuri as Literary Journalist

1. It is important to distinguish this more globally acknowledged genre of writing from what, for instance, Marvin Marcus refers to as literary journalism in his discussion of Bundan coterie writing, that is, contemporary writing about Japan's literati in the Meiji period and later. While such texts might qualify loosely as "journalism" under the parameters we will set, since they were both current and of (limited) public interest, my use of the expression *literary journalism* refers to stories about true events that are more broadly relevant to the public at large. One could, of course, object that writing about, say, the Vietnam War suffers from the same defect, but I would respond that an event like the Vietnam War is relevant to a far wider public. Obviously, some distinctions of this type are of degree, while others are of quality. See Marcus, "The Social Organization of Modern Japanese Literature," esp. 53–55.

2. See Cawelti, *Adventure, Mystery, and Romance.*

3. More remains in my own memory, thirty years after the fact, from reading Vidal's *Julian* than from Suetonius's *The Twelve Caesars,* though this admission is unlikely to bring joy to my classics professors at the University of Texas.

4. Kramer, "Breakable Rules for Literary Journalists," in Sims and Kramer, eds., *Literary Journalism,* 21.

5. While there is a legitimate genre of poetry that deals with current events—the poetry of World War I, for instance, or popular verse about social injustice in the mid-twentieth century—theoretical writing on the subject of literary journalism tends, fairly or not, to focus predominantly on works of prose. In Japan one might cite some of the verse written in the immediate aftermath of the atomic bombings of Hiroshima and Nagasaki, or the Kantō earthquake of 1923.

6. See Mayer, "The Reception of *A Journal of the Plague Year* and the Nexus of Fiction and History in the Novel"; also see Kramer, "Breakable Rules for Literary Journalists," in Sims and Kramer, Literary Journalism, 21. The work's factuality would be called into question, among other reasons, by virtue of the fact that the plague outbreak of which Defoe purports

to tell—as the work's physician-narrator—took place when he was just five years old.

7. Davis, *Factual Fictions,* 45–46.

8. Hutcheon, *A Poetics of Postmodernism,* 105.

9. Frus, *The Politics and Poetics of Journalistic Narrative,* 2.

10. Yagoda, preface to Kerrane and Yagoda, eds., *The Art of Fact,* 14.

11. Kramer, "Breakable Rules for Literary Journalists," in Sims and Kramer, eds., *Literary Journalism,* 23.

12. Sims, ed., *Literary Journalism in the Twentieth Century,* 13. Cf. Sims, "The Art of Literary Journalism," in *Literary Journalism,* ed. Sims and Kramer.

13. Fishken, "The Borderlands of Culture," 133.

14. Many, "Literary Journalism, 64–65.

15. Honda, *The Impoverished Spirit of Contemporary Japan,* 219–20.

16. Honda, *Masukomi ka, jānarizumu ka,* 133.

17. Ibid., 163.

18. Murakami Gen'ichi, *Kisha kurabu tte nan da!?,* 69.

19. Farley, "Japan's Press and the Politics of Scandal," 137–38. Cf. Yamamoto, "The Press Clubs of Japan."

20. de Lange, *A History of Japanese Journalism,* 185–86.

21. Though I shall refer to this work in subsequent pages by its English title *Underground,* it is important to remind readers that the English translation of this work was combined with its sequel, *Yakusoku sareta basho de: Underground* 2. I shall distinguish between these two works as *Underground* and *Underground* 2.

22. Murakami, *Andāguraundo,* 709.

23. Ibid., 15.

24. Ibid., 15–16.

25. Murakami, *Yakusoku sareta basho de,* 12.

26. Ibid., 17.

27. Murakami, *Andāguraundo,* 692.

28. Murakami, *Yakusoku sareta basho de,* 16.

29. Ibid., 38.

30. Ibid., 34.

31. Some might say the same of the American press. Significantly, it was Gore Vidal who wrote one of the first works of journalism dissenting from public fervor over the 9/11 attacks and their causes, in *Perpetual War for Perpetual Peace: How We Got to Be So Hated.* He notes at the outset of that work that his initial remarks on the 9/11 attacks had to be published in Italy, because no American periodical was willing to print them just then.

32. A similar impulse drives so-called counterfactual histories, in which one or more crucial decisions are changed to see what would have been. The difference is that counterfactual histories work explicitly with historical

events, showing how seemingly trivial, often chance events might have changed the course of human history.

33. Murakami Ryū, *Kibō no kuni no ekusodasu,* 420.

34. Kawamoto, "*Umibe no Kafka* jōge," 203.

35. Numano, Uchida, and Tokō, "Murakami Haruki no 'ketsudan,'" 167.

36. Reported in "*Shōnen A,*" a book whose authors are identified only as "the Mother and Father of 'Shōnen A,'" 8.

37. Takayama, "*Shōnen A,*" 23.

38. The conversation took place at the University of California at Berkeley in October 2008.

39. Yamaguchi, "Truancy Doubles in Japan over Past Decade."

40. Murakami, *Afutādāku,* 77–78.

41. Ibid., 78–79.

42. Ibid., 79.

43. These, and the accounts by other major writers, may be found in *Kantō daishinsai* (The great Kantō earthquake), esp. 202–63.

44. I am greatly indebted to Dr. Alex Bates for introducing me to this remarkable text, and for assisting me in locating one of the few surviving copies at Waseda University.

45. Kawakami, "Kamisama," 112.

46. Kawakami, "Kamisama 2011," 104.

47. Ibid., 106.

48. Ibid., 114.

49. Murakami, *1Q84,* 1:226–27.

50. Kawamoto, "'Monogatari' no tame no bōken," 63.

51. Murakami, *Underground 2,* 113.

52. Murakami, *Kaze no uta o kike,* in *MHZ,* 1:15.

5. Forbidden Dreams from "Over There"

1. Kōnosu Yukiko likens this to the sorts of titles found in such seventeenth- and eighteenth-century novels as Bunyan's *Pilgrim's Progress,* which contain "the name, hometown, activities, and situation" of the main character, and she suggests, only half facetiously, that the full English title of Murakami's new novel should be "The Pilgrim's Progress of Colourless Tsukuru Tazaki from This World to That Which Is to Come, delivered under the similitude of a dream, wherein is discovered the manner of his setting out, his dangerous journey, and safe arrival at the desired country." See Kōnosu, "Dare ga Shirayukihime o koroshita ka?," 179.

2. Andō, "Rekishi to kioku, genjitsu to yogen," 290.

3. Murakami , *Shikisai o motanai Tazaki Tsukuru to, kare no junrei no toshi,*

20; hereafter cited as *Tazaki Tsukuru;* hereafter page numbers are given parenthetically in the text.

4. Andō, "Rekishi to kioku, genjitsu to yogen," 292. The Japanese term used is *saisei.*

5. Ibid., 293.

6. Chesterton is suggested by Kōnosu, "Dare ga Shirayukihime o koroshita ka?" (183), while Auster's *Ghosts*—which does bear certain thematic similarities to Murakami fiction in general—is noted by both Kōnosu, "Dare ga Shirayukihime o koroshita ka?," and Numano, "Shikisai, hiyū, nosutarujia." *Ghosts* is the second novel in Auster's *New York Trilogy* (1985–86), which also includes *City of Glass* and *The Locked Room.*

7. Numano connects the color and light imagery in this text, among other things, to Johann Wolfgang von Goethe's nineteenth-century study of colors, and Rudolf Steiner's later theories relating colors to human "astral" forms, arguing that "Steiner saw life, souls, and spirits in the glow of various colors, and behind the glitter of those colors, he saw the angels." See Numano, "Shikisai, hiyū, nosutarujia," 169. The texts to which Numano refers, though he does not cite them, are Goethe, *Zur Farbenlehre* (1810; Theory of colors); and Steiner, *Goethes Weltanschauung* (1897; Goethe's view of the world).

8. Here, too, it is useful to recall Frazer's discourse on the tradition of killing divine kings in certain cultures, particularly those in which the length of the king's reign is determined in advance. See Frazer, *The Golden Bough,* esp. 647–68.

9. Huxley, *The Doors of Perception,* 20–22; hereafter page numbers are given parenthetically in the text.

10. Kōnosu, "Dare ga Shirayukihime o koroshita ka?," 184.

11. For more in this regard, see Jung, *Collected Works of C. G. Jung,* vol. 8, esp. 237–80.

12. Jung, "Freud and Psychoanalysis," in the *Collected Works of C .G. Jung,* vol. 4, 28.

13. In this, of course, their "perfect circle" mirrors social conventions that forbid "inappropriate" relationships, not only incest but extramarital affairs and the like, due to the social chaos that would result.

Epilogue

1. Murakami, *Moshi bokura no kotoba ga uisukii de atta nara,* 9.

2. Murakami, *Henkyō/kinkyō,* 30.

3. Ibid., 31; emphasis in the original.

4. Murakami and Itoi, *Yume de aimashō,* 3.

5. Murakami, *Wakai dokusha no tame no tanpen shōsetsu annai,* 18–20.

6. Miyawaki, "Hon'yaku o meguru bōken," 200.

7. Koshikawa, Numano, and Niimoto, "Murakami Haruki yaku o yomu," 304.

8. Miyawaki, "Hon'yaku o meguru bōken," 198.

9. Readers interested in this topic may find useful José Ortega y Gasset's essay, "The Misery and the Splendor of Translation," 93–112.

10. This is described in some detail by Kazamaru in *Ekkyō suru "Boku,"* who, among other things, carries out a detailed comparison of Murakami's translation style vis-à-vis that of Shibata Motoyuki in Paul Auster's short story "Auggie Wren's Christmas Story." See esp. 248–50.

11. Koshikawa, Numano, and Niimoto, "Murakami Haruki yaku o yomu," 286.

12. See Benjamin, "The Task of the Translator," 71–82.

13. Koishikawa, Numano, and Niimoto, "Murakami Haruki yaku o yomu," 286.

14. Ibid., 292–93.

BIBLIOGRAPHY

Andō Reiji. "Ō o koroshita ato ni: Kindai to iu shisutemu ni aragau sakuhin *1Q84*" [After killing the king: *1Q84* as a text that challenges the modern system]. In *Murakami Haruki 1Q84 o dō yomu ka* [How to read Murakami Haruki's *1Q84*?], edited by Kawade Shobō Editorial Board. Tokyo: Kawade Shobō Shinsha, 2009.

———. "Rekishi to kioku, genjitsu to yogen: Murakami Haruki *Shikisai o motanai Tazaki Tsukuru to, kare no junrei no toshi* ni tsuite" [History and memory, reality and prophesy: On Murakami Haruki's *Colorless Tsukuru Tazaki and his years of pilgrimage.*] *Shinchō* 110, no. 6 (2013).

———. "Renzoku to furenzoku" [Connections and disconnections]. *Shinchō* 107, no. 6 (2010).

Andō Reiji, Matsunaga Miho, Karube Tadashi, and Suwa Tetsushi. "Murakami Haruki *1Q84* o tokoton yomu" [Thoroughly reading Murakami Haruki's *1Q84*]. *Gunzō* 64, no. 8 (2009).

Auster, Paul. *Ghosts.* New York: Penguin, 1987.

Bailey, Paul J. *Postwar Japan: 1945 to the Present.* Oxford: Blackwell Publishers, 1996.

Barnaby, Karin, and Pellegrino D'Acierno. *C. G. Jung and the Humanities: Toward a Hermeneutics of Culture.* Princeton, N.J.: Princeton University Press, 1990.

Barnstone, Willis. *The Poetics of Translation: History, Theory, Practice.* New Haven, Conn.: Yale University Press, 1993.

Barthes, Roland. *A Barthes Reader.* Edited by Susan Sontag. New York: Hill and Wang, 1982.

———. *Elements of Semiology.* Translated by Annette Lavers and Colin Smith. New York: Hill and Wang, 1967.

———. *Image—Music—Text.* Translated by Stephen Heath. New York: Hill and Wang, 1977.

———. *The Pleasure of the Text.* Translated by Richard Miller. New York: Hill and Wang, 1975.

Baudrillard, Jean. *The Illusion of the End.* Translated by Chris Turner. Stanford, Calif.: Stanford University Press, 1994.

———. *Selected Writings.* Edited by Mark Poster. Stanford, Calif.: Stanford University Press, 1988.

———. *Simulacra and Simulation.* Translated by Sheila Faria Glaser. Ann Arbor: University of Michigan Press, 1994.

Benjamin, Walter. "The Task of the Translator." In *The Translation Studies Reader,* edited by Lawrence Venuti. London and New York: Routledge, 2000.

Bulfinch, Thomas. *The Age of Fable or, Beauties of Mythology.* Revised and edited by Rev. J. Loughran Scott. Philadelphia: David McKay, 1898. Orig. pub. 1855.

Campbell, Joseph. *The Hero with a Thousand Faces.* Bollingen Series 17. Princeton, N.J.: Princeton University Press, 1949.

———. *The Masks of God: Creative Mythology.* New York: Arkana, 1968.

———. *An Open Life: Joseph Campbell in Conversation with Michael Toms.* Edited by John Maher and Dennie Briggs. New York: Larson Publications, 1988.

———. *The Power of Myth.* With Bill Moyers. New York: Anchor Books, 1991.

Cawelti, John G. *Adventure, Mystery, and Romance: Formula Stories as Art and Popular Culture.* Chicago: University of Chicago Press, 1976.

———. "The Concept of Formula in the Study of Popular Literature." *Journal of Popular Culture* no. 3 (1969).

Chang Mingmin. "Taiwanjin no Murakami Haruki: 'Bunka hon'yaku' to shite no Murakami Haruki genshō" [The Taiwanese people's Murakami Haruki: The Murakami Haruki phenomenon as cultural translation]. In *Higashi Ajia ga yomu Murakami Haruki* [Murakami Haruki as read in East Asia], edited by Fujii Shōzō. Tokyo: Wakakusa Shobō, 2009.

Chesterton, G. K. *The Scandal of Father Brown.* London: Cassell and Company, 1935.

Clavell, James. *Shōgun.* New York: Atheneum, 1975.

———. *Tai-Pan.* New York: Atheneum, 1966.

Davis, Lennard. *Factual Fictions: The Rise of the English Novel.* New York: Columbia University Press, 1983.

Dawson, Christopher. *Religion and Culture.* New York: Meridian Books, 1958.

de Lange, William. *A History of Japanese Journalism: Japan's Press Club as the Last Obstacle to a Mature Press.* Surrey: Japan Library, 1998.

Derrida, Jacques. "From *Des Tours de Babel.*" In *Theories of Translation: An Anthology of Essays from Dryden to Derrida,* edited by Rainer Schulte and John Biguenet. Chicago: Chicago University Press, 1992.

Dil, Jonathan. "Murakami Haruki and the Search for Self-Therapy." Ph.D. thesis. University of Canterbury, New Zealand, 2007.

Eco, Umberto. *Baudolino.* Translated by William Weaver. New York: Vintage, 2003.

———. *Foucault's Pendulum.* Translated by William Weaver. New York: Ballantine, 1988.

———. *The Mysterious Flame of Queen Loana.* Translated by Geoffrey Brock. New York: Harcourt, 2005.

———. *The Name of the Rose.* Translated by William Weaver. New York: Warner Books, 1983.

———. *The Prague Cemetery.* Translated by Richard Dixon. New York: Houghton Mifflin Harcourt, 2011.

Eliade, Mircea. *Myth and Reality.* Translated by Willard R. Trask. New York: Harper and Row, 1963.

Faris, Wendy, and Lois Parkinson Zamora, eds. *Magical Realism: Theory, History, Community.* Durham, N.C.: Duke University Press, 1995.

Farley, Maggie. "Japan's Press and the Politics of Scandal." In *Media and Politics in Japan,* edited by Susan J. Pharr and Ellis S. Krauss. Honolulu: University of Hawai'i Press, 1997.

Fisher, Susan. "An Allegory of Return: Murakami Haruki's *The Wind-Up Bird Chronicle.*" *Comparative Literature Studies* 37, no. 2 (East-West Issue) (2000).

Fishken, Shelley Fisher, "The Borderlands of Culture: Writing by W. E. B. Du Bois, James Agee, Tylie Olsen, and Gloria Anzaldúa," in *Literary Journalism in the Twentieth Century,* edited by Norman Sims. New York: Oxford University Press, 1990.

Frazer, James. *The Golden Bough: A Study of Magic and Religion.* Auckland, New Zealand: The Floating Press, 2009. Orig. pub. 1890.

Freud, Sigmund. *Civilization and Its Discontents.* Translated by James Strachey. New York and London: Norton, 1961.

———. *A General Introduction to Psychoanalysis.* Translated by Joan Riviere. New York: Horace Liveright, 1924.

———. *New Introductory Lectures on Psycho-Analysis.* Translated by W. J. H. Sprott. New York: Norton and Co., 1933.

Fromm, Erich. *Psychoanalysis and Religion.* New Haven: Yale University Press, 1950.

Frus, Phyllis. *The Politics and Poetics of Journalistic Narrative: The Timely and the Timeless.* Cambridge: Cambridge University Press, 1994.

Frye, Northrop. *Anatomy of Criticism: Four Essays.* Princeton, N.J.: Princeton University Press, 1957.

Fujii Shōzō, ed. *Higashi Ajia ga yomu Murakami Haruki* [Murakami Haruki as read in East Asia]. Tokyo: Wakakusa Shobō, 2009.

Fukuda Kazuya. "Bōryokuron no shōsoku" [The latest on the violence theory]. *Shinchō* 107, no. 6 (2010).

———. "Gendaijin wa sukuwareuru ka—Murakami Haruki *1Q84*" [Can contemporary people be saved?—Murakami Haruki's *1Q84*]. Parts 1 and 2. *Shinchō* 106, no. 8 (part 1); *Shinchō* 106, no. 9 (part 2) (2009).

———. "Genjitsuteki na mono, gutaiteki na mono: Murakami Haruki *Umibe no Kafka* ni tsuite" [Real things, concrete things: On Murakami Haruki's *Kafka on the Shore*]. *Bungakukai* 56, no. 11 (2002).

———. "Sofutobōru no yō na shi no katamari o mesu de kirihiraku koto" [Cutting through the hardness of softball-like death with a scalpel]. *Shinchō* 91, no. 7 (1994).

Furukawa Hideo. "Murakami Haruki no 'miru chikara' o omoinagara" [While thinking on Murakami Haruki's "power of vision"]. *Subaru* 34, no. 1 (2012).

Fuse Hidetoshi. "Murakami Haruki no 'shitai'" [The "corpses" of Murakami Haruki]. *Subaru,* December 1995.

Garon, Sheldon. *Molding Japanese Minds: The State in Everyday Life.* Princeton, N.J.: Princeton University Press, 1997.

Goethe, Johann Wolfgang von. *Theory of Colours.* Translated by Charles Lock Eastlake. Cambridge, Mass.: Massachussetts Institute of Technology Press, 1970. Orig. pub. 1810 as *Zur Farbenlehre.*

Gotō Masaharu. "*Andāguraundo* o megutte" [Concerning *Underground*]. *Bungakukai* 51, no. 6 (1997): 256–60.

Graves, Robert. *The Greek Myths.* 2 vols. New York: Penguin Books, 1960.

Greene, Graham. *The Quiet American.* London: William Heinemann, 1955.

Haipātekusuto: Murakami Haruki [Hypertext: Murakami Haruki]. Special issue of *Kokubungaku* 43, no. 3 (1998).

Hamilton, Edith. *Mythology: Timeless Tales of Gods and Heroes.* New York: Mentor, 1969.

Hatanaka Yoshiki. "Murakami Haruki no namae o meguru bōken" [A wild Murakami Haruki name chase]. *Yuriika* 21, no. 8 (1989).

Hawking, Stephen. *A Brief History of Time: From the Big Bang to Black Holes.* New York: Bantam Dell, 1988.

Hesiod. *The Homeric Hymns and Homerica.* Edited by G. P. Goold. Translated by Hugh G. Evelyn-White. Cambridge, Mass.: Harvard University Press, 1982. Orig. pub. 1914.

Hidaka Rokurō. *The Price of Affluence: Dilemmas of Contemporary Japan.* Translated and edited by Gavan McCormack et al. Tokyo: Kodansha International, 1984.
Hirano Jun. *Zero no rakuen: Murakami Haruki to Bukkyō* [The zero paradise: Murakami Haruki and Buddhism]. Tokyo: Rakkōsha, 2008.
Hisai Tsubaki. *Nejimakidori no sagashikata* [How to search for the Wind-Up Bird]. Tokyo: Ōta Shuppan, 1994.
Honda Katsuichi. *The Impoverished Spirit of Contemporary Japan.* Edited by John Lie. Translated by Eri Fujieda, Masayuki Hamazaki, and John Lie. New York: Monthly Review Press, 1993.
———. *Masukomi ka, jānarizumu ka* [Mass communications or journalism?]. Tokyo: Asahi Shinbunsha, 2000.
Hukami Haruka. *Murakami Haruki no uta* [The song of Murakami Haruki]. Tokyo: Seikyōsha, 1990.
Hutcheon, Linda. *A Poetics of Postmodernism: History, Theory, Fiction.* New York: Routledge, 1988.
———. *The Politics of Postmodernism.* New York: Routledge, 1989.
Huxley, Aldous. *The Doors of Perception and Heaven and Hell.* New York: Harper and Row, 1990. Orig. pub. 1954.
———. *Time Must Have a Stop.* London: Triad/Granada, 1982. Orig. pub. 1945.
Ida Makiko. "Murakami-shi no hōhōron" [On Mr. Murakami's method]. *Bungakukai* 51, no. 6 (1997).
Imai, Kiyoto. *OFF no kankaku* [The OFF sensation]. Tokyo: Kokken Shuppan, 1990.
Inoue Yoshio. *Murakami Haruki to Nihon no "kioku"* [Murakami Haruki and Japan's "memory"]. Tokyo: Shinchōsha, 1999.
Ishiguro, Kazuo, and Ōe Kenzaburō. "The Novelist in Today's World: A Conversation." In *Japan in the World,* edited by Masao Miyoshi and H. D. Harootunian. Durham, N.C.: Duke University Press, 1993.
Ishihara Chiaki. "Murakami Haruki to Natsume Sōseki: Kokumin sakka no manazashi" [Murakami Haruki and Natsume Sōseki: The view of the people's writer]. *Bungei shunjū* 91, no. 7 (2013).
Itō Ryūtarō. "Idai na manneri Haruki no 'Kafka'" [Haruki's gigantic mannerly "Kafka"]. *Aera* no. 46 (2002).
Itō Yoshirō. *"Shōnen A" no kokuhaku* [The confessions of "Shōnen A"]. Tokyo: Shogakukan, 1999.
Iwamiya Keiko. *Shishunki o meguru bōken: Shinri ryōhō to Murakami Haruki no sekai* [A wild adolescence chase: Psychotherapy and the world of Murakami Haruki]. Tokyo: Nihon Hyōronsha, 2004.

Iwamoto, Yoshio. "A Voice from Postmodern Japan: Murakami Haruki." *World Literature Today*, Spring 1993.
Jameson, Fredric. *Postmodernism, or The Cultural Logic of Late Capitalism.* Durham, N.C.: Duke University Press, 1991.
Jung, Carl. *Analytical Psychology: Its Theory and Practice.* New York: Pantheon, 1968.
———. *The Basic Writings of C. G. Jung.* Edited by Violet Staub de Laszlo. New York: The Modern Library, 1959.
———. *The Collected Works of C. G. Jung.* 20 vols. Princeton, N.J.: Princeton University Press, 1972.
———. *Memories, Dreams, Reflections.* Translated by Richard and Clara Winston. New York: Pantheon Books, 1961.
———. *Modern Man in Search of a Soul.* Translated by W. S. Dell and Cary F. Baynes. New York: Harcourt, Brace and World, 1933.
———. *The Portable Jung.* Edited by Joseph Campbell. New York: Penguin, 1971.
———. *Psyche and Symbol.* Edited by Violet S. de Laszlo. New York: Doubleday and Company, 1958.
———. *The Undiscovered Self.* Translated by R. F. C. Hull. Princeton, N.J.: Princeton University Press, 1990.
Kaikō Takeshi. *Aa, nijūgo-nen: 1958–1983* [Ah, twenty-five years: 1958–1983]. Tokyo: Ushio Shuppansha, 1983.
———. *Betonamu senki* [Vietnam war diary]. In vol. 11, *Kaikō Takeshi zenshū* [Complete works of Kaikō Takeshi]. 22 vols. Tokyo: Shinchōsha, 1992.
———. *Into a Black Sun.* Translated by Cecelia Segawa Seigle. Tokyo: Kodansha International, 1980.
———. "Janguru no naka no zetsubō" [Despair in the jungle]. In vol. 11, *Kaikō Takeshi zenshū* [Complete works of Kaikō Takeshi]. 22 vols. Tokyo: Shinchōsha, 1992.
———. *Kagayakeru yami* [Shining darkness] (translated as *Into a Black Sun*). In vol. 6, *Kaikō Takeshi zenshū* [Complete works of Kaikō Takeshi]. 22 vols. Tokyo: Shinchōsha, 1992.
———. "Kiroku, jijitsu, shinjitsu" [Records, reality, and truth]. In vol. 13, *Kaikō Takeshi zenshū* [Complete works of Kaikō Takeshi]. 22 vols. Tokyo: Shinchōsha, 1992.
———. *Saigon no jūjika* [Crosses of Saigon]. In vol. 11, *Kaikō Takeshi zenshū* [Complete works of Kaikō Takeshi]. 22 vols. Tokyo: Shinchōsha, 1992.
———. "Saigon kara" [From Saigon]. In vol. 11, *Kaikō Takeshi zenshū* [Complete works of Kaikō Takeshi]. 22 vols. Tokyo: Shinchōsha, 1992.

Kamata Tōji. *Shintai to uchūshi* [Bodies and the cosmic text]. Kōdansha Gakujutsu Bunkō No. 1128. Tokyo: Kōdansha, 1994.
Kantō daishinsai [The great Kantō earthquake]. Edited by Gendaishi no kai. Tokyo: Sōfūkan, 1996.
Karatani Kōjin. "The Discursive Space of Modern Japan." In *Japan in the World,* edited by Masao Miyoshi and H. D. Harootunian. Durham, N.C.: Duke University Press, 1993.
———. *Kindai Nihon no hihyo: Showa-hen* [Modern Japanese criticism: Shōwa volume]. 2 vols. Tokyo: Fukutake Shoten, 1990.
———. *Shūen o megutte* [On endings]. Tokyo: Fukutake Shoten, 1990.
Katō Hiroichi. "Ishō no mori o aruku" [Walking the forests of vision]. *Gunzō* 44, no. 11 (1989).
Katō Norihiro. *Haisengo-ron* [A post-defeat study]. Tokyo: Kōdansha, 1997.
———. "Jihei to sakoku" [Self-absorption and national isolation]. In *Siiku & fuaindo Murakami Haruki* [Seek and find Murakami Haruki], edited by Murakami Ryū. Tokyo: Seidōsha, 1986.
———. "'Ketachigai' no shōsetsu" [A "different class" of novel]. *Bungakukai* 63, no. 8 (2009).
———. "Murakami Haruki no tanpen o eigo de yomu" [Reading Murakami Haruki's short fiction in English]. Part 1. *Gunzō* 64, no. 9 (2009).
———. "'Masaka' to 'yareyare'" ["Masaka" and "Yareyare"]. *Gunzō* 43, no. 8 (1988).
———. *Murakami Haruki o meguru bōken* [A wild Murakami Haruki chase]. Tokyo: Kawai Shobō, 1991.
———. *Murakami Haruki: Ierō pēji* [Murakami Haruki: Yellow pages]. Tokyo: Arachi Shuppansha, 1996.
———. "*Umibe no Kafka* to kan'yūteki na sekai" [*Kafka on the Shore* and the metonymical world]. *Gunzō* 58, no. 2 (2003).
Katō Norihiro and Nakazawa Shin'ichi. "Yūrei no ikikata" [How spirits live]. *Shisō no kagaku* no. 515 (1994).
Kawai Hayao. "Gūzen no shinjitsu: *Tōkyō kitanshū*" [Accidental truths: *Strange tales of Tokyo*]. *Shinchō* 102, no. 11 (2005).
———. "Kyōkai taiken o monogataru: Murakami Haruki *Umibe no Kafka* o yomu" [Narrating experiences from the border: Reading Murakami Haruki's *Kafka on the Shore*]. *Shinchō* 99, no. 12 (2002).
———. *Mukashibanashi to Nihonjin no kokoro* [Ancient tales and the Japanese mind]. Tokyo: Iwanami Gendai Bunko, 2002.
Kawai Toshio. *Murakami Haruki no "monogatari": Yume tekisuto to shite yomitoku* [Murakami Haruki's "narrative": Interpretive reading of the dream text]. Tokyo: Shinchōsha, 2011.

———. "Sekai no monogatari to watashi no monogatari" [The world's story and my story]. *Shinchō* 107, no. 6 (2010).

Kawakami Hiromi. "Kamisama 2011" [The gods, 2011]. *Gunzō* 66, no. 6 (2011).

———. "Kamisama" [The gods]. *Gunzō* 66, no. 6 (2011).

Kawamoto Saburō. *Murakami Haruki-ron shūsei* [Collected essays on Murakami Haruki]. Tokyo: Wakakusa Shobō, 2006.

———. "'Monogatari' no tame no bōken" [A wild "story" chase]. *Bungakukai* 39, no. 8 (1985): 34–86.

———. "Murakami Haruki o meguru kaidoku" [Deciphering Murakami Haruki]. In *Siiku & fuaindo Murakami Haruki* [Seek and find Murakami Haruki], edited by Murakami Ryū. Tokyo: Seidōsha, 1986.

———. "*Umibe no Kafka* jōge" [*Kafka on the Shore*, vols. 1 and 2]. In *Murakami Haruki sutadiizu bukku 3* [Murakami Haruki studies book 3], edited by Murakami Haruki Ronshūsei. Tokyo: Wakakusa Shobō, 2006.

Kawamura Minato. "Amerika kara tōku hanarete—9.11 ikō to *Umibe no Kafka*" [Far from America—post-9/11 and *Kafka on the Shore*]. In *Murakami Haruki sutadiizu 2005–2007* [Murakami Haruki studies 2005–2007], edited by Imai Kiyoto. Tokyo: Wakakusa Shobō, 2008.

———. *Murakami Haruki o dō yomu ka* [How to read Murakami Haruki?]. Tokyo: Sakuhinsha, 2006.

Kawamura Minato and Ōsugi Shigeo. "Murakami Ryū to Murakami Haruki: 25-nen no bungaku kūkan" [Murakami Ryū and Murakami Haruki: 25 years of literary space]. *Gunzō* 55, no. 7 (2000).

Kazamaru Yoshihiko. *Ekkyō suru "Boku"—Murakami Haruki, hon'yaku buntai to katarite* ["Boku" crosses the border—Murakami Haruki, translation style and the narrator]. Tokyo: Shironsha, 2006.

———. *Murakami Haruki tanpen saidoku* [Rereading Murakami's short fiction]. Tokyo: Misuzu Shobō, 2007.

Kerrane, Kevin, and Ben Yagoda, eds. *The Art of Fact: A Historical Anthology of Literary Journalism.* New York: Simon and Schuster, 1998.

Kim Yang-su. "Kankoku ni okeru Murakami Haruki no juyō to sono kontekusuto" [Murakami Haruki's reception and its context in South Korea]. Translated by Matsuzaki Hiroko. In *Higashi Ajia ga yomu Murakami Haruki* [Murakami Haruki as read in East Asia], edited by Fujii Shōzō. Tokyo: Wakakusa Shobō, 2009.

Kiyoshi Mahito. *Murakami Haruki no tetsugaku wārudo* [Murakami Haruki's philosophical world]. Tokyo: Haruka Shobō, 2011.

Kobayashi Masaaki. "Kurai parodii: Furoito genshō to shite no Murakami Haruki" [Dark parody: Murakami Haruki as a Freudian phenomenon].

In *Modan to posutomodan* [Modern and postmodern], edited by Komori Yōichi and Toyama Takeo. Tokyo: Iwanami Shoten, 2003.

Komori Yōichi. "Kōmura Toshokan to shomotsu no meikyū" [The Kōmura Library and the labyrinth of the text." In *Murakami Haruki sutadiizu 2005–2007* [Murakami Haruki studies 2005–2007], edited by Imai Kiyoto. Tokyo: Wakakusa Shobō, 2008.

Komori Yōichi and Toyama Takeo. *Modan to posutomodan* [Modern and postmodern]. Tokyo: Iwanami Shoten, 2003.

Kondo, Dorinne. "Multiple Selves: The Aesthetics and Politics of Artisanal Identities." In *Japanese Sense of Self*, edited by Nancy Rosenberger. Cambridge: Cambridge University Press, 1992.

Konishi Keita. *Murakami Haruki no ongaku zukan* [Music in the world of Murakami Haruki]. Tokyo: Japan Mix, 1995.

Kōnosu Yukiko. "Dare ga Shirayukihime o koroshita ka? Tazaki Tsukuru to, sono karafuru na jinsei" [Who killed Snow White? Tazaki Tsukuru and his colorful life]. *Bungakukai* 67, no. 6 (2013).

Koschmann, J. Victor. *Revolution and Subjectivity in Postwar Japan*. Chicago: University of Chicago Press, 1996.

Koshikawa Yoshiaki, Numano Mitsuyoshi, and Niimoto Ryōichi. "Murakami Haruki yaku o yomu [Reading Murakami Haruki translations]. *Bungakukai* 57, no. 6 (2003).

Koyama Tetsurō. *Murakami Haruki o yomitsukusu* [Reading Murakami Haruki to death]. Tokyo: Kōdansha Gendai Shinsho no. 2071, 2010.

Kurata Mitsuhiro. "Reitōko no pinbōru" [Pinball in a freezer]. *Shisō no kagaku* no. 521 (1995).

Kurihara Yūichiro. "Sedai o tagaete rifurein sareta sōshitsu to sogai: Murakami Haruki *Shikisai o motanai Tazaki Tsukuru to, kare no junrei no toshi*" [The refrain of generational loss and alienation: Murakami Haruki's *Colorless Tsukuru Tazaki and his years of pilgrimage*]. *Subaru* 35, no. 6 (2013).

Kuroko Kazuo. *Murakami Haruki to dōjidai bungaku* [Murakami Haruki and contemporary literature]. Tokyo: Kawai Shuppan, 1990.

———. *Murakami Haruki: Za rosuto wārudo* [Murakami Haruki: The lost world]. Tokyo: Daisan Shokan, 1993.

———. *Sensō/henkyō/bungaku/ningen: Ōe Kenzaburō kara Murakami Haruki made* [War/frontiers/literature/humanity: From Ōe Kenzaburō to Murakami Haruki]. Tokyo: Bensei Shuppan, 2010.

———. *"Sōshitsu" no monogatari kara "tenkan" no monogatari e* [From stories of "loss" to stories of "change"]. Tokyo: Benseisha, 2007.

MacCannell, Juliet Flower. *Figuring Lacan: Criticism and the Cultural Unconscious*. London: Croom Helm, 1986.

Many, Paul. "Literary Journalism: Newspapers' Last, Best Hope." *Connecticut Review* 18, no. 1 (1996).

Marcus, Marvin. "The Social Organization of Modern Japanese Literature." In *The Columbia Companion to Modern East Asian Literature,* edited by Joshua Mostow. New York: Columbia University Press, 2003.

Maruya Saiichi and Miura Masashi. "Motoori Norinaga kara Murakami Haruki made" [From Motoori Norinaga to Murakami Haruki]. *Bungakukai* 49, no. 1 (1995).

Matsumoto Ken'ichi. *Toshi Shōsetsu kara sekai bungaku e* [From urban novels to world literature]. Tokyo: Daisan Bunmeisha, 2010.

———. "'Watashi' ni nani ga dekiru ka" [What can "I" do?]. *Kōkoku hihyō* no. 3 (1982).

Mayer, Robert. "The Reception of *A Journal of the Plague Year* and the Nexus of Fiction and History in the Novel." *English Literary History* no. 57 (1990).

McGee, Patrick. *Telling the Other: The Question of Value in Modern and Postcolonial Writing.* Ithaca, N.Y.: Cornell University Press, 1992.

McGowan, John. *Postmodernism and Its Critics.* Ithaca, N.Y.: Cornell University Press, 1991.

Miyawaki Toshifumi. "Hon'yaku o meguru bōken: Murakami Haruki to Amerika bungaku" [A wild translation chase: Murakami Haruki and American literature]. In *Eibei bungaku no rivābu: Kyōkai o koeru ishi* [English and American literature reverb: Border-crossing will], edited by Suzue Akiko and Ueno Tatsurō. Tokyo: Kaibunsha, 2004.

Mukai Satoshi. "Shudai ni shisshite monogatari o ushinau" [Sacrificing the story to a theme]. *Bungakukai* 47, no. 1 (1993).

Murakami Gen'ichi. *Kisha kurabu tte nan da!?* [What are press clubs!?]. Tokyo: Kadokawa Shoten, 2001.

Murakami Haruki. *1Q84* [1Q84]. 3 vols. Tokyo: Shinchōsha, 2009–10.

———. *1Q84.* Translated by Philip Gabriel and Jay Rubin. New York: Vintage, 2013.

———. *After Dark.* Translated by Jay Rubin. New York: Vintage, 2008.

———. *After the Quake.* Translated by Jay Rubin. New York: Vintage, 2003.

———. *Afutādāku* [After dark]. Tokyo: Kōdansha, 2004.

———. *Andāguraundo* [Underground]. Tokyo: Kōdansha, 1997.

———. *Blind Willow, Sleeping Woman.* Translated by Philip Gabriel and Jay Rubin. New York: Knopf, 2007.

———. *Colorless Tsukuru Tazaki and His Years of Pilgrimage.* Translated by Philip Gabriel. New York: Knopf, 2014.

———. *Dance Dance Dance.* Translated by Alfred Birnbaum. New York: Vintage, 1995.
———. *The Elephant Vanishes.* Translated by Alfred Birnbaum and Jay Rubin. New York: Knopf, 1993.
———. *Fushigi na toshokan* [The weird library]. Tokyo: Kōdansha Bunko, 2008.
———. *Hard-Boiled Wonderland and the End of the World.* Translated by Alfred Birnbaum. New York: Vintage, 1991.
———. *Hashiru koto ni tsuite kataru toki ni Boku no kataru koto* [What I talk about when I'm talking about running]. Tokyo: Bungei Shunjū, 2007.
———. *Henkyō/kinkyō* [Frontiers near and far]. Tokyo: Shinchōsha, 1998.
———. *Kafka on the Shore.* Translated by Philip Gabriel. New York: Vintage, 2006.
———. *Kami no kodomotachi wa mina odoru* [All god's children can dance; English translation published as *After the Quake*]. Tokyo: Shinchōsha, 2000.
———. *Kokkyō no minami, taiyō no nishi* [South of the border, west of the sun]. Tokyo: Kōdansha, 1992.
———. *Moshi bokura no kotoba ga uisukii de atta nara* [If our words were whiskey]. Tokyo: Heibonsha, 1999.
———. *Murakami Haruki, Kawai Hayao ni ai ni iku* [Murakami Haruki goes to meet Kawai Hayao]. Tokyo: Shinchō Bunkō, 1996.
———. "Murakami Haruki rongu intabyū" [Murakami Haruki long interview]. *Kangaeru hito* no. 33 (2010).
———. *Murakami Haruki zensakuhin, 1979–1989* [Complete works of Murakami Haruki, 1979–1989]. 8 vols. Tokyo: Kōdansha, 1991.
———. *Nejimakidori kuronikuru* [Wind-up bird chronicle]. Tokyo: Shinchōsha, 1994–96.
———. *Norwegian Wood.* Translated by Jay Rubin. New York: Vintage, 2000.
———. "Rongu intabyū: *Umibe no Kafka* o kataru" [Long interview: Narrating *Kafka on the Shore*]. *Bungakukai* 57, no. 4 (2002).
———. *The Scrap: Natsukasi no 1980-nendai* [The scrap: The nostalgic 1980s]. Tokyo: Bungei Shunjū, 1987.
———. *Shikisai o motanai Tazaki Tsukuru to, kare no junrei no toshi* [Colorless Tsukuru Tazaki and his years of pilgimage]. Tokyo: Bungei Shunjū, 2013.
———. *South of the Border, West of the Sun.* Translated by Philip Gabriel. New York: Vintage, 2000.
———. *The Sputnik Sweetheart.* Translated by Philip Gabriel. New York: Vintage, 2002.
———. *Supūtoniku no koibito* [The Sputnik sweetheart]. Tokyo: Kōdansha, 1999.

———. *Tōkyō kitanshū* [Strange tales of Tokyo]. Tokyo: Shinchōsha, 2005.
———. *TV piipuru* [TV people]. Tokyo: Bungei Shunjū, 1990.
———. *Umibe no Kafka* [Kafka on the shore]. Tokyo: Shinchōsha, 2002.
———. *Underground.* Translated by Alfred Birnbaum and Philip Gabriel. New York: Vintage, 2001.
———. *Wakai dokusha no tame no tampen shōsetu annai* [A guide to short fiction for young readers]. Tokyo: Bungei Shunjū, 1997.
———. *What I Talk About When I Talk About Running.* Translated by Philip Gabriel. New York: Vintage, 2009.
———. *A Wild Sheep Chase.* Translated by Alfred Birnbaum. New York: Plume, 1989.
———. *The Wind-Up Bird Chronicle.* Translated by Jay Rubin. New York: Knopf, 1997.
———. *Yagate kanashiki gaikokugo* [Ultimately, a sad foreign language]. Tokyo: Kōdansha, 1994.
———. *Yakusoku sareta basho de: Underground 2* [At the place that was promised: Underground 2]. Tokyo: Bungei Shunjū, 1998.
———. *Yume o miru tame ni mainichi Boku wa mezameru no desu* [I awaken every morning in order to dream]. Tokyo: Bungei Shunjū, 2010.
———. *Zatsubunshū 1979–2010* [Collected essays 1979–2010]. Tokyo: Shinchōsha, 2011.
Murakami Haruki and Itoi Shigesato. *Yume de aimashō* [Let's meet in a dream]. Tokyo: Kōdansha Bunko, 1986.
Murakami Haruki. Special series: Gunzō Japanese Writers, no. 26. Tokyo: Shōgakukan, 1997.
Murakami Haruki. Edited by Kimata Satoshi. Wakakusa Shobō, 1998.
Murakami Haruki 1Q84 o dō yomu ka [How does one read Murakami Haruki's *1Q84*?]. Tokyo: Kawade Shobō Shinsha, 2009.
Murakami Haruki no sekai [The world of Murakami Haruki]. Special issue of *Yuriika* 21, no. 8. Tokyo: Seidosha, 1989.
Murakami Haruki: 1Q84 e itaru made, soshite korekara . . . [Murakami Haruki: To *1Q84* and beyond . . .] Special issue of *Yuriika* 42, no. 15. Tokyo: Seidosha, 2010.
Murakami Ryū. *In za miso sūpu* [In the miso Soup]. Tokyo: Yomiuri Shimbunsha, 1997.
———. *Kibō no kuni no ekusodasu* [Exodus to the promised land]. Tokyo: Bungei Shunjū, 2000.
———. *Kyōseichū* [Symbiotic worm]. Tokyo: Kōdansha, 2000.
———. *Rabu & Poppu* [Love & pop]. Tokyo: Gentōsha, 1996.
Murakami Tomohiko. "Mada shinenai de iru 'Kōbe' no tame ni" [For the Kobe that cannot die]. *Shisō no kagaku* no. 135 (1990).

Nagata Mikihiko. *Daichi wa furuu* [The great earth shakes]. Tokyo: Shun'yōdō, 1923.

Nakagami Kenji to Murakami Haruki [Nakagami Kenji and Murakami Haruki]. Special issue of *Kokubungaku* 30, no. 3 (1985).

Nakamura Mitsuharu. "Yukue fumei jinbutsu kankei" [Missing human relationships]. *Kokubungaku* 43, no. 3 (1988).

Napier, Susan. *The Fantastic in Modern Japanese Literature: The Subversion of Modernity.* London: Routledge, 1996.

———. "The Magic of Identity: Magic Realism in Modern Japanese Fiction." In *Magical Realism: Theory, History, Community,* edited by Wendy B. Faris and Lois Parkinson Zamora. Durham, N.C.: Duke University Press, 1995.

———. "Meet Me on the Other Side: Strategies of Otherness in Modern Japanese Literature." In *Representing the Other in Modern Japanese Literature: A Critical Approach,* edited by Rachael Hutchinson and Mark Williams. London: Routledge, 2006.

Noda Masaaki. "Kakusareta dōki: Nonfuikushon sakka kara fuikushon sakka e" [The hidden motive: From nonfiction writer to fiction writer]. *Gunzō* 52, no. 5 (1997).

"*Noruwei no Mori* no himitsu" [The Secret of *Norwegian Wood*]. *Bungei shunjū* 67, no. 5 (1989).

Numano Mitsuyoshi. "Ima dōshite sekai bungaku na no ka?" [Why is it now world literature?]. *Bungei* 51, no. 1 (2012).

———. "Murakami Haruki wa sekai no 'ima' ni tachimukau" [Murakami Haruki faces the "now" of the world]. *Bungakukai* 48, no. 7 (1994).

———. "Shikisai, hiyū, nosutarujia: Torauma to tadashisa o meguru shizuka na monogatari" [Color, metonymy, nostalgia: A quiet tale of trauma and right]. *Bungakukai* 67, no. 6 (2013).

———. "Yomioetara mō 200Q no sekai" [Once you finish reading it's already the year 200Q]. *Bungakukai* 63, no. 8 (2009).

Numano Mitsuyoshi and Suzumura Kazunari. "'Nejimakidori' wa doko e tobu ka?" [To where will the "wind-up bird" fly?]. *Bungakukai* 49, no. 10 (1995).

Numano Mitsuyoshi, Uchida Tatsuru, and Tokō Kōji. "Murakami Haruki no 'ketsudan'" [Murakami Haruki's "resolve."] *Bungakukai* 64, no. 7 (2010).

Oda Makoto. *Fukai oto* [A deep sound]. Tokyo: Shinchōsha, 2002.

Odaka Shūya. *Kindai bungaku igo: "Naikō no sedai" kara mita Murakami Haruki* [After modern literature: Murakami Haruki seen by the "introverted generation"]. Tokyo: Sakuhinsha, 2011.

Ōe Kenzaburō. *Man'en gannen no futtobōru* [Football in the year 1860; translated as *The Silent Cry*]. Tokyo: Kōdansha, 1971.

———. *The Silent Cry*. Translated by John Bester. Tokyo: Kōdansha International, 1981.
Oka, Yoshitake. "Generational Conflict after the Russo-Japanese War." In *Conflict in Modern Japanese History: The Neglected Tradition,* edited by Tetsuo Najita and J. Victor Koschmann. Princeton, N.J.: Princeton University Press, 1982.
Okamura Akihiko. *Minami Vetonamu sensō jūgunki* [Record of an embedded reporter in the South Vietnam War]. Tokyo: Iwanami Shinsho, no. 548 (1965).
———. *Zoku Minami Vetonamu sensō jūgunki* [War memoir of the South Vietnamese war]. Tokyo: Iwanami Shinsho, no. 608 (1966).
Okuyama Michiaki. "Spiritual Quests in Contemporary Japanese Writers before and after the AUM Affair: Ōe Kenzaburō and Murakami Haruki around 1995." *Nanzan Bulletin* no. 25 (2001).
Ortega y Gasset, José. "The Misery and the Splendor of Translation." In *Theories of Translation: An Anthology of Essays from Dryden to Derrida,* edited by Rainer Schulte and John Biguenet. Chicago: University of Chicago Press, 1992.
Plato. *Lysis, Symposium, Gorgias*. Translated by W. R. M. Lamb. Cambridge, Mass.: Harvard University Press, 1961.
Pynchon, Thomas. *Gravity's Rainbow*. New York: Penguin, 1973.
Rubin, Jay. *Haruki Murakami and the Music of Words*. London: Vintage, 2005.
———. "Sekkusu to rekishi to kioku" [Sex, history, and memory]. *Shinchō* 92, no. 2 (1995).
Rubin, Jay, and Komori Yōichi. "*1Q84* to Sōseki o tsunagu mono" [Things that connect *1Q84* with Sōseki]. *Gunzō* 65, no. 7 (2010).
Rubin, Jay, and Ōno Kazumoto. "Naze sekai de yomareru no ka: *1Q84* hon'yakusha ga kataru" [Why is he read throughout the world? The translator of *1Q84* talks]. *Bungei shunjū* 88, no. 7 (2010).
Rushdie, Salman. *Midnight's Children*. London: Penguin, 1980.
Saitō Eiji. "Gendai no gōsuto sutōrii" [A modern ghost story]. *Shinchō* 90, no. 2 (1993).
Saitō Tamaki. *Bungaku no chōkō* [Literary symptoms]. Tokyo: Bungei Shunjū, 2004.
Sano Shin'ichi. "Nonfuikushon no setsujitu na kadai" [The urgent problem of nonfiction]. *Bungakukai* 51, no. 6 (1997).
Seats, Michael. *Murakami Haruki: The Simulacrum in Contemporary Japanese Culture*. New York: Lexington Books, 2006.
Sekine Makihiko. "Aimu natto raiku eburibadii erusu" [I'm not like everybody else]. *Shisō no kagaku* no. 511 (1994).

Sengoku Hideyo. *Airon o kakeru seinen: Murakami Haruki to Amerika* [The youth plying the iron: Murakami Haruki and America]. Tokyo: Sairyūsha, 1991.

Shibata Motoyuki, Fujii Shōzō, Numano Mitsuyoshi, and Yomota Inuhiko, eds. *A wild Haruki chase: Sekai wa Murakami Haruki o dō yomu ka* [A wild Haruki chase: How does the world read Murakami Haruki?]. Tokyo: Bungei Shunjū, 2006.

Shibata Motoyuki and Numano Mitsuyoshi. "Ōsutā, Murakami Haruki, Sarinjā" [Auster, Murakami Haruki, Salinger]. *Shinchō* 99, no. 10 (2002).

Shibata Shōji. *Nakagami Kenji to Murakami Haruki: <Datsu 60-nendai>teki sekai no yukue* [Nakagami Kenji and Murakami Haruki: Whereabouts of the "post-1960s-esque" world]. Tokyo: Tokyo Gaikokugo Daigaku Shuppankai, 2009.

Shimamura Teru. "'Kuronosu' to no kōsō: *Nejimakidori kuronikuru* no kōdo" [Battle with "Cronos": The code of *The Wind-Up Bird Chronicle*]. In *Murakami Haruki sutadiizu 04* [Murakami Haruki studies 04], edited by Kuritsubo Yoshiki and Tsuge Teruhiko. Tokyo: Wakakusa Shobō, 1999.

Shimizu Yoshinori. "'Chichi' no kūi" ["Father" vacancy]. *Bungakukai* 63, no. 8 (2009).

———. "'Ritoru piipuru' to wa nani ka" [What are the "Little People"?]. In *Murakami Haruki 1Q84 o dō yomu ka* [How to read Murakami Haruki's *1Q84*?], edited by Kawade Shobō Editorial Board. Tokyo: Kawade Shobō Shinsha, 2009.

"Shōnen A": Kono ko o unde . . . ["Youth A": That we gave birth to this child . . .] "Shōnen A" no Fubo [parents of "Youth A"]. Tokyo: Bungei Shunjū, 1999.

Siegle, Robert. *The Politics of Reflexivity: Narrative and the Constitutive Poetics of Culture.* Baltimore: Johns Hopkins University Press, 1986.

Sims, Norman, ed. *Literary Journalism in the Twentieth Century.* New York: Oxford University Press, 1990.

Sims, Norman, and Mark Kramer, eds. *Literary Journalism: A New Collection of the Best American Nonfiction.* New York: Ballantine Books, 1995.

Snyder, Stephen. "Two Murakamis and Marcel Proust: Memory as Form in Contemporary Japanese Fiction." In *In Pursuit of Contemporary East Asian Culture,* edited by Xiaobing Tang and Stephen Snyder. Boulder, Colo.: Westview Press, 1996.

Steiner, Rudolph. *Goethes Weltanschauung* [Goethe's view of the world]. Berlin: Philosophisch-anthroposophischer verlag, 1921. Orig. pub. 1897.

Strecher, Matthew. "At the Critical Stage: A Report on the State of Murakami Haruki Studies." *Literature Compass* 8, no. 11 (2011).

———. "Beyond 'Pure' Literature: Mimesis, Formula, and the Postmodern

in the Fiction of Murakami Haruki." *Journal of Asian Studies* 57, no. 2 (1998).
———. *Dances with Sheep: The Quest for Identity in the Fiction of Murakami Haruki.* Ann Arbor, Mich.: Center for Japanese Studies/University of Michigan Press, 2002.
———. "Magical Realism and the Search for Identity in the Fiction of Murakami Haruki." *Journal of Japanese Studies* 25, no. 2 (1999).
———. "Murakami Haruki: Japan's Coolest Writer Heats Up." *Japan Quarterly* 45, no. 1 (1998).
———. *Murakami Haruki's* The Wind-Up Bird Chronicle: *A Reader's Guide.* London and New York: Continuum Publishers, 2002.
———. "A Spatial Odyssey or It's All Greek to Me." In *Cultural Interactions and Interpretations in a Global Age,* edited by Ji Fengyuan, Lin Jinghua, and Susan Bouterey. Christchurch, New Zealand: Canterbury University Press, 2011.
Strecher, Matthew, Chieko Katō et al. *Shinri to jōhō* [Psychology and information]. Tokyo: Index Press, 2011.
Sugai Senri. "'Kōryū no naratorojii' o koete" [Going beyond "exchange narratology"]. *Kokubungaku kaishaku to kanshō* 76, no. 7 (2011).
Suter, Rebecca. *The Japanization of Modernity: Murakami Haruki between Japan and the United States.* Cambridge, Mass.: Harvard University Asia Center, 2008.
Suzuki Tomoyuki. *Murakami Haruki to monogatari no jōken* [Murakami Haruki and the conditions of the story]. Tokyo: Seikyūsha, 2009.
Suzumura Kazunari. "Jishin no ato, Murakami Haruki no Kōbe o iku" [After the quake, going to Murakami Haruki's Kobe]. *Bungakukai* 65, no. 8 (2011).
———. *Mada/sude ni: Murakami Haruki to "hādo-boirudo wandārando* [Encore/Déjà: Murakami Haruki and the "hard-boiled wonderland"]. Tokyo: Yosensha, 1990.
———. *Murakami Haruki kuronikuru 1983–1995* [Murakami Haruki chronicle]. Tokyo: Yosensha, 1994.
———. *Murakami Haruki senki: 1Q84 no jeneshisu* [Murakami Haruki war journal: The genesis of *1Q84*]. Tokyo: Sairyūsha, 2009.
Takayama Fumihiko. *"Shōnen A": 14-sai no shōzō* ["Youth A": Portrait of a 14-year-old]. Tokyo: Shinchōsha, 1998.
Takeda Tōru. "Murakami sakuhin ni arawareta 'ore'" [The appearance of "Ore" (I, vulg.) in the Murakami work]. *Chūō kōron* 128, no. 6 (2013).
Tanaka Kazuo. "Posutomodan bungaku to shite no watakushi-shōsetsu" [The I-novel as postmodern literature]. *Kokubungaku kaishaku to kanshō* 76, no. 6 (2011).

Tanaka Masashi. "Naibu to gaibu o kasaneru sentaku—Murakami Haruki *Umibe no Kafka* ni mirareru jikoaiteki imēji to taikōteki ronri" [Internal and external superimposed options—narcissistic images and regressive logic visible in Murakami Haruki's *Kafka on the Shore*]. *Kōnan Daigaku kiyō*, 2006.

Tanaka Minoru. "'100% no ai' no uragiri: Murakami Haruki *Rekishinton no yūrei* no shinsō no hihyō" [Betrayal of "100% love": A deep critique of Murakami Haruki's *Ghosts of Lexington*]. *Kokubungaku kaisyaku to kanshō* 76, no. 7 (2011).

———. "<Genbun> to <katari> saikō": Murakami Haruki *Kami no kodomotachi wa mina odoru*" [Rethinking <original text> and <narration>: A deep critique of Murakami Haruki's *All children of the gods dance*]. *Kokubungaku kaisyaku to kanshō* 76, no. 7 (2011).

Tanaka Yasuo. *Kōbe shinsai nikki* [Kobe earthquake diary]. Tokyo: Shinchō Bunko, 1996.

Tatsumi Takayuki. *Nihon henryū bungaku* [Japanese slipstream literature]. Tokyo: Shinchōsha, 1998.

Toews, John. "Intellectual History after the Linguistic Turn: The Autonomy of Meaning and the Irreducibility of Experience." *American Historical Review* 94, no. 4 (1987).

Tōyama Yoshitaka. "Doitsu ni okeru gendai Nihon bungaku no juyō" [The reception of contemporary Japanese literature in Germany]. In *Murakami Haruki sutadiizu 2000–2004* [Murakami Haruki studies, 2000–2004], edited by Imai Kiyoto. Tokyo: Wakakusa Shobō, 2000.

Tsuge Teruhiko. "Media to shite no 'ido': Murakami Haruki wa naze Kawai Hayao ni ai ni itta ka" [The "well" as media: Why did Murakami Haruki go to meet Kawai Hayao?]. *Kokubungaku* 43, no. 3 (1998).

Uchida Tatsuru. "Kyōkaisen to shishatachi to kitsune no koto" [Borderlines, the dead, and foxes]. *Bungakukai* 67, no. 6 (2013).

———. *Mō ichido Murakami Haruki ni go-yōjin* [Once again a caution to Murakami Haruki]. Tokyo: Artes, 2010.

Ueno Chizuko, et al. *Danryū bungakuron* [Theory of men's literature]. Tokyo: Chikuma Shobō, 1992.

Van Wolferen, Karel. *The Enigma of Japanese Power.* New York: Knopf, 1989.

Vidal, Gore. *Burr.* New York: Random House, 1973.

———. *Julian.* Boston: Little, Brown, 1964.

———. *Lincoln.* New York: Random House, 1984.

———. *Perpetual War for Perpetual Peace: How We Got to Be So Hated.* New York: Thunder's Mouth Press/Nation Books, 2002.

Watanabe Mieko. *Katarienu mono: Murakami Haruki no rezubian hyōshō*

[Things that cannot be told: Murakami Haruki's lesbian representations]. Tokyo: Ochanomizu Shobō, 2009.

White, Hayden. *The Content of the Form: Narrative Discourse and Historical Representation.* Baltimore: Johns Hopkins University Press, 1987.

———. *Metahistory: The Historical Imagination in Nineteenth-Century Europe.* Baltimore: Johns Hopkins University Press, 1973.

Williams, David. *Japan: Beyond the End of History.* New York: Routledge, 1994.

Yamaguchi, Mari. "Truancy Doubles in Japan over Past Decade." *The Columbian* (Vancouver, Wash.), August 11, 2002.

Yamamoto, Taketoshi. "The Press Clubs of Japan." *Journal of Japanese Studies* 15, no. 2 (1989).

Yamasaki Makiko. *Murakami Haruki no honbun kaikō kenkyū* [Study of revisions of original editions by Murakami Haruki]. Tokyo: Wakakusa Shobō, 2008.

Yamawaki Ayako. "Tachiagaru jijitsu no 'monogatari'" [Real "stories" that stand up]. *Aera* 10, no. 13 (1997).

Yokoo, Kazuhiro. *Murakami Haruki: Kyūjū nendai* [Murakami Haruki: The nineties]. Tokyo: Daisan Shokan, 1994.

———. *Murakami Haruki to Dosutoēfusukii* [Murakami Haruki and Dostoyevsky]. Tokyo: Kindai Bungeisha, 1991.

Yoshida Haruo. *Murakami Haruki, tenkan suru* [Murakami Haruki, about face]. Tokyo: Sairyūsha, 1997.

———. *Murakami Haruki to Amerika: Bōryokusei no yurai* [Murakami Haruki and America: The advent of violence]. Tokyo: Sairyūsha, 2001.

Yoshida Tsukasa. "AUM wa wagatomo" [The AUM is our friend]. *Bungakukai* 51, no. 6 (1997).

Yoshikawa Yasuhisa. *Murakami Haruki to MURAKAMI HARUKI: Seishin bunseki suru sakka* [Murakami Haruki and MURAKAMI HARUKI: A psychoanalyzing writer]. Tokyo: Minerva Shobō, 2010.

INDEX

Matthew Carl Strecher is associate professor of Japanese language and literature at Winona State University in Minnesota. He is the author of *Dances with Sheep: The Quest for Identity in the Fiction of Murakami Haruki* and *Haruki Murakami's* The Wind-Up Bird Chronicle: *A Reader's Guide*.